With gratitude to the A.E.C.
for giving me the opportunity to serve, as well as
the time & to author this book.

To: Carl Wallen, President
11/4/92

[signature]

GOOD NEWS STUDIES

Consulting Editor: Robert J. Karris, O.F.M.

Volume 36

Peter in Matthew

Discipleship, Diplomacy, and Dispraise . . . with an Assessment of Power and Privilege in the Petrine Office

Arlo J. Nau

Foreword by
Martin E. Marty

A Michael Glazier Book
THE LITURGICAL PRESS
Collegeville, Minnesota

A Michael Glazier Book published by The Liturgical Press

Cover design by David Manahan, O.S.B.

Cover illustration: Detail of "Transfiguration" by Giuseppe Cesari; Musée du Louvre

1 2 3 4 5 6 7 8 9

Library of Congress Cataloging-in-Publication Data

Nau, Arlo J., 1928–
Peter in Matthew : discipleship, diplomacy, and dispraise — with an assessment of power and privilege in the Petrine office / Arlo J. Nau.
p. cm. — (Good news studies)
"A Michael Glazier Book."
Includes bibliographical references and index.
ISBN 0-8146-5700-1
1. Bible. N.T. Matthew—Criticism, interpretation, etc.
2. Peter, the Apostle, Saint. I. Title. II. Series.
BS2575.2.N38 1992
226.2'092—dc20 92-24116
CIP

To my late parents,
the Rev. and Mrs. J. H. Nau,
and to my brother Harold,
martyred in World War II

Contents

Foreword

There is nothing so useless as an answer to an unasked question. That truism applies also to problems: I must have a problem about which I consult, if I am to welcome an offered solution. Or: I must be *given* a problem before I can welcome the solution.

Author Arlo Nau gives me such a problem, and it is likely he will give one to many other readers. One can go through decades, as I have, hearing Matthew when the Gospel is read at the Eucharist; reading Matthew in the study; studying Matthew in class with other readers—yes, one can do all that and not be ready for the problem and, thus, the tentative solution to it, proposed here.

The problem has to do with Peter, a central figure in one portion of the Gospel of Matthew. Now, on second thought, one *does* have, *has* had some problems with that disciple all along—particularly as he is portrayed in Matthew. The problem about the problem is that until someone brings it to focus it can just lie there, inert in the back of the mind. Its dimensions can be vaguely disconcerting, potentially disruptive of one's thinking. But the pericope ends, the study session is over, the class disperses, and Peter goes away. "Some day," one thinks, "I will bring this issue to the front of my mind. I will consult the commentaries and the experts, and deal with it."

That second thought, or set of thoughts, has to do with the portrait of Peter in this First Gospel. This could be good advice for a reader to take: before you read Nau's book, read this Gospel again, but as if for the first time. Pretend you never heard of

Peter. Picture the assignment of scripting a film about him, or writing a biography based on the few Petrine chapters.

Then, the issue will become clear. The problem with the clear picture is that it is clearly self-contradictory. Why does the evangelist pay attention to such an obviously important figure, only to—dare we say it, anticipating the plot—put him down? Put him down he does. That is, if we had only the portrait of Peter in Matthew, in spite of or even including the words "You are Peter, and on this rock I will build my church," we would have to say that Matthew the writer-editor is mixed up, or has mixed motives. Nau uses words like "ambivalent," "helter-skelter," a "rollercoaster ride" for the reader. Can't this Matthew, who Nau presumes wrote at Antioch, Syria, around 85 C.E., make up his mind?

Answer: he has done so, if Nau has him right. After promising that he will use simple language—and after keeping it, remarkably in a work of scholarship, most of the time—Nau speaks of Matthew's form of discourse as "encomiastic dispraise." To what shall we liken this?

Try a celebrity roast, minus the conventionally debased and debasing humor. Everyone appears in tuxedos and formals, ready to go through the motions of honoring the designated guest. The gestures and sounds are of the sort that ordinarily go with acts of honoring. But what comes out are insults, acts of putting someone in his or her place.

We are trained to know what encomia are. They are useful for praise. But why use the same rhetorical game to utter dispraise, as at a roast?

Nau's answer is ingenious, thoughtful, credible. Forewords are not the places to give the plot away. The author comes to the point in nuanced ways which I would only mess up if I tried to condense them. But one can say something here and now, and in any case, about the post-plot. Why did Nau write this book, given this viewpoint and set of tentative conclusions? He makes very clear the answer to that question.

As I read Nau's reconstruction of Matthew's purposes, I thought of the figure of John the Baptist in Mathias Gruenewald's great Isenheim altarpiece. John is pointing at Jesus on the cross, identified with the legend: "He must increase, so I must decrease."

Whatever happened to the reputation of Peter, at least among the believers up in Antioch where this Matthew is editing the stories and preparing a Gospel, it is crowding the place of Jesus. So Matthew does to Peter what John the Baptist did for himself in the painting. He points beyond the disciple to Jesus: he must increase; Peter must decrease.

How write that without being a revolutionary, an unheard disruptive figure? Nau's answer: Matthew does so through his choice of stories and ways of telling them, covertly but effectively, while using this standard Hellenic form of rhetoric, the encomium of praise. Matthew's readers in the Greekified world would catch on at once.

There is an ironic twist, however. If Nau is correct, Matthew failed in his mission. And Peter, a great one, an inner core disciple, maybe even a first among equals, acquired over time what Nau calls a "church-political" status which was inimical to Matthew's purpose. As a result, there have been at least 1800 years of problems, of misunderstanding. Years marked by tears and, Nau reminds us, bloodshed.

It is a measure of the advance of ecumenical progress and an indication of the degree of acceptability with which honest critical readings of the New Testament can occur that a faithful Catholic house, The Liturgical Press, is publishing this work. However I may have described the book in these anticipatory paragraphs, it is not destructive biblical criticism. Publishers do not have to put "Imprimatur" and "Nihil Obstat" on their books, and this publisher is not necessarily identifying with all the argument or the conclusions. But it is quite likely that The Liturgical Press, like the readers of The Liturgical Press books, including this one, has gone ahead because it can discern at once the book's ambitious and constructive purpose.

Martin E. Marty
The University of Chicago

Preface

Scholarship is for ordinary people. Such is the working principle of this book.

While the following pages treat a subject that is exegetically complex and emotionally freighted, every effort has been made to keep the prose simple and the technicalities to a minimum. Technical terms are defined and foreign words translated. Of course, some exegetical jargon is unavoidable. New Testament scholars with their broader backgrounds will naturally have an easier time of it, but students, pastors, and parishioners should also be able to follow the argument with, perhaps, only occasional recourse to a dictionary or one of the standard reference works.

All biblical quotations are taken from the Revised Standard Version of the Bible (1952, 1971). Although the NRSV was published while this book was in preparation, reference works employing the NRSV were not available for consultation. Important, or just interesting, changes in translations between the two versions will be noted where appropriate.

The scholarly neutral designations B.C.E. (Before the Common Era) and C.E. (Common Era) are used with dates instead of the conventional B.C. (Before Christ) and A.D. (Anno Domini). The designations "par." or "parr." following text locations denote one or more parallels in other Synoptic Gospels.

For clarity's sake, a distinction between MATTHEW, the first Gospel, in upper case letters, and Matthew, the evangelist, in lower-case letters, has been implemented. The same method has been used to distinguish between other canonical works and their respective authors. Of course, lower case letters and numbers are consistently employed to indicate chapter and verse locations.

Where Greek is quoted, please note that the transcription of Greek letters in this book is as follows: a "w" represents an *omega,* "ee" an *eta,* "xs" a *xi,* "ps" a *psi,* and "th" a *theta.* Aspiration is indicated by an initial "h." All other letters should be self-evident from their English equivalents.

The footnotes should be read, or at least scanned. Besides bibliographic information and some hints to alternative views which would interest New Testament scholars particularly, they also contain occasional comments of an anecdotal nature which should help to color and flavor everyone's reading pleasure. The bibliographic information in the notes is given in short form, just enough to identify the work in the bibliography where full publication facts are provided.

My thanks to the Arizona Ecumenical Council for granting me a leave of absence from my tasks as Administrator permitting me to concentrate on this manuscript, and to the members of an informal local Advisory Editorial Committee: My wife Lynn, who heard my arguments *ad nauseam;* Mr. Bernard Backman, advisor and confidant; Drs. Linell Cady and Charles Emerson of Arizona State University's Department of Religious Studies; Dr. Holt Graham, emeritus Professor of New Testament Studies at the United Seminary of the Twin Cities, New Brighton, Minnesota; Dr. David Keller, Director of the Department for Ministry Development for the Episcopal Diocese of Arizona; the Rev. Mr. Thomas Parker, Director of the Fuller Seminary Extension Program in Phoenix; and the Rev. Dr. James Standiford, Pastor of University United Methodist Church, Tempe.

A word of special appreciation for their encouragement and counsel is extended to two highly respected friends of longstanding, Dr. Robert C. Dentan, emeritus Professor of Old Testament at the General Theological Seminary, New York City, and Dr. Martin Marty, noted author and Church historian at the University of Chicago.

Students in several of my classes at Arizona State University-West and at the Inter-Church Center, Phoenix, were also more helpful than they will ever know.

Perhaps a potential word of thanks may be directed to you, the readers, as well. This book is meant to initiate a dialog. If you would be so kind as to send me your written responses I would be most appreciative.

Arlo J. Nau, Th.D.
5144 N. 6th Street
Phoenix, Arizona 85012

ANTIOCH, SYRIA, AND VICINITY

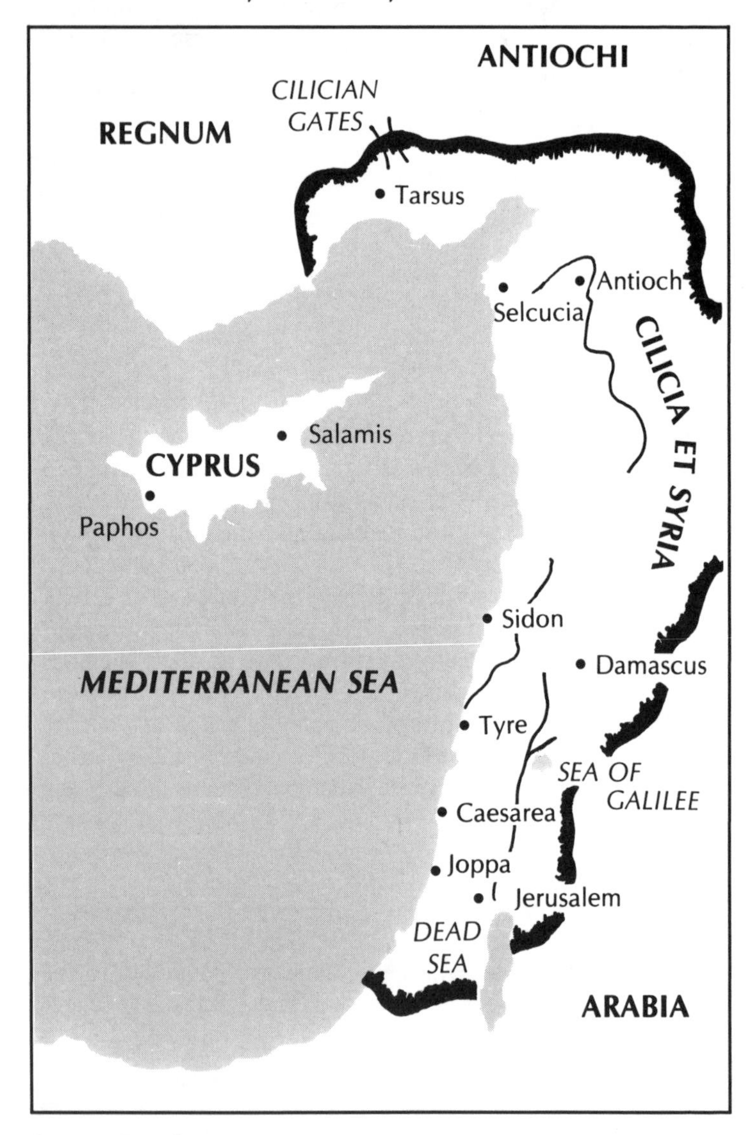

Roman Provinces

Cities and Town •

1

The Problem in Context

Make no mistake, this book is primarily about MATTHEW, the First Gospel, (henceforth in capital letters), and Matthew, the first evangelist, (in lower-case letters), although Peter, the first disciple, will undoubtedly attract a disproportionate amount of attention. Peter is simply too captivating a figure to treat cursorily or dispassionately.

In this volume, the significant Petrine material in MATTHEW will be used as a study sample—a fascinating and at times exasperating test case—in an attempt to define more precisely the literary art, editorial intentionality and theological focus of Matthew, the first evangelist. Such information should enable students of the New Testament to read this Gospel with increased competence and benefit, especially where Peter is concerned, but surely in other areas as well.

MATTHEW and Matthew: Questions of Provenance

MATTHEW, the Gospel, is quite familiar to everyone.[1] As the first Gospel listed in the New Testament, and as one of the longer

[1]See the bibliography for a list of some of the more available commentaries on MATTHEW. Of these, I would select the following for special mention: Ulrich Luz, *Matthew 1–7,* trans. Wilhelm C. Linss (German, 1985, English, 1989). While not yet complete, it is already the most detailed and thorough; W. C. Allen, *St. Matthew,* in the *International Critical Commentary* (1907), is old, but contains much useable information; John Paul Meier, *Matthew* (1980) is very read-

and more complete works, MATTHEW is undoubtedly also one of the most influential of all canonical writings. Many favorite passages are found here: the Christmas Story told from Joseph's point of view and featuring the Visit of the Wisemen (1:18–2:23), the Sermon on the Mount (chapters 5–7), including the Beatitudes (5:3-11), the Lord's Prayer (6:9-13), and the Golden Rule (7:12), and finally the Great Commission in 28:18-20.

As to the location and date of the Gospel's composition, Antioch in Syria in the years 80 to 90 of the first Christian century are the leading candidates among scholars today.[2]

Ignatius of Antioch, early in the second century C.E., was the first to quote MATTHEW, or at least reflect common MATTHEAN traditions.[3] The Alexandrian theologian Origen, shortly thereafter, simularly associated Peter with Antioch, naming him its first bishop.[4] This combination, of course, neatly coincides with the Petrine interest evidenced in the First Gospel, strongly suggesting Antiochan provenance.

able. Also helpful: *The Vision of Matthew* (1978), by the same author. M. D. Goulder, *Midrash and Lection in Matthew* (1974) 476–485, and Robert H. Gundry, *Matthew. A Commentary on His Literary and Theological Art* (1982) 641–649, have invaluable vocabulary-frequency lists.

[2]Accepting Antioch as the location for MATTHEW'S composition are Feine, Behm, Kümmel, *Introduction to the New Testament* (1965) 84; B. H. Streeter, *The Four Gospels* (1930) 500ff.; and John Meier, *Vision* (1983) 15. G. Strecker, *Weg* (1971) 37, suggests Phoenicia; Sjef von Tilborg, *Jewish Leaders in Matthew* (1972) thinks of Alexandria; Sherman E. Johnson, *St. Matthew* (1951) 241, considers Edessa or Apamea in Eastern Syria; H. D. Slingerland, "Transjordanian Origin," in *The Journal for the Study of the New Testament* (1979) 18–28, opts for Pella; H. B. Green, *Matthew* (1975) 32, says somewhere "near Palestine." As for the proposed date of composition John P. Meier, in Raymond E. Brown and John P. Meier, *Antioch & Rome* (1983) 45, says 80–90 C.E. W. C. Allen, *St. Matthew* (1907) lxxxiv and lxxxv, suggests 65–75 C.E. U. Luz, *Matthew 1-7,* (1989) 93, says 80 C.E. Strecker, *Weg* (1971) says 90–95 C.E. Kilpatrick, *Origin* (1946) 90–100 C.E.

[3]For the "Letters of Ignatius," see *The Apostolic Fathers,* ed. Jack Sparks; Evidences that Ignatius was familiar with MATTHEW are found in "Smyrneans" 1:1 (Matt 3:15), "Polycarp" 2:2 (Matt 10:16b), "Ephesians" 5 and "Smyrneans" 8 (Matt 18:20), "Trallians" 11 and "Philadelphians" 3 (Matt 15:13). Casual references to Peter are found in "Romans" 4 and "Smyrneans" 3. Cf. also Raymond Brown and John P. Meier, *Antioch and Rome* (1983) esp. 24f.

[4]Origen, "Homily on Luke," VI, c., in Migne, *Patrologiae cursus copletus.* Series *Graeca,* XIII, col. 1814ff.

Furthermore, since MATTHEW is based on MARK, as is generally assumed by Synoptic scholars, this First Gospel could not have been composed before 66 to 70 C.E., the proposed dates for MARK, or later than the first decade of the second century when Ignatius composed his celebrated seven letters to the Churches of Asia Minor.

Antioch on the Orontes (cf. map, p. xvi) and 85 C.E., then, are the assumed location and approximate time of composition of MATTHEW in this book.

These were the "glory years" for Antioch.[5] It was the third largest city in the Roman Empire, an imperial residence, and a vast cultural and commercial center. It enjoyed a cosmopolitan population of approximately one-half million people dominated politically and culturally by Greeks and Romans, but consisting mostly of Syrians, a wide ethnic assortment of slaves and not a few diaspora Jews. Some of these Jews were residents of long-standing in Antioch, but others were of more recent arrival, escapees from the Roman conquest of Palestine and the destruction of Jerusalem in 70 C.E.

There is undoubtedly more to debate about the appropriate outline of MATTHEW. Among the many suggestions of the various commentators, three general types of outlines have emerged as the more popular. These may be labled the Markan, the chiastic or concentric, and the five-book or structural models.

Jack Dean Kingsbury may be cited as representative of the first type.[6] He detects salvation-historical shifts at 4:17 and 16:21 as indicated by Matthew's use of the rare introductory phrase "From that time he began. . . ." (*Apo tote eerxsato*) at these locations. In effect, this perspective mirrors a similar arrangement in MARK where the parallel to Matt 16:21, Mark 8:31, is also seen as dividing the Second Gospel. This design, with Peter's Confession at Caesarea Philippi (Matt 16:13-20) and Jesus' statement of the Great Commission (Matt 28:16-20) concluding the two major sections, contributes to an overall Christological emphasis and focus in the First Gospel.

[5]Cf. Raymond Brown and John P. Meier, *Antioch and Rome* (1983) 30–32; Also Michael H. Crosby, *House of Disciples* (1988) 36–38.

[6]J. D. Kingsbury, *Matthew: Structure, Christology and Kingdom* (1975) 7–25.

The chiastic, or concentric circles type of outline takes special notes of Matthew's preference for inclusios, similar phrases or themes which begin and end both larger sections and smaller subsections of the Gospel. For example, the interpretation of the name Emmanuel in Matthew 1:23 as "God with us" and Jesus' climactic promise "Lo, I am with you always" in Matthew 28:20 may be seen as a set of inclusios bracketing the entire book. This chiastic proposal has the advantage of accounting for the several themes repeated at different locations throughout the First Gospel, but, if we may take Peter F. Ellis' 1974 work *Matthew, His Mind and His Message,* as a case in point, the various associations of passages and themes needed to construct the multi-level chiasm are very subtle, witnessing perhaps more to the cleverness of the commentator than to the intentions of the author.[7]

The third suggestion is the oldest, but also the most enduring. It was proposed by B. W. Bacon in the first decades of the twentieth century.[8] Bacon took special note of the five extended discourses featured in the First Gospel, each concluding with the conventional phrase: "When Jesus had finished all these sayings. . . ." (Matt 7:28, 11:1, 13:53, 19:1 and 26:1). Basing his thoughts on this observation, Bacon maintained that the First Gospel was designed to be seen as a New Testament Pentateuch. Thematically, this suggestion did not stand the test of scholarly examination, but structurally the five-book division of the Gospel has proved too valid and just plain handy to be abandoned. According to this scheme, the five sermons in chapters 5–7, 10, 13, 18, and 23–25 act as ribs or stays in a piece of rattan with biographical vignettes or theological emphases interwoven around and between them. To use another analogy, MATTHEW may be viewed as the facade of a classical Greek temple with the birth narratives forming the foundation, the five sermons the pillars,

[7]Peter F. Ellis, *Matthew: His Mind and His Message* (1974) 10–12. Ulrich Luz, *Matthew 1–7* (1989) 40, speaks of Matthew's preference for "chiastic rings."

[8]Among those using the five-book divisions are B. W. Bacon, *Studies in Matthew* (1930); Green, *Matthew* (1975); and Meier, *Vision* (1978). Michael H. Crosby, *House of Disciples* (1988) 54–55, uses the five-book outline, but sees a chiastic arrangement between them. Cf. U. Luz, *Matthew 1-7* (1989) 35, for a discussion of MATTHEW's structure. Also Kingsbury, *Matthew* (1975) 3, n. 13 for a long list of older works which espouse the five-book structural outline.

and the resurrection accounts the roof. The sermons are recognizably topical, but the open spaces between the sermonic columns, while exhibiting a certain coloration consistent with the discourses, are not thematically restricted.

It is primarily convenience that prompts our general espousal of this third approach in the pages to follow. Chapter 6, however, will feature a more intentional theological analysis of MATTHEW's Book IV, 13:52–18:35.

We may be faulted for our Greek temple analogy when it comes to a consideration of the cultural ambiance of the First Gospel. A majority of scholars see MATTHEW as a "Jewish" book, written for a Jewish Christian congregation.[9] As supportive evidence, they can point to the genealogy in 1:2-17, tracing Jesus' lineage back only to Abraham, the Patriarch of Israel. Some of the sayings, parables, and miracle stories also exude a heavy Semitic aroma. Further, the Gospel contains some sixty Old Testament allusions, including eleven quotations introduced by the formula: "This was to fulfill what the Lord had spoken by the prophet. . . . "[10] Jewish terms and customs are generally not explained, leading scholars to surmise that no explanations were thought necessary since such commonplaces would be immediately recognized by a Jewish readership.[11]

Nevertheless, I would argue that the Greek temple metaphor is valid. MATTHEW does have a definite hellenistic patina about it also. The book is, after all, written in Greek and displays a distinct concern for the Gentile community, as the concluding Great Commission makes obvious. In addition, the Gospel contains several rather egregious errors involving the Old Testament and

[9]Scholars accepting the view that MATTHEW is essentially Jewish in nature include Luz, *Matthew 1–7* (1989) 79–82; David E. Orten, *The Understanding Scribe* (1989) 18, 24; Eduard Schweizer, *The Good News According to Matthew* (1975) 15–17; O. Lamar Cope, *Matthew: A Scribe Trained for the Kingdom of Heaven* (1976) 51.

[10]Matt 1:23; 2:6f., 15, 17f., 23; 4:14-16; 8:17; 12:17-21; 13:35; 21:4f., 27:9f.

[11]E.g., hand-washing, Matt 15:2/Mark 7:2f.; phylacteries, Matt 23:5. Bar-Jonah, Matt 16:17; Gethsemane, Matt 26:36; Beelzebul, Matt 10:25; but some terms are defined: Golgotha, Matt 27:33. Others are simply not transferred from Matthew's MARCAN source. The two Hebrew passages in Matthew 1:24 and 27:46 are translated.

Jewish tradition which tend to cast additional doubt upon the contention for an over-all Semitic ethos. Note, for example, the reference to "Zachariah, the son of Barachiah," in 23:35, when clearly "Zechariah, the son of Jehoiada the priest" (2 Chronicles 24:20-22) is meant.[12] Would a Hebrew community have permitted such an elementary mistake to slip by?

We may deduce, then, that MATTHEW's readership and community constituted a *corpus mixtum* with both Jewish and Gentile Christians interspersed.

The question could perhaps be more properly posed as one of authorship. Who was "Matthew?" The Gospel, of course, is anonymous. Very early on, it was ascribed to "Matthew," probably because Matthew 9:9 alone employs that name for the tax-collector whom Jesus called to discipleship, instead of "Levi" as in MARK and LUKE (Mark 2:14 and Luke 5:27). It was popular among these earlier commentators to assume that Levi/Matthew, the disciple, had inserted his own better known Greek name here in Matthew 9:9 as a way of identifying himself as the eye-witness author of the First Gospel. It is more common today, however, to believe that since the name "Levi" did not appear in any subsequent list of the disciples, the first evangelist, whoever he was, chose to exchange it with the name of the known companion of Jesus, "Matthew," for the simple reason that *Maththaios* so closely resembles the Greek word for "disciple," *matheetees.*[13]

Of greater credibility today is the suggestion that the identification of "a scribe trained for the kingdom" in Matthew 13:52 may be the author's autobiographical self-designation in the First Gospel because the description of a scribe as one who "brings out of his treasure what is new and what is old" corresponds so closely with the evangelist's own editorial practice.[14]

[12]Other problematic references: There is no known Old Testament prophecy to match Matthew 2:23. MATTHEW is the only Gospel which links arch rivals "Pharisees and Sadducees" in opposition to Jesus, cf. 16:1, 6, 11, 22:34. Cf. also Matthew's literalistic interpretation in Matthew 21:2 of the obvious collective "ass . . . colt" combination from Zechariah 9:9 as two distinct animals.

[13]Cf. Crosby, *House* (1988) 44.

[14]Cf. O. Lamar Cope, *Matthew, A Scribe Trained for the Kingdom,* The Catholic Biblical Quarterly Monograph Series 5 (1976) 130, final paragraph; also David E. Orton, *The Understanding Scribe* (1989) 165. Perhaps the best example of this

But the question remains: Was Matthew a Jew or a Gentile? Ernst Von Dobschütz, in 1928, declared the evangelist not only a Jew, but a converted rabbi.[15] On the contrary, John Paul Meier, more recently, has argued that Matthew's antipathy toward Jewish leaders as well as those several editorial errors in Jewish nomenclature and tradition suggest that the first evangelist was a Gentile, well-versed, but not grounded in the Hebrew Scriptures.[16] No doubt the current majority view, with which I concur, is that the author was a hellenistic Jewish Christian, whose home traditions and training were Jewish, but whose first language and formal education were Greek.[17] The first evangelist, then, was not Matthew, the disciple, but an unnamed second or third generation Jewish Christian of the diaspora living somewhere within the environs of Antioch, Syria, and writing in the ninth decade of the first century C.E. However, we shall continue to use the name Matthew, in lower-case letters, to designate the evangelist because of its familiarity and convenience.

The Peter of History: A Biographical Collage

Peter, the disciple, represents more of an enigma, in the New Testament generally and especially in MATTHEW.

Without question, Peter is simultaneously one of the most attractive, frustrating, intriguing, and confusing figures in the entire Bible. He is identified 214 times under four different names:

principle is found in the Sermon on the Mount where statements "by them of old time" are contrasted with Jesus' new perspectives.

[15]Ernst von Dobschütz, "Matthäus als Rabbi und Katechet," *ZNW,* 27 (1928) 338–348.

[16]J. P. Meier. *Vision* (1978) 22. In agreement are K. Clark, "The Gentile Bias of Matthew," *JBL* 66 (1947) 165–172; Strecker, *Weg* (1971) 15–35; Ernest L. Abel, "Who Wrote Matthew?" *New Testament Studies* 17 (1970–1971) 138–152, solves the problem by claiming two "Matthews," one Jewish and one Greek.

[17]H. Benedict Green, *Matthew* (1975) 30. He also lists Bacon, Kilpatrick, Davies, and Stendahl as agreeing. Luz, *Matthew 1–7* (1989) 94, says Matthew "possessed a Jewish-influenced feeling for style, a good Greek linguistic feeling, and a synagogue education.

Peter,[18] Simon,[19] Cephas,[20] and, in two widely separated Aramaic renditions as Simeon (Acts 15:14 and 2 Pet 1:1). St. Paul apparently knew him best by his transliterated Aramaic nickname, Cephas (1 Cor 1:12, 9:5, Gal 1:18, 2:11; exception: Gal 2:7-8), while John, in the fourth Gospel, consistently refers to him as Simon Peter, combining both his Hebrew and Greek designations.

Appropriately, Peter's father is also known by two very different appellations, Jonah, *Iwna,* in Matthew 16:17 and John, *Iwannees,* in John 1:42 and 21:15, 16, 17.[21]

Peter heads every list of the twelve disciples in the New Testament,[22] as well as every subgroup such as MARK'S familiar "inner circle" consisting of Peter, James, and John, and occasionally, Andrew (cf. Mark 14:33, 13:3). Matthew 10:2 explicitly designates Peter *prwtos,* "first."

That Peter was a fisherman by trade, and a married man, is learned from Mark 1:16 and 29 parr. Aside from the fact that his wife accompanied him on some of his missionary travels, (1 Cor 9:5) nothing is known of his immediate family, only that on at least one occasion he shared a house with his mother-in-law (Matthew 8:14-16).

[18]Greek: *Petros,* derived from the Greek feminine noun *petra,* rock. It is a translation of the Aramaic *Keepha.* Since "Peter" is not found in pre-first-century onomastica, it must have originally been a sobriquet, or nickname, "Rocky." Nicknames are usually translated while proper names are transliterated. The great frequency of "Peter" as a proper name in post-first-century times is a tribute to the prominence of the first disciple. Augustine Stock in his article: "Is Matthew's Presentation of Peter Ironic?" (1987) 65, suggests that the nickname was given to Simon before his introduction to Jesus, but see Mark 3:16 and John 1:42.

[19]Greek *Simwn.* Transliteration of the Aramaic proper name of very similar pronunciation, cf. Acts 15:14 and 2 Peter 1:1.

[20]*Cephas,* Greek transliteration of the Aramaic *Keepha,* rock. It is used especially in Paul's letters. It is the equivalent of "Peter." It is not found in MATTHEW.

[21]The variation in names may indicate the existence of different traditions. "Jonah" could also have mnemonic theological value associating Peter with the Old Testament prophet. Terrence Smith, *Petrine Controversies in Early Christianity* (1985) 2, n. 6, calls attention to R. Eisler, *Jesus Basileus* (1929) 67f. and O. Cullmann, *The State in the New Testament* (1957) 16–17, who were of the opinion that Jonah was not a proper name, but indicated that Peter belonged to the Zealots.

[22]Matt 10:2-4, Mark 3:16-19, Luke 6:14-16, Acts 1:13.

That he was somewhat older and slower of foot could also be deduced from the Fourth Gospel's observation that the "disciple whom Jesus loved" outdistanced Peter in a race to the empty tomb on the first Easter morning (John 20:4). This would be true, of course, only if we accept the tradition as historically reliable and not altered to fit some ulterior editorial, or Church-political, purpose in John's Gospel favoring the shadowy "beloved disciple" over Peter, "the big fisherman."[23]

A latent penchant for violence is similarly attributed to Peter in this Fourth Gospel where in a gratuitous attempt to defend Jesus he is specifically designated as the disciple who drew his sword and cut off the ear of Malchus, the high priest's servant (John 18:10f. cf. Matthew 26:51).

In one observation, however, all New Testament witnesses seem to agree: Peter was irrepressibly vocal. In fact, this is probably where his troubles began. He is often cast as the spokesman for the disciples,[24] receiving both instruction and correction from Jesus in return. Mark 9:6 portrays him as something of a babbler at the transfiguration, not realizing what he was saying. He was capable of bold confession (Matt 16:16 par.) and of cowardly denial (Mark 14:66-72 parr.). He could boast of his prowess: "Even though they all fall away, I will not," and "If I must die with you, I will not deny you" (Mark 14:29 and 31 parr.), and then shortly thereafter he would sleep while Jesus suffered in the garden (Mark 14:37 parr.) and flee along with the other disciples when his Lord was arrested (Mark 14:50 par.).

Peter's role in the resurrection accounts is equally disconcerting. In one of the earliest creedal statements in the New Testament, 1 Corinthians 15:5, the risen Jesus is reported to have "appeared to Cephas, then to the twelve." Yet, in JOHN, Jesus' first appearance was to Mary Magdalene (John 20:14), and only several days later in Galilee to Peter and a small band of disciples at the Sea of Tiberias (John 21:1-19). While there, however, Peter

[23]Cf. Raymond E. Brown, *The Community of the Beloved Disciple* (1979) and Kevin Quast, *Peter and the Beloved Disciple* (1989).

[24]Cf. Mark 1:36, 10:28, 11:21; Matt 15:15. On one exceptional occasion, Matthew 17:24, Peter even speaks for Jesus.

is magnanimously rehabilitated by Jesus, given the commission to feed Jesus' metaphorical sheep and lambs.

Similarly, in LUKE, two Emmaus travelers are the first to recognize the resurrected Christ (24:13ff.). Even though in 24:34 Jesus' disciples are able to report: "The Lord is risen indeed and has appeared to Simon," curiously no account to support that claim is provided, indicating, perhaps, more of a theological than historical interest on the part of the evangelist.

MARK notes Peter's post-Easter presence indirectly, but importantly. The young man dressed in white at the empty tomb instructs the women to "go tell the disciples *and Peter* that he (Jesus) is going before you to Galilee" (Mark 16:7).[25] Such specificity, however brief, speaks volumes about Peter's unique standing among his peers in the Second Gospel.

It is only when we come to MATTHEW that we find no Easter or post-Easter story explicitly involving Peter at all. His name never appears after the account of his denials. If anything, compared to the other Gospels, MATTHEW'S description of the resurrection and of post-Easter events in Galilee betrays a noticeable Petrine vacuum. Isn't that interesting? And disturbing!

Unfortunately, this enigmatic portrayal of Peter does not end even with Jesus' resurrection/ascension and the disintegration of the disciples as an identifiable social unit. Luke, in the first twelve chapters of Acts, describes Peter as the temporary leader of the Christian community in Jerusalem, tending to the physical and spiritual needs of the mother Church. As such, he preaches a powerfully effective sermon on the first New Testament Pentecost (Acts 2:14-42). The sick find comfort in having just his shadow fall upon them (Acts 5:15). On more than one occasion, he is imprisoned and miraculously released (Acts 5:19; 11:7). He is seen at several nearby locations, such as Joppa, (Acts 9:36ff.) and Ceasarea Maritima (10:24ff.), where he receives radically new revelations. But then, suddenly, in 12:17, Luke reports cryptically that Peter "departed and went to another place." No one knows

[25]It is generally agreed by scholars that MARK ends with 16:8. Mark 16:9-20 obviously consists of a later collection of brief resurrection appearance narratives based on MATTHEW, LUKE, and JOHN. These may not be used to illustrate Mark's editorial intentions.

with any precision why he left or where he went, but indications are that he traveled extensively throughout the eastern Mediterranean area visiting local Jewish-Christian enclaves of the new, expanding Church (cf. Gal. 2:7-8). For example, according to Galatians 2:11-14, in an incident of special interest to this study, he surfaced on one occasion at Antioch in Syria where, as Paul relates, he and Peter engaged in a serious altercation over the propriety or impropriety of Jewish dietary laws in a religio-social setting that included Gentile Christians.

Peter, as Cephas, is a prominent figure also in Corinth in the mid-50s of the first century. There he is identified as the patron leader of one of the congregation's four competing factions (1 Cor 1:12). There is nothing here, however, to either confirm or deny that the first disciple was ever physically present in that Greek city.

As far as the New Testament is concerned, Peter is last seen back in Jerusalem attending the Apostolic Council, detailed in Acts 15. There his advice is sound and accepted, but his status appears somewhat reduced. James, the brother of Jesus, and the acclaimed first "bishop" of Jerusalem, makes all the final decisions (Acts 15:19ff.).

It is left to the extra-biblical correspondent Clement of Rome, writing about 95 C.E., to author the final page of the Petrine biography. He recalls that Peter "having borne his witness, went to a place of glory he deserved."[26] A widely accepted tradition infers that Peter suffered martyrdom in Rome under Emperor Nero around 64 C.E.[27]

This complex biographical portrait of Peter is bound to generate numerous questions in the mind of any serious reader of the

[26]Clement of Rome, "Clement," 5:4 in *The Faith of the Early Fathers,* trans. W. A. Jurgens, 7f. According to *World Book Encyclopedia* (1981) "P" vol. 15, 588, Clement was the fourth bishop of Rome, 88–96 C.E. If our dates for the composition of MATTHEW are correct, Clement was a contemporary of the first evangelist.

[27]Cf. H. Benedict Green, *The Gospel According to Matthew* (1975) 243; Erich Dinkler, "Die Petrus-Rom-Frage," *Theologische Rundschau* (1959) 189–230; Kurt Aland, "Wann Starb Petrus?" *New Testament Studies* (1955–1956) 267–275. Eusebius, *Ecclesiastical History,* Book III, chap. 1, records the tradition that Peter was crucified upside down at his own request.

New Testament. What kind of a person was the real Peter anyway? Was he an unsophisticated fisherman or an accomplished "fisher of men?" (Matt 4:19) Was his confession of Jesus as the Messiah worthy of high commendation, as in MATTHEW (16:17) or unworthy of repetition, as in MARK (8:29-30). Was he truly *a Petros,* a "rock" empowered by God (Matt 16:18-19), or was he a *skandalon,* a "stumbling-block" to Jesus, as Matthew 16:23 declares? Whether intentionally so, or not, the New Testament keeps its readers guessing.

The Peter of Tradition: A Church-Political Phenomenon

Another part of the puzzle, and perhaps also of its solution, is a recognition of and sensitivity to the extraordinary Church-political shading of Peter's character, evidenced already in the canonical New Testament, but found elaborated in several extra-canonical works, later pseudepigrapha and subsequent Church history. This Petrine Church-political dimension will haunt our analysis as well.

In those early post-resurrection years described in the New Testament, the "Kingdom of God" was in large part only an idea without an institution, an ark without an anchor. With Jesus gone some kind of authority or rallying point was needed to give the "church" unity, integrity, and identity. The disciples, the companions of Jesus during his ministry, were naturally prime candidates. The several references in the New Testament to the disciples arguing over which of them would be the greatest, and jockeying for positions of privilege in the kingdom, seem to both reflect and anticipate the fact that Church-politics began very early indeed within the Christian community and would be endemic to the Church throughout its history (Mark 10:37, Luke 22:24).

More specifically, reference has already been made to Peter's candidacy, along with those of Paul, Apollos, and Christ, for preeminence among the various factions in the Corinthian congregation (1 Cor 1:12). Similarly, there has been occasion to note the apparent rivalry between Peter and the "beloved disciple" for the allegiance of the Johannine community (John 21:20-24).

The LUKE-ACTS presentation is more balanced in describing the relationship between Peter and Paul. In the Third Gospel, Peter is accorded prominence, if not preeminence, among the disciples. The call to be a fisher of men is addressed exclusively to him instead of shared with Andrew, James, and John, as in the other Synoptics (cf. Luke 5:10 parr.). Again, in Luke 22:32, Peter is singled out as the one who, after his conversion, should "strengthen your brethren." However, in Acts, Luke's sequel to his Gospel, Paul dominates while Peter fades "to another place" (12:17). Apparently, Luke, pursuing a salvation-historical design, wished to portray Paul as Peter's successor rather than competitor in bringing the Gospel to the wider Mediterranean world. This approach would be consistent with Luke's apparent apologetic purposes to impress his Gentile readers (Theophilus, 1:1) with a picture of harmonious development within the early Christian movement. Or, if Luke had an internal Church-political motive, it could only have been to promote peace among competing factions loyal to one or the other of the two most celebrated apostles.

Of course, one other Gospel, MATTHEW, our target text, has strong Church-political overtones as well, most obvious in the "You are Peter" passage of 16:17-19. We will forego further comment on this subject at this time, however, since the nature and intent of Matthew's treatment of Peter as a potential Church leader will constitute the major burden of this book in the pages and chapters that follow.

A final New Testament circumstance deserves consideration. As Terrence V. Smith in his 1985 work on *Petrine Controversies in Early Christianity*[28] suggests, the two anachronous epistles credited to Peter may well have been accepted into the New Testament canon specifically to afford the first disciple a literary role balancing at least to some extent the predominance of Paul's genuine letters and the deutero-Pauline pastoral epistles. As 2 Peter 3:16 observes rather judgmentally, Paul's writings contain "some things . . . hard to understand."

[28]On 1 PETER, see T. Smith, *Controversies* (1985) 150–156, and Feine, Behm, Kümmel, *Introduction to the New Testament,* 14th ed. (1965) 297ff. On 2 PETER, cf. T. Smith, *Controversies,* 65–101; and Feine, Behm, Kümmel, *Introduction,* 302ff.

Even after the deaths of the disciples/apostles, in the post-biblical world, their memories were able to serve as tangible models with which the faithful could identify. As such, these heroes of the faith could posthumously continue to provide the fledgling Christian movement with substance, structure, character, and continuity. Unfortunately, partisan loyalties also continued to complicate the process, theologically and organizationally.[29]

Consistent with Paul's Galatians 2:11ff. recollection of his confrontation with Peter in Antioch, an early tradition preserved by the second-century Alexandrian theologian Origen, as previously noted, records that the first disciple later became the first bishop of the Christian community in that same Syrian city.[30] Although the "bishop" ascription may have been a bit premature, there is no reason to doubt that Peter spent some time in Antioch in the 50s of the first Christian century, preceding either Evodius, an otherwise unknown figure, or St. Ignatius, or both, as leader of the Christian community there.[31]

If this is true, however, it is perhaps noteworthy and not a little surprising that Ignatius, while quite clearly familiar with MATTHEW, or at least MATTHEAN traditions, never refers to Peter as his predecessor in any of his famous seven letters to the Churches of Asia Minor. Nor does he ever quote Matthew 16:13-19 in support of his well-known efforts to establish the mon-

[29]We also see some of the urgency of the situation in the selection of Matthias as the replacement for Judas in Acts 1:21.

[30]Cf. Origen, "Homily on Luke," VI, c, J.-P. Migne, *Patrologiae,* Series Graece, XIII, col. 1814ff. According to *A Catholic Dictionary,* ed. Donald Attwater (1958) 381, the western Church, except for the Benedictines, observes Peter's episcopal ascendancy at Antioch annually on February 22. Philip H. Pfatteicher, *Festivals and Commemorations* (1980) 52f., acknowledges that in more recent years many Churches have combined this observance with that of Peter's elevation at Rome on January 18. Traditionally, this date was known as the Festival of the Chair of Peter. Today, it is observed more universally as the Festival of the Confession of Peter which initiates the Week of Prayer for Christian Unity, January 18–25.

[31]*The Oxford Dictionary of the Christian Church,* 2nd ed., eds. F. L. Cross and E. A. Livingstone (1957) sub voce, 688, estimates Ignatius' elevation c. 69 C.E. Glanville Downey, *A History of Antioch* (1961) p. 286, suggests an intervening twenty-nine-year "episcopate" of Evodius, delaying Ignatius' elevation to c. 83 C.E. If these dates are correct, MATTHEW must have been written during Ignatius' episcopacy.

episcopacy as the God-ordained polity for his Church. Why not? The proposed Petrine precedents would surely have helped his cause, and he certainly had ample opportunity.[32]

Several of the forty-eight tractates found among the thirteen-volume Gnostic library discovered at Nag Hammadi, Egypt, in 1945,[33] reflect an even more polemical character, indicating that Peter remained locked in a Church-political battle for supremacy in the role of patron saint or mythopoeic patriarch in many second- to fourth-century rival Christian/Gnostic communities, especially in the East. Here Peter's chief competitors interestingly enough were Paul, James, and Thomas. Paul was championed especially by the proto-Gnostic, Marcion.[34] Those who favored a dynastic and hierarchical polity, on the other hand, proposed James and Judas Thomas, both of whom were projected as brothers of Jesus in *The Gospel of Thomas.*[35] Saying #12 in this work, for example, reads:

> The disciples said to Jesus: We know you will go away from us. Who is it that will (then) be great over us? Jesus said to them: In the place to which you have come, you will go to James the Just, for whose sake heaven and earth came into existence.

[32]An ideal location to quote Matthew 16:17-19 would have been "Smyrneans" 9:1.

[33]*The Nag Hammadi Library in English,* gen. ed. James M. Robinson (1977). For a handy review of this and other related literature, see T. Smith, *Controversies* (1985). R. Pesch, *Simon Petrus* (1980) covers essentially the same material in German. A new work by Robert B. Eno, *The Rise of the Papacy* (1990) focuses on Patristic evidence.

[34]Marcion was a super-Paulinist heretic from Pontus in Asia Minor. He died ca. 160 C.E. He is credited with compiling one of the first "New Testament" canons, consisting of ten letters ascribed to Paul and the Gospel of Luke—all purged of any leanings toward Judaism. He established a movement which rivaled the developing "catholic" Church in the late second and third centuries. Tertullian was the chief adversary of Marcionism in the mid-third century. Cf. Virgilius Ferm, *An Encyclopedia of Religion* (The Philosophical Library, New York, 1945) 468. Also Tertullian, "Adversus Marcionem" 4:3, 2. Also footnote 14, 142 of Jurgens' *The Faith of the Early Fathers,* and Jaroslav Pelikan, *The Emergence of the Catholic Tradition 100–600,* vol. 1 (1971) 113.

[35]See the "Gospel of Thomas" trans. B. M. Metzger in *Synopsis Quattuor Evangeliorum,* ed. Kurt Aland, 7th ed. (1971) 517–530. Judas Thomas is here presented as Jesus' twin brother. Cf. Matthew 13:55 for a reference to Judas as a "brother" of Jesus and to John 11:16 for the identification of Thomas as the "Twin."

The reconstructed text of the so-called *Kerygmata Petrou,* on the contrary, promoted Peter depicting him as successfully engaging in a series of debates and contests with Simon Magus, the infamous magican of Acts 8:9-24, but usually identified here as a surrogate for Paul.[36]

It wasn't until late in the second century and early in the third that European and North African proponents recaptured Peter for the western, Latin, Church. By that time, Rome had become established as the site of Peter's martyrdom.[37] Aided and abetted by a developing theory of apostolic succession,[38] it was a relatively easy step to credit the Roman bishop with all the powers and privileges of his distinguished predecessor.

Significantly, however, it was not the Roman bishops who first made these claims for themselves. Rather, it was Irenaeus, the renowned bishop of Lyons, in Gaul,[39] and two North African

[36]The "Kerygmata Petrou" is a hypothetical document reconstructed from the "Pseudo-Clementine Homilies." See T. Smith, *Controversies,* 59–61; also Hennecke-Schneemelcher, *Apocrypha,* 94–127. Other Petrine literature includes the "Preaching of Peter," "Gospel of Peter," "Acts of Peter," "Acts of Peter and the Twelve Apostles," "The Epistle of Peter to Philip," etc. See Smith, *Controversies* (1985); R. Pesch, *Simon-Petrus* (1980) and Hennecke-Schneemelcher, *Apocrypha* (1964).

[37]Cf. O. Cullmann, *Peter, Disciple-Apostle-Martyr* (1953, 2nd rev. ed. 1962). In chap. 3, "Peter the Martyr," 71–157, Cullmann reviews the literary, historical, and archeological evidence in support of the tradition that Peter died in Rome. *A Catholic Dictionary,* ed. Donald Attwater (1958) 381, dates Peter's martyrdom in 67 C.E. Cf. also D. W. O'Connor, *Peter in Rome* (1969).

[38]The concept, or doctrine, of apostolic succession is central to the polity of the Roman Catholic, Anglican, Episcopal, and Orthodox Churches. It provides that Jesus in commissioning his apostles in Matthew 28:18-20, and Peter specifically in Matthew 16:17-19, imbued them with a special charism, or authority of office, which they, in turn, passed on to their successors by the laying on of hands. Ordinarily only such properly ordained clergy are authorized to administer the sacraments and rites of the Church. There are various adaptations of this teaching among other episcopally structured denominations. Non-episcopal Churches usually stress the "priesthood of all believers," (1 Pet 2:9) according to which all Christians technically share all the spiritual privileges, but delegate them to the clergy for their public performance. This is generally known as a "Call System." Hans Küng discusses the Apostolic Succession at length in *Structures of the Church* (1964) 154–190.

[39]Irenaeus, "Against Heresies," *The Ante-Nicene Fathers,* III,18,4 and III,21,8. Also Pelikan, *Emergence* (1971) 118. Irenaeus quotes only Matthew 16:17 in support of his thesis.

bishops, Tertullian and Cyprian,[40] who, while under attack from divergent elements at home and Gnostic forces in the East, opted to champion their western compatriot in Rome as possessing superior ecclesiastical qualifications and authority.

The cause was helped along considerably when Optatus, bishop of Numidia, North Africa,[41] coined the linguistically ludicrous, but winsomely powerful sequence: *Cephas* (transliterated form for the Aramaic *Keepha,* Peter/rock), *Cephalee* (Greek for "head"), *Caput* (Latin for the pontifical hood). It was the equivalent of "Peter = Preeminence = Pope," only in three different languages. The alliteration, we can imagine, was cacophanous for the educated, but clever and irresistibly appealing to the masses.

In mid-third century, Pope Stephen I was the first Roman bishop explicitly to appropriate to himself and to his see all the accumulated prerogatives of Peter.[42] In effect, he became a Peter redivivus, the Peter of Matthew 16:17-19 reborn. With that, the Church-political case for Petrine primacy in the West was successfully on its way.

The exegetical underpinning for such action, however, would take a little longer—more than one thousand years, as a matter of fact. Following the lead of the celebrated bishop of Hippo, St. Augustine, the dominant interpretation of Matthew 16:18 for centuries taught that the "rock" upon which Christ would build his Church referred to Christ himself or at least to Peter's confession of Christ as "the Son of the living God" in Matthew

[40]Tertullian, "Adversus Marcionem," 4,21,6; 22,6; 34,16. Cyprian, "The Dress of Virgins," in *Saint Cyprian, Treatises, The Ante-Nicene Fathers.* These two bishops emphasize Matthew 16:18-19. Later, Tertullian became a Montanist and rescinded all former allegiances to Rome. Cf. W.H.C. Frend, *The Early Church* (1965, 1982) 81. Also Pelikan, *Emergence* 101. Re Cyprian, see his "Unity of the Church," chap. 4. Also, Pelikan, *Emergence* (1971) 119. Like Tertullian, Cyprian also later modified his position observing that all the disciples in Matthew 18:18 received the same powers as Peter.

[41]Bishop Optatus of Numidia, Liber 2, "Contra Parmenian," in Migne, *Patrologiae,* Series *Latina,* 11, 974A. Also Yves Congar, "Céphas-Cephalè-Caput," in *Revue Du Moyen Age Latin,* 8 (1952) 5–42.

[42]Stephen I was the bishop of Rome from 254–257 C.E. T. Smith, *Controversies,* 20f. and O. Cullmann, *Peter* (1953) 217–222, believe it may have been an even earlier bishop of Rome, Callistus, 217–222 C.E., who claimed the Petrine prerogatives.

16:16.[43] Luther and Calvin championed essentially this same view in Reformation times.[44] But then in the period of the Counter-Reformation came an entirely different and yet definitive answer in the incisive observation of the Roman Catholic scholar Robert Cardinal Bellarmine.[45] He reasoned that the best explanation of the perplexing Greek gender dissonance in Matthew 16:18, where *petra,* "rock," a feminine noun, has no identifiable antecedent even though it appears to relate to *Petros,* the masculine proper name, "Peter," is to understand that an original Aramaic source must have existed behind the translated Greek text. In Aramaic, the language spoken in Palestine during Jesus' lifetime, both the words for "Peter" and "rock," *Keepha . . . keepha,* are masculine. *Petros,* then, could well be the intended antecedent for *petra.* On this basis Bellarmine concluded that Jesus had in fact designated Peter as the rock upon which he, Christ, would build his Church, giving to this celebrated disciple the keys to the Kingdom of Heaven. This explanation and interpretation made good exegetical sense. With that, the concept of the "Petrine Office" was now not only Church-politically, but also theologically, well-grounded.

[43]St. Augustine, "The Retractions," Book 1, chap. 20, in *The Fathers of the Church,* 60, 90. See also Jean de Launoy, "Epistola VII, Gulielmo Voello," in *Omnia Opera,* Tom 5, 101–115. Launoy, in 1666, reviewed all available writings of the Church Fathers, East and West. He found that forty-four Fathers had identified *petra* with Peter's confession in Matthew 16:16, seventeen with Peter himself, sixteen with Christ, and eight as designating all the disciples. Launoy's findings, of course, were hotly disputed.

[44]According to Luther's hermeneutic principle which provided that only "Scripture interprets Scripture," the "rock" in Matthew 16:18 must refer to Christ since it clearly does so in 1 Corinthians 10:4c. Cf. *Luther's Works* (1970) vol. 39, 86f., "On the Papacy in Rome," trans. Eric W. and Ruth C. Gritsch; vol. 40, 325f., "The Keys," trans. Earl Beyer and Conrad Bergendorf; and in the same volume, 27, "Concerning the Ministry," trans. Conrad Bergendorf. Calvin's comment is that if Peter is the rock it must be in the sense of a "living stone" as mentioned in 1 Peter 2:5. Cf. John Calvin, *Institutes of the Christian Religion,* 2, IV, VI, 372. For a general discussion of Petrine literature in Reformation times, see Bernard Ramm, "The Exegesis of Matt. 16: 13-20 in the Patristic and Reformation Period," *Foundations,* 5 (1962) 206–216.

[45]Robertus Bellarminus, "De summo pontifice," Tom 1, *Operum,* 542–577. Cf. also Joseph A. Burgess, *A History of the Exegesis of Matthew 16:17-19 from 1781 to 1965* (1976) 58–59. For an interesting biography read James Broderick *Robert Bellarmine* (1961).

Even many Protestant theologians had to agree.[46] At least Bellarmine's solution left the fundamental doctrine of biblical inerrancy intact. Although the Roman Catholic claims for papal primacy were rejected out of hand, the Petrine office, as a concept, tended to lend legitimacy also to Protestant clericalism and Church polity, even where the supporting traditions of apostolic succession and hierarchical structure were not present.

What had begun as a humble quest for localized religious integrity and stability in the early Antiochan Church had in succeeding centuries become nothing short of a Church-political phenomenon of global significance. Assisted along the way by the niceties of scholastic systematic theology and later Thomistic dogmatic theology,[47] plus a few more questionable but opportunistic medieval inventions, such as the "Pseudo-Isidoran Decretals" and the "Donations of Constantine,"[48] a kind of Petrine apotheosis took place. The past became present and reified in universal proportions. Peter become Pope, the "Prince of the Apostles" and the "Vicar of Christ." As such, he had found a new home in Rome, making it the religious capital of the world. "Peter's bark" (cf. Matt 14:30) became the Church and the big fisherman a secular monarch, ruling for a while over several papal states[49]

[46]Especially exegetical scholars. It is the only possibility that makes grammatical sense.

[47]"Thomistic theology" refers to the writings of Thomas Aquinas, especially his *Summa Theologiae,* which is viewed as the standard authority in the Roman Catholic Church. Aquinas is often esteemed as the "Angelic Doctor."

[48]Around 850 C.E. a collection of canons passed by earlier councils began to circulate. The collator is unknown, but the work was erroneously attributed to Bishop Isidore of Seville. The list contained both genuine and forged decretals. Significantly, the forged ones were attributed to first-century councils and bishops and ascribed special powers and privileges to the clergy as prescribed by Peter and other apostles. One of the forged documents is referred to as the "Donation of Constantine." It quotes Emperor Constantine as bequeathing jurisdictional powers to the priests, also properties, in the West. The forgeries, now acknowledged, were very helpful in the ninth and tenth centuries in supporting various pontifical claims, especially authority over secular rivals. Cf. *Lutheran Cyclopedia,* ed. in chief, Erwin L. Leuker (1954) 861f.

[49]A band of states stretching across the "leg" of Italy which were, off and on, under the control of the popes from the eighth to the nineteenth centuries. They originated as the "Donation of Pepin," King of the Franks. The accompanying secular involvements on the part of several popes during this extended period proved to be an embarrassment to the Church.

and even today over Vatican City.[50] The son-in-law of Mark 1:30 suddenly became celibate. And finally, in a particularly controverted action, the aborted Vatican Council I of 1869–1870[51] declared the successors of Peter infallible when speaking *ex cathedra*[52] in matters of faith and morals. Peter had come a long way from the courtyard of Caiaphas' judgment hall (Mark 14:66ff.).

It should be noted that immense good was accomplished along the way by this appropriation of Petrine prerogatives and the centralization of power in the Roman see. The Roman pontiffs in large measure fulfilled the imperial role in the West when Emperor Constantine chose to move his capital east to Constantinople in 324 C.E.[53] Much of classical Roman culture was preserved. Vast areas of the world were Christianized.[54] The liturgical heri-

[50]The official residence of the pope and the site of St. Peter's Basilica located on Vatican Hill on the banks of the Tiber River in Rome. These 108.7 Vatican City acres are all that is left of the papal states. According to a Treaty of Conciliation and Concordat (1929 and 1947) signed with the Italian government, the popes retain sovereignty over Vatican City and receive an annual endowment from the state for its maintenance.

[51]The council was aborted because of the outbreak of the Franco-Prussian War. Fifty-six bishops had left before the canon on infallibility was passed. Canon 218, 1, reads:

"The Roman Pontiff, the successor to the primacy of Saint Peter, not only has the primacy of honour but the supreme and juridical power over the universal Church in regard to faith and morals as well as in what pertains to discipline and government of the Church which is spread through the whole world. 2. This power is truly episcopal power, ordinary and immediate, over each and every individual church as well as over each and every one of the pastors and faithful, and independent of any human authority." The Council was never reconvened.

[52]"From the official chair, or seat of authority." The privilege has been used infrequently, but its mere existence in the background adds considerable force to all papal pronouncements and encyclicals. This "chair" concept has also assumed great liturgical significance in Roman Catholicism. In a bronze monument above the altar in the apse of St. Peter's Basilica is a chair which is said to have been used by Peter while serving as bishop. In some areas, January 18 is still celebrated as the Feast of St. Peter's Chair marking the traditional date of Peter's assumption of the episcopal office in Rome.

[53]Cf. M. Cary and H. H. Scullard, *A History of Rome,* 3rd ed. (1975) 524. For more detail on this period, cf. W.H.C. Frend, *The Early Church* (1965, 1982) 219–224.

[54]The most familiar names to come to mind are the legendary St. Patrick (389–461) who is credited with the conversion of Ireland; St. Augustine of Can-

tage of the Christian Church was immeasurably enriched.[55] Ecumenically speaking, the Roman pontiff for centuries was the most successful symbol of Christian unity history has known. Through the years, the "Holy Father" has stood as a stabilizing force around the world lifting up concerns for peace, hope, and human rights.

Unfortunately, today one also hears the anguished cries of some Catholic liberationist theologians,[56] scholars whose academic freedom has been breached,[57] and advocates for lay and women's rights in the Church who have come to consider Rome an insensitive and oppressive ecclesiastical power. For many, the "Pontifex Maximus," i.e., the "Great Bridge-builder," has become a roadblock to social, theological, and ecumenical progress.[58]

terbury (died 604 C.E.), who did the same for England; Jacque Marquette (1637–1675) in mid-western United States and Eusebio Fransisco Kino (1645–1711) in Arizona and the American Southwest.

[55]We think of the pericopic system of prescribed daily and Sunday Scripture readings credited to St. Jerome (347–420); The order of the Roman Mass, which developed between the fourth and the seventh centuries, and remains basic to most western liturgical worship; Gregorian music, or plainsong, named after its patron compiler, Pope Gregory I (540–604), was used for worship almost exclusively between the fourth and twelfth centuries and remains the basis for most religious chants today. Cf. sub voce, *Lutheran Cyclopedia* (1954) and Ferm, *An Enclyclopedia of Religion* (1945).

[56]Fr. Leonardo Boff, a Brazilian Franciscan priest and a noted exponent of liberation theology, was silenced for one year on May 9, 1985, for comments critical of the hierarchical structure in the Roman Catholic Church made in his book *Church, Charism and Power* (1985).

[57]New Testament scholar Anton Vögtle received a *monitum* in 1961. In 1979 the heralded theologian and scholar Hans Küng, had his authorization to teach as a member of the Roman Catholic faculty at Tübingen withdrawn. Charles Curran, moral theologian at The Catholic University in Washington, D.C., was also forbidden to teach in 1987. Another popular priest, Fr. Matthew Fox, was similarly silenced for one year, 1988–1989. While this book was in preparation in the summer 1990, a further furor developed over a new Vatican document banning public dissent from established Roman Catholic doctrine on the part of Roman Catholic clergy and theologians. Cf. "Instruction on the Ecclesial Vocation of the Theologian" issued by the Congregation for the Doctrine of the Faith in Rome on May 24, 1990.

[58]On April 28, 1967, Pope Paul VI admitted: "The Pope, as we well know, is undoubtedly the gravest obstacle in the path of ecumenism." Cf. J.M.R. Tillard, O.P., in *The Bishop of Rome* (1985) 17–18.

Some negative effects of Petrine clericalism are felt throughout Protestant Christendom as well, especially, perhaps, among ecumenists who while encouraged by so much interdenominational cooperation in recent years consistently find their further efforts to build community stymied when it comes to questions of legitimate ministry and ecclesial authority.

Of greater importance for our immediate exegetical purposes, however, is the development of what I have come to refer to as the "Matthew 16:17-19 syndrome." This "You are Peter" text, supported by Luke 22:32 and John 21:15-19, has itself become the bedrock upon which the massive Petrine edifice has been built, directly or indirectly affecting concepts of Church polity and ministry in many, if not all, denominations. This text is often read at the ordination of pastors and at the elevation of bishops and popes. It is used to undergird and legitimize official ecclesiastical statements and actions. Appropriately, the words from verse 18: "You are Peter and on this rock I will build my church," are engraved in gold around the cupola of St. Peter's Basilica in Rome.[59] This passage has become so inviolate and institutionalized that one feels guilty, even unscholarly, just to question it. It is so dominant as the cornerstone of the Petrine office that any attempt to reinterpret it is normally either ignored or constrained to conform. The literature brims with examples.[60]

After all that has been said, then, it is no wonder that in any discussion of Peter in MATTHEW, or anywhere else for that matter, the first disciple will almost always dominate the conversation. His stature, achieved and ascribed, is too pervasive and imposing to avoid. We shall have to try to control the temptation to be intimidated by this Petrine phenomenon if we are to remain objective in our exegetical research and review. There will

[59]Cf. Hans Conzelmann, *History of Primitive Christianity* (1973) 42.

[60]Note the unproved euphemistic references to Peter as "archetypal man of faith," H. B. Green, *Matthew* (1975) 248; as "representative disciple," in Daniel Patte, *The Gospel According to Matthew* (1985) 212; Even the word "variegated," to describe MATTHEW's Petrine passages in Brown, Donfried and Reumann, *Peter in the New Testament* (1973) 107, seems an unnecessarily guarded term for "contradictory." Perhaps most obvious is the hasty retreat by Augustine Stock, "Is Matthew's Presentation of Peter Ironic?" *Biblical Theology Bulletin* 17 (1989) 68: Cf. chap. 2, p. 35, below.

be occasion enough in chapter 8 to discuss further the Church-political implications of our conclusions re the role of Peter in MATTHEW for Church dogma, practice and inter-Church relations today.

This cursory reprise of the principals—MATTHEW, Matthew and Peter—reveals that what we are dealing with in broad terms in this book is a Gospel which most scholars assume is quite well-known and understood, an author about whose identity and perspective there is still some question, and a larger-than-life subject overburdened with complicating extraneous baggage of an extremely sensitive Church-political nature.

The time has now come for a statement of the problem in more specific, exegetical terms.

2

The Problem in Detail

At issue in this research is what the editors Brown, Donfried, and Reumann, in the 1973 publication *Peter in the New Testament* cautiously refer to as the "variegated" portrayal of Peter in MATTHEW,[1] or what Joachim Jeremias in 1971 less discretely described as the "juxtaposition of conflicting traditions" about Peter in the first Gospel.[2] A brief glance at the Visualization (fig. 1, 25)[3] will illustrate what they had in mind.

The MATTHEAN depiction of Peter is a literary, emotional, and theological rollercoaster for anyone who sensitively reads the First Gospel cover-to-cover. Using a hypothetical "Plain of Discipleship" to denote what might be expected as appropriate behavior for a disciple, the Visualization reveals that in Peter's case negatives follow positives with dizzying rapidity. Blessings turn

[1]*Peter in the New Testament,* eds. Raymond Brown, Karl Donfried, and John Reumann (1973) 107.

[2]Joachim Jeremias, *New Testament Theology I,* trans. John Bowden (1971) 307, n. 1. This footnote was determinative in motivating me to research the role of Peter in Matthew. It said to me that as late as 1971 the MATTHEAN passages so long assumed to be basic to the Petrine office were still not understood. In other words, the celebrated Petrine office which undergirds the ecclesial systems espoused by most of Christendom to one degree or another was itself built on stilts! The question begged for comprehensive research.

[3]This visualization is admittedly somewhat subjective and personal. It represents my reading of the Petrine portrayal in MATTHEW. It is intended to provide a frame of reference for the reader who may raise or lower the convolutions "to taste."

Figure 1

Visualization: Peter in MATTHEW

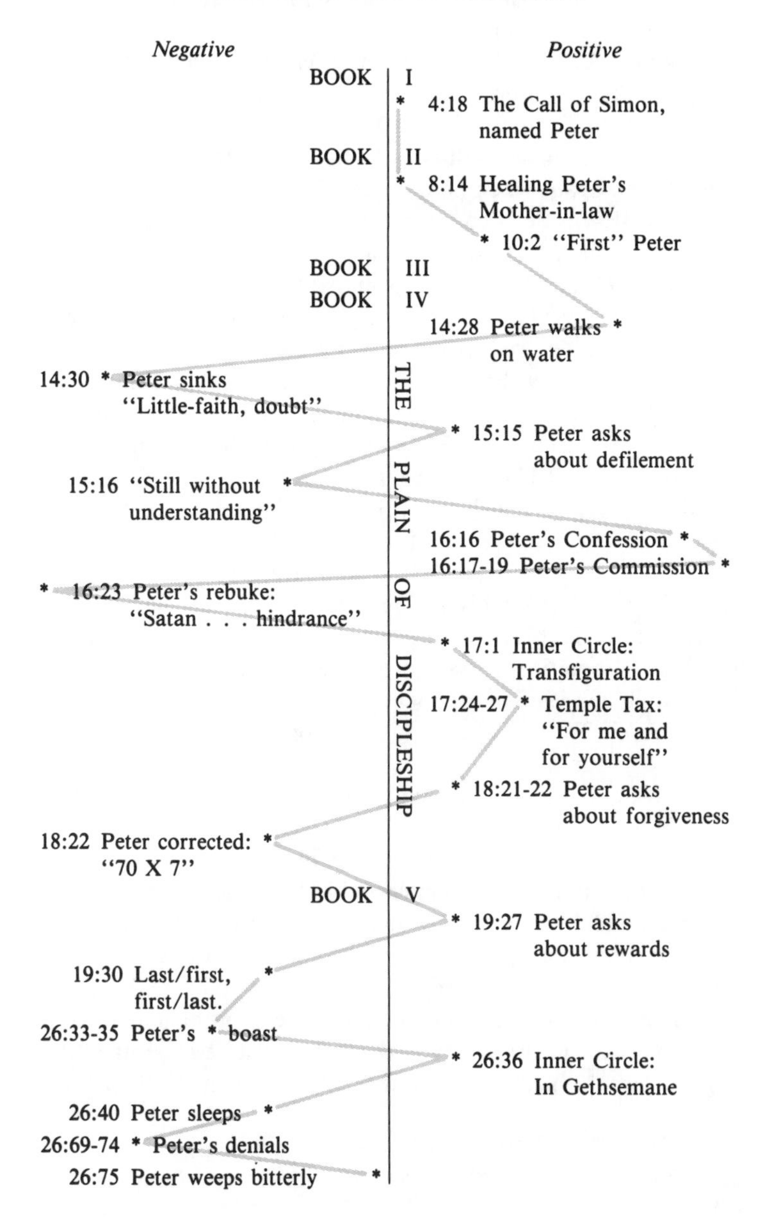

to curses and confessions to denials. What began with promises (4:18f.) ends literally in tears (26:75).

Only in MATTHEW is Peter specifically designated "first," 10:2, but then omitted from any active role in the accounts of the crucifixion, resurrection, or post-Easter Church. Only in MATTHEW is Peter credited with the ability to walk on water only to sink again when he observes the wind (14:28-30)! Only in MATTHEW is Peter commended as personally inspired by God (16:17) and then, just six verses later, condemned as Satan and a "hindrance" (16:23, RSV). Only in MATTHEW is the authority to "bind and loose" given exclusively to Peter, in 16:19, and then, two chapters later, redistributed to all the disciples, in 18:18.

Another curiosity the Visualization suggests is the concentration of Petrine references in chapters 14 to 18, corresponding to MATTHEW'S traditional Book IV. Eight of the fifteen Petrine pericopes in MATTHEW appear in these five chapters alone.

What is going on here? Why this special interest in Peter in the first place? Why such radical fluctuation in portrayal? Why the focus on Peter in one section and comparative nonchalance toward him in others? How did Matthew really want his readers to view Peter? Is this another example of what David Orton detects as a "dramatic reversal" in Matthew's literary art,[4] or what Bruce Malina, a leading exponent of applying social science categories to New Testament study, calls "normative dissonance" in nascent Christianity?[5]

One would have thought that with all the ink—to say nothing of the blood—spilled on the subject of Peter through the centuries, and with all the confident claims by his proponents of his preeminence among the disciples and in the Church, these questions would all have been answered beyond any doubt long ago. But such is not the case, not even with these most fundamental, and most frequently quoted passages found only in the First Gospel. Whether we like it so, or not, the Peter problem in MATTHEW persists. Georg Strecker, the highly regarded German theologian, calls the inconsistent description of Peter in Matthew *"ein*

[4]Cf. David Orton, *The Understanding Scribe* (1989) 156.

[5]Cf. Bruce J. Malina, "Normative Dissonance and Christian Origins," *Semeia,* 35 (1986) 35–55.

noch offenes Problem," a still open question.[6] Our analysis and discussion, then, are not only timely, but urgent.

Representative Responses

Undoubtedly, the best evidence of this lingering exegetical discomfort with past and prevailing interpretations of the role of Peter in MATTHEW is seen in the number and diversity of proposed scholarly solutions to the quandary. The following is a cursory review of some of the most representative.

First, of course, there is the accepted traditional answer, more dogmatic than exegetical, previously described as the Matthew 16:17-19 syndrome.[7] It piously assumes that Matthew, the disciple/evangelist, was an eye-witness of the events which he faithfully recorded in the First Gospel. As for Peter, he had his faults. Yet, despite all, he was the first disciple and the one who possessed divinely inspired and delegated ecclesiastical authority. MATTHEW, accordingly, is a pro-Peter Gospel with 16:17-19 the dominant passage—naming and commissioning Peter as the head of the Church. Everything else about Peter in the First Gospel, and in the entire New Testament for that matter, is, therefore, to be understood as consistent with this central text. History, if nothing else, it is assumed, has proven this position correct. Who would contest the wisdom of the ages?

What is intellectually discomforting about this perspective is the tremendous subconscious hold this syndrome continues to exert upon many scholars who do not otherwise even subscribe to the concept of the Petrine office. For example, there is a widespread assumption, found most often in the commentaries, and in pastors' sermons, that everything Matthew included in his text he also unilaterally endorsed, that Peter's prominence in the First Gospel necessarily translates into his preeminence in the Church, and that what is proposed in one situation, or pericope, applies

[6]Georg Strecker, *Weg* (1971) 198. Erich Dinkler, "Die Petrus-Rom Frage," *Theologische Rundshau,* 25 (1959) 195, also says resignedly that any study focusing on the role of Peter in Matthew *bleibt unfruchtbar,* i.e., remains fruitless.

[7]Cf. chap. 1, p. 22, above.

in all.[8] Fortunately, the scholars whose views are summarized in the next paragraphs, did not, in general, succumb to this predilection.

The first real challenge to the entrenched view came late in the eighteenth century, and then understandably only anonymously. A German scholar, later identified as Friedrich Andreas Stroth, wrote an article entitled "On Interpolations in Matthew's Gospel" in which he suggested that since the Peter Walking on the Water episode (14:28-31) and the elevated 16:17-19 "You are Peter" passage did not appear in the other canonical Gospels, MARK, LUKE, or JOHN, they probably were not original but later additions to the text from early apocryphal writings dating from the period of emergent Catholicism.[9] This radical interpolationist perspective, as one can imagine, caused quite a theological stir. It would have provided a quick fix to the variegated portrait of Peter in MATTHEW, but since no early manuscripts of the First Gospel could be found which actually omitted these critical passages, support for Stroth's position soon waned. His challenge, however, at least served to break the thick ice of the centuries relative to the curious role of Peter in MATTHEW. It was an idea that in time would spawn numerous progeny.[10]

In the mid-nineteenth century the perspectives of the "Tübingen School" dominated the discussion. Using as a methodological guide the dialectics of Hegel, which tended to see all history and life in constant conflict between theses and antitheses, this

[8]Some of this orientation, of course, is also due to the parameters of the various exegetical methods employed. Form-criticism, for example, was preoccuppied with individual traditions and had little concept of the Gospels as literary wholes.

[9]Friedrich Andreas Stroth, "Von Interpolationem im Evangelium Matthäe," *Reportorium für Biblische and Morganländische Litteratur* (1781); Cf. also Burgess, *History,* 43–45 for a review of the Roman Catholic response by T. A. Dereser (Thaddaeus a S. Adamo), *Commentatio Biblica in effatum Christi, Matth. XVI 18, 19* (1789).

[10]Cf. Adolf von Harnack, "Tatian's Diatessaron und Marcion's Kommentar zum Evangelium bei Ephraem Syrus," *Zeitschrift für Kirchengeschichte,* 4 (1881) 484–485. For somewhat more recent examples, see W.L. Dulière, "La péricope sur le 'Pouvoir des clés," *La Nouvelle Clio,* 6 (1954) 76–90, and Henri Clavier, "Brèves Remarques sur less Commentaire Patristique de Matth. 16:18a," *Studia Patristique,* 1 (1957) 260–261.

Tübingen school under Ferdinand Christian Baur determined that a contest for dominance between Peter and Paul was the critical social and religious reality of the first and second centuries.[11] Each piece of New Testament literature, therefore, could be categorized on the basis of its *Tendenz,* i.e., whether it favored Peter or preferred Paul. Gustav Volkmar was a Tübingen scholar who focused on the Gospels. MATTHEW, largely on the basis of its Petrine negatives, Volkmar adjudged pro-Pauline.[12] Imagine the reaction generated by this revolutionary view.

The Tübingen perspective was represented somewhat belatedly in the United States in the writings of B. W. Bacon, a professor at Yale in the early twentieth century.[13] Using redaction-critical methods almost fifty years before their time, he studied the three larger uniquely MATTHEAN Petrine passages, 14:28-31, 16:17-19, and 17:24-27. His conclusion: Matthew, the evangelist, was portraying Peter as a surrogate Paul dispensing Pauline answers to questions and conditions prevailing in his MATTHEAN community.

B. H. Streeter, writing in the 1920s, thought he discovered a different dialectic.[14] The real contest, he surmised, was between the followers of Paul and those of James, the Lord's brother and bishop of Jerusalem (Acts 1:19). In MATTHEW, amid all the pros and cons, Peter was being presented as the compromise candidate to fill the leadership role in the Antiochan congregation.

Meanwhile, a new scholarly trajectory was forming on the European continent. The *Religionsgeschichtliche Schule,* or History-of-Religions School, was looking for parallels to New Testament conventions and phenomena in other primitive religions, mystery

[11]Ferdinand Christian Baur, "Die Christuspartei in der korintischen Gemeinde" (1831), printed in *Theologische Jahrbücher,* 10 (1851) 294–296. Also *Das Christentum und die Christliche Kirche der drei ersten Jahrhunderte* (1860) 126–131.

[12]Cf. G. Volkmar, *Die Religion Jesu* (1857) as discussed in T. Smith, *Controversies* (1985) 31f.

[13]B. W. Bacon, "Petrine Supplements in Matthew," *The Expositor,* 8th Series, 73 (1917) 1–23.

[14]B. H. Streeter, "The Petrine Compromise," in *The Four Gospels* (1930) 511-516. J. P. Meier in *Antioch & Rome* (1983) 57–72, adopts the same view calling it a Matthean Petrine "synthesis."

cults, and rites of homeopathic medicine.[15] They found several, including the use of sobriquets such as "Peter," and of thematic metaphors such as "keys" and "binding and loosing." In the long run, their discoveries did not contribute much to anyone's exegetical understanding of the texts except to cast doubt upon the originality, uniqueness, and significance of many of the MATTHEAN Petrine passages.

The celebrated Marburg professor Rudolf Bultmann was a student of the History-of-Religions School, but his primary interest and contribution was in the recognition, classification, and dating of various literary forms.[16] Accordingly, he concluded that the 16:17-19 passage, while a genuine response of Jesus to Peter's confession in Mark 8:27-29, originated in the post-Easter period of the Jerusalem Christian community where Peter's leadership as described in the early chapters of Acts subsequently became recognized. Matthew had simply misplaced the tradition, retrojecting it within Jesus' Galilean ministry. The conflicting nature of the Petrine accounts, however, did not trouble Bultmann unnecessarily. To form-critics, like himself, such inconsistency simply reflected the diverse origins of the various traditions which the evangelists rather mechanically reproduced.[17]

Bultmann's student Günther Bornkamm, took a different tack.[18] He contended that the 16:17-19 tradition could not have been original with Jesus because it presupposes the resurrection and the delayed *parousia,* or return of Christ. It was, therefore,

[15]Cf. Frederick Cornwallis Conybeare, *Myth, Magic and Morals, A Study of Christian Origins* (1910) 245–246. For an interesting exchange of views, see Otto Immisch, "Matthäus 16,18. Laienbemerkungen zu der Untersuchung Dells," *ZNW,* XV (1914) 1ff. and A. Dell, "Zur Erklärung von Matthäus 16:17-19," in *Zeitschrift für die neutestamentliche Wissenschaft und die Kunde des Urchristentums,* XVII, 1 (1916) 27–32.

[16]Rudolf Bultmann, *The History of the Synoptic Tradition,* trans. John Marsh (German, 1921, English, 1963) 5–7. Also "Die Frage nach dem messianishen Bewusstsein Jesus und das Petrus Bekenntnis," *Exegetica* (1967) 1–7 (first published in 1919–1920).

[17]This circumstance undoubtedly also prompted Jeremias' statement that "a redaction-critical analysis of the first Gospel cannot achieve success," *New Testament Theology,* vol. 1 (1971) 307, n. 1.

[18]Günther Bornkamm, "The Risen Lord and the Earthly Jesus, Matthew 28:16-20," *The Future of Our Religious Past* (1978) 203–229, esp. 220f.

a construct of early Palestinian Christianity. The ambiguity that appears in MATTHEW is the result of the theological clash which occurred when this Palestinian traditon interfaced with the more egalitarian, charismatically oriented Hellenistic Christianity.

In addition, Bornkamm attempted to resolve the apparent conflict between Jesus' bestowal of the power to bind and loose first upon Peter in 16:19, and then on the rest of the disciples in 18:18. In the first instance, he concluded, primarily on contextual grounds, that the power of the keys was general. Peter was given authority over the universal Church. While in the second case, only jurisdiction over local communities was intended.[19] While very attractive to systematic theologians, such a fine-line distinction, especially where the very same phraseology is employed, was exegetically unprovable.

Oscar Cullmann also took a page from Bultmann's book.[20] Using tradition-critical methods, he agreed that 16:17-19 was an original Jesus saying, but misplaced in MATTHEW. However, he believed it fit much better with the quasi-commissioning passage and situation described in Luke 22:31-34 where Jesus had told Peter, after his conversion, to "strengthen your brethren."

Cullmann deserves credit for producing the first comprehensive, book-length, exegetical and historical study of Peter in the New Testament. His intention to provide a framework for dialogue which could lead to increased ecumenical rapproachment between Protestants and Roman Catholics was also commendable.[21] But his efforts were short-lived. Redaction-criticism, as a new method of doing exegesis was capturing the scholarly limelight in those post-World War II years with such promising results

[19]Günther Bornkamm, "The Authority to 'Bind' and 'Loose' in the Church in Matthew's Gospel," *Jesus and Man's Hope,* 1 (1971) 37–50.

[20]Oscar Cullmann, *Peter, Disciple-Apostle-Martyr,* trans. Floyd V. Filson (1953; 2nd rev. ed., 1962).

[21]For the Roman Catholic response, see esp. Otto Karrer, "Apostolische Nachfolge und Primat. Ihre biblischen Grundlagen im Lichte der neueren Theologie," *Zeitschrift für Katholische Theologie,* 77 (1955) 129–168. For alternate Protestant/Roman Catholic responses see *Begegnung der Christen. Studien evangelischer und katholischer Theologen,* eds. Maximilian Roesle and Oscar Cullmann (1960). In English, see O. Karrer, *Peter and the Church, An Examination of Cullmann's Thesis* (1963).

that all prevailing assumptions, including Cullmann's, were up for review.

G. D. Kilpatrick was one of the first to publish a redaction-critical study of the First Gospel, including its Petrine portrayal.[22] He isolated the five uniquely MATTHEAN Peter passages, 14:28-30, 15:15, 16:17-19, 17:24-27, and 18:21, and concluded that in them Matthew consciously associated Peter with legal rulings in the Church.

Georg Strecker was more thorough and sensitive to Matthew's vacillating description of Peter.[23] The result of his study, accordingly, was a novel, double perspective: Matthew was stereotyping the disciples to correspond generally with the members of his own community while simultaneously depicting Peter to represent the typical individual Christian among them who displayed the same kind of negative and positive characteristics. For the first time, a serious attempt had been made to account for Matthew's apparent ambivalence in dealing with the first disciple.

Building on Strecker, the respected American MATTHEAN authority, Jack Dean Kingsbury, listed the many terms and phrases, traditional and redactional, in the First Gospel which served to parallel Peter and the disciples.[24] Matthew was certainly equating Peter with the Twelve. Nevertheless, the identification of Peter as "first" in 10:2 must be taken seriously. Matthew's personal view, therefore, according to Kingsbury, was that Peter was *primus inter pares,* the "first among equals," within the circle of his fellow disciples, and in Matthew's community.

In the final two decades of the twentieth century, biblical scholarship has again sought fresh insights through the use of new exegetical methodologies. Structural and rhetorical-criticism have now replaced redaction-criticism as the favored approach with many exegetes.[25] Both can be helpful techniques. In terms of the

[22]G. D. Kilpatrick, *Origins* (1946) 36–40.

[23]Georg Strecker, *Der Weg der Gerechtigkeit* (1962; 3rd expanded ed., 1971) 198–206.

[24]Among Kingsbury's many publications, the most significant for our purposes is "The Figure of Peter in Matthew's Gospel as a Theological Problem," *JBL,* 98, 1 (1979) 67–83.

[25]Cf. E. P. Sanders and Margaret Davies, *Studying the Synoptic Gospels* (1989) 224–251.

Matthean treatment of Peter in the First Gospel, however, little that is new or distinctive has surfaced to date. Daniel Patte's 1987 *The Gospel According to Matthew,* subtitled "Structural Commentary on Matthew's Faith," for example, is, from my perspective, remarkably traditional in this regard.[26] We shall have much more to say about rhetorical-critical contributions to our study later on.

Representative Responses: Roman Catholic

Most of the responses reviewed to this point have been those of Protestant scholars, or scholars whose religious commitments are unknown or incidental. The reason for such one-sidedness is due to the dogmatic restrictions placed upon Roman Catholic exegetes prior to 1943. In that year, however, Pope Pius XII issued the encyclical *Divino Afflante Spiritu* which permitted Catholic scholars henceforth to use the same exegetical methods and tools as their Protestant counterparts.[27] Roman Catholic authors were quick to catch up, and with their vested interest in the Petrine office did so with some of the most amazing results.

Anton Vögtle was probably the first to gain notoriety.[28] In 1957 he published a detailed, two-part study of Matthew 16:13-20 in which he argued that 16:17 commending Peter upon his confession was not an original saying of Jesus at all, but a redactionally composed passage based on 11:27. The idea never generated much excitement outside Catholic circles, but as an inside challenge to

[26]Daniel Patte, *The Gospel According to Matthew. A Structural Commentary on Matthew's Faith* (1987).

[27]"*Divino Afflante Spiritu,* Encyclical Letter on Promotion of Biblical Studies, Pope Pius XII," National Catholic Welfare Conference (September 30, 1943). It declares: "Let the interpreter then, with all care and without neglecting any light derived from recent research, endeavor to determine the peculiar character and circumstances of the sacred writer, the age in which he lived, the sources written or oral to which he had recourse and the forms of expression he employed," 18. Since the encyclical was issued during World War II, little note was taken of it at the time, but subsequently its import has been far-reaching indeed.

[28]Anton Vögtle, "Messiasbekenntnis und Petrusverheissung. Zur Komposition Mt. 16:13-23 par.," *Biblische Zeitschrift,* N.F. 1 (1957) 252–272, and 2 (1958) 85–103.

the very foundations of the inviolable Petrine office, it was intolerable. An official *monitum,* or admonition, was issued by the Vatican on June 20, 1961, to silence Vögtle and anyone with similar notions.[29] Once again the Petrine syndrome had prevailed.

But not for long. With the advent of Vatican Council II in 1962, the *monitum* was soon forgotten. A new window of academic freedom had opened. Clerical collegiality, rather than unilinear papal authority, was now under active consideration.[30]

In 1963 Paul Gaechter accordingly took courage to go a step beyond Vögtle and question whether the other two verses, 18 and 19, of Matthew 16, with their mixed metaphor of keys binding and loosing instead of opening and locking, could have been a true saying of the historical Jesus.[31]

A decade later, in June 1972, Hubert Frankemölle, while addressing the graduates of the department of Catholic theology at the University of Münster, posed an even more direct challenge to the traditional Petrine office by asking the rhetorical question: Is there criticism of ecclesial offices in MATTHEW?[32] The implied answer: In view of all the negatives heaped upon Peter in the First Gospel, it would certainly appear so. The first evangelist, then, was not only depicting Peter as an average individual Christian whose faith tended to vacillate, à la Strecker, but was apparently aiming his arrows directly at the religious leaders, the elders or overseers of the various house churches which together comprised the Antiochan Christian community and of whom better things should have been expected.

Similar sentiments have become relatively commonplace in the literature and among Roman Catholic exegetes since then. Perhaps most stunning, however, are the views expressed by Au-

[29]Cf. Burgess, *History,* 163.

[30]Vatican Council II opened in October 1962 and continued in two- or three-month segments each year until December 8, 1965. Cf. esp. "The Constitution of the Church," chap. 3, "Hierarchical Structure of the Church," in *De Ecclesia, The Constitution of the Church of Vatican Council II,* ed. Edward H. Peters (1965).

[31]Paul Gaechter, *Das Matthäus-Evangelium* (1963), sub. 16:17–19.

[32]Hubert Frankemölle, "Amtkritik im Matthäus-Evangelium?" *Biblica,* 54 (1973) 247–262.

gustine Stock, O.S.B., in his 1989 *Biblical Theology Bulletin* article entitled "Is Matthew's Presentation of Peter Ironic?" He says of the Peter/rock reference in 16:18:

> . . . Peter is anything but trustworthy bedrock on which one could build . . . Matthew's overall description of Peter suggests that he might more fittingly be likened to the loose sand of 7:24-27 that cannot bear the weight of a house. "This raises the suspicion that there is an ironic intention in v. 18, and, indeed, in the most extreme form of irony, where the words mean the opposite of what they seem to say. . . . "[33]
>
> Matthew's gospel presents a broad picture of Peter that can be summed up as "good beginning—poor ending."[34]

Once having voiced such devastating conclusions, however, Stock, undoubtedly sensing the threatening stares of the 16:17-19 syndrome, quickly retreats to the earlier wordplay on *prwtos/ Petros,* "first/Peter," in 10:2, and reassures his readers:

> Peter's position and prerogatives are too solidly grounded to be compromised by this discussion. When the evidence of the Second Testament as a whole is combined, it is legitimate to speak of "primacy" . . . It can also be argued that people indulge in ironic wordplay on the names of persons for whom they have affection rather than otherwise.[35]

[33]Augustine Stock, "Is Matthew's Presentation of Peter Ironic?" *Biblical Theology Bulletin* (1989) 66. Stock here affirms and quotes an address given by the Dutch Catholic theologian, Bas Van Iersel, delivered at Nijmegen, Holland, April 25, 1986.

[34]*Ibid.*, 68.

[35]*Ibid.*, loc. cit. J. P. Meier in *Antioch & Rome* (1983) 71f., expresses his discomfort even with his own understanding of Matthew's treatment of Peter, although he puts the blame on Matthew: "The ambivalence of Matthew's approach to church authority may be explained partly by the various traditions with which Matthew must work, partly by the fact that his church is a church in transition . . . but perhaps most of all by Matthew's own indecisiveness about how much authoritative leadership is good for his church. He admires the rock of 16:18-19 but seems unable or unwilling to have a local counterpart to this figure of universal ecclesiastical stability. Matthew's ambivalent treatment of church leadership may serve as a healthy reminder that we cannot expect the evangelist to have provid-

Stock's quandary may well summarize the persisting state of MATTHEAN scholarship as far as Peter is concerned. Major cracks have appeared in the traditional theological foundations of the Peter-phenomenon, yet the 16:17-19 syndrome tenaciously endures, continuing to victimize its adherents and detractors alike.

Another surprising evidence of the delicacy of this Peter problem in MATTHEW is that despite the number of studies listed above there is a continuing paucity of thorough, rigorous, exegetical analyses of the subject. Hundreds of thousands of pages employing devotional and systematic categories have been written on the exalted role of Peter in the Church, but nowhere to my knowledge, with the single exception of Cullmann's *Peter: Disciple-Apostle-Martyr* (1953, 1962), is this crucial issue of Peter in MATTHEW researched exegetically in larger compass than in a journal article or, perhaps, one chapter in a book. While doctoral dissertations have been written on Peter in MARK, LUKE-ACTS, JOHN, and PAUL,[36] there was none on Peter in MATTHEW before my own in 1983.[37] Why this avoidance? The topic is too fundamental in terms of comprehending MATTHEW and in furthering the cause of ecumenical relationships to permit the mere complexity of the problem or one's denominational investments to overwhelm one's exegetical inquisitiveness.

Statement of Thesis

It is my intention in this volume, therefore, to start over and try again to understand and identify Matthew's procedure, perspective and purpose in describing Peter in such apparently am-

ed a perfect solution to each and every problem that the crises at Antioch put before him."

[36]Cf. Teruo Kobayashi, "The Role of Peter According to the Theological Understanding of Paul, Mark, and Luke-Acts," microfilmed manuscript submitted to the Division of Biblical Studies in the Graduate School of Drew University, Madison, New Jersey (1962), and Wolfgang Dietrich, "Das Petrusbild der Lukanischen Schriften" (1972). Cf. also Kevin Quast, *Peter and the Beloved Disciple* (1989).

[37]Arlo J. Nau, "A Redaction-Critical Analysis of the Role of St. Peter in the Gospel of St. Matthew," submitted to the combined Biblical Studies Faculties of the Toronto School of Theology and the University of Toronto (1983).

bivalent terms. Along the way, several of the preceding scholarly suggestions will be further evaluated and either gratefully affirmed or regretfully discarded. In the end, by means of a comprehensive and methodologically consistent analysis, employing primarily redaction and rhetorical critical strategies, I believe it can be demonstrated that Matthew, artfully applying the rubrics of a mature form of "encomiastic dispraise," current in his day, is diplomatically seeking to neutralize Peter's traditional prominence within the Antiochan community, and to equate him with the other disciples, with the ultimate ecclesiological/Christological goal to present Jesus as the unrivaled head of the developing Church.

We now consider the evidence.

3

The Evidence: Source-Criticism

While redaction-criticism, focusing upon the contributions of Matthew, the redactor, or editor, will be the over-arching exegetical method employed in this study (cf. chap. 4), it does not stand alone. It cannot. Redaction-criticism is based on and assumes the prior discoveries of grammatical, textual, source, form, and tradition criticisms. In addition, in an investigation as comprehensive as this one, encompassing Matthew's treatment of Peter throughout the First Gospel, it will be necessary to incorporate many of the holistic perspectives of story, audience, and rhetorical analysis as well. In short, we will need to enlist the aid of every exegetical tool available to us.[1]

There are a few fundamental assumptions. The third editon of *The Greek New Testament,* edited by Aland, Black, Martini, Metzger, and Wikgren and published by the United Bible Society, 1966, will be accepted as the basic text. The Revised Standard Version of the Bible[2] as the most consistent English

[1]If unfamiliar with the various exegetical methods, cf. the Guides to Biblical Scholarship series, published by Fortress Press. Perhaps most helpful for this study: Edgar Krentz, *The Historical Critical Method*; Edgar V. Mcknight, *What is Form Criticism*?; Norman Perrin, *What is Redaction Criticism*?; and Burton L. Mack, *Rhetoric and the New Testament*. Also the well-written chapters on "Form Criticism" and "Redaction Criticism" in E. P. Sanders and Margaret Davies, *Studying the Synoptic Gospels* (1989) 123–223.

[2]*The Holy Bible*, Revised Standard Version (New Testament, 1946). The New Revised Standard Version of the Bible (1990) was released while this book was in preparation. Substantive changes in translation are noted in the text.

translation of the Greek text, and the version used by most commentators and in resource and reference works currently available, will also be employed to provide relevant quotations. Thirdly, together with the vast majority of New Testament scholars today, we shall adopt the Two-Source Hypothesis whereby MATTHEW is understood to have been composed in large measure from materials taken from MARK and the Sayings Source, Q, as the best answer to the so-called Synoptic Problem.[3] If, when and where there are alternatives worth considering they will be duly noted.

We begin in this chapter, then, by applying the rubrics of source-criticism as fundamental to our study. We need to know something about the origins and general character of the materials the editor—in this case the first evangelist—had on hand out of which to frame and fashion his Gospel. Fortunately, this is a relatively easy task with MATTHEW. Consistent with the Two-Source Hypothesis, MARK clearly provides the narrative framework for the First Gospel, and Q most of the teaching material. Together they comprise approximately 75 percent of MATTHEW, leaving only one quarter to be comprised of traditions from Matthew's own community and compositions from his own hand.[4]

[3]The Two-Source Hypothesis is undoubtedly the most popular solution to the Synoptic Problem dealing with the relationship between the Synoptic Gospels, MATTHEW, MARK, and LUKE. It theorizes that MARK and a "Sayings Source," called "Q," were the two written sources used by Matthew and Luke in compiling their Gospels. "Q" stands for the German: *Quelle*, "source." It is reconstructed from materials common to MATTHEW and LUKE, but not found in MARK. It consists largely of sayings attributed to Jesus: axioms, parables, commands, chriae. The Beatitudes, Matthew 5:3-12/Luke 6:20-23, and the Lord's Prayer, Matthew 6:9-15/Luke 11:2-4, belong to this double tradition. Cf. B. H. Streeter, *Oxford Studies in the Synoptic Problem* (1911); John S. Kloppenborg, *The Formation of Q* (Philadelphia, 1987). Chap. 3, 51–66, in E. P. Sanders and Margaret Davies, *Studying the Synoptic Gospels* (1989), illustrates the Two-Source Hypothesis. For a more detailed discussion of other proposals, see 67–119 in the same work.

[4]H. Benedict Green, *The Gospel According to Matthew* (1975) 3, says: "Mt reproduces 90% of the subject-matter of Mk in language largely identical with that of Mk." Paul Feine, Johannes Behm, Werner Georg Kümmel, *Introduction to the New Testament* (1966) 77, says: "Approximately half of Matthew has no parallel in Mark. Of this about five ninths is also found in Luke. The remaining four ninths is special material."

Peter in MARK

Approximately the same proportions, i.e., three fourths to two thirds, of the MARCAN Petrine references are retained in MATTHEW (cf. the Visualization of Peter in MARK, fig. 2, p. 41). MARK has fifteen pericopes, or vignettes, which involve Peter, or at least employ one of his names. Matthew reproduces ten of them:

1. The Call to Become Fishers of Men (Mark 1:16-20/Matt 4:18-22)
2. Healing Peter's Mother-in-law (Mark 1:29-31/Matt 8:14-17)
3. The Call of the Twelve Disciples (Mark 3:14-19/Matt 10:2-4)
4. Peter's Confession at Ceasarea Philippi (Mark 8:27-30/Matt 16:13-16)
5. The Satan-Saying (Mark 8:31-33/Matt 16:21-23)
6. The Transfiguration (Mark 9:2-8/Matt 17:1-8)
7. Peter Asks About Rewards (Mark 10:28-31/Matt 19:27-30)
8. Peter's Boast (Mark 14:26-31/Matt 26:30-35)
9. Asleep in Gethsemane (Mark 14:32-42/Matt 26:36-46)
10. Peter's Denials (Mark 14:66-72/Matt 26:69-75)

In addition, upon closer inspection, we note that one of the passages into which Matthew has inserted Peter by name, 15:15 (15:10-20), is also basically MARCAN. It is the pericope on What Defiles a Man. Here Matthew has simply exchanged Peter for MARK'S "disciples" as the one who asks Jesus to explain the parable.

Obviously, Matthew also omits, in whole or in part, five other MARCAN Petrine references:

1. Mark 1:35-38, Simon and the Disciples Search for Jesus
2. Mark 5:21-24, 35-43, The Healing of Jairus' Daughter
3. Mark 11:20-25, The Withered Fig Tree
4. Mark 13:3-4, The Prediction of the Destruction of the Temple
5. Mark 16:7, The Announcement at the Empty Tomb

What effect these omissions will have upon Matthew's Petrine portrayal, however, will have to be assessed later.

Looking back over the entire Petrine portrait in MARK, then,

Figure 2

Visualization: Peter in MARK

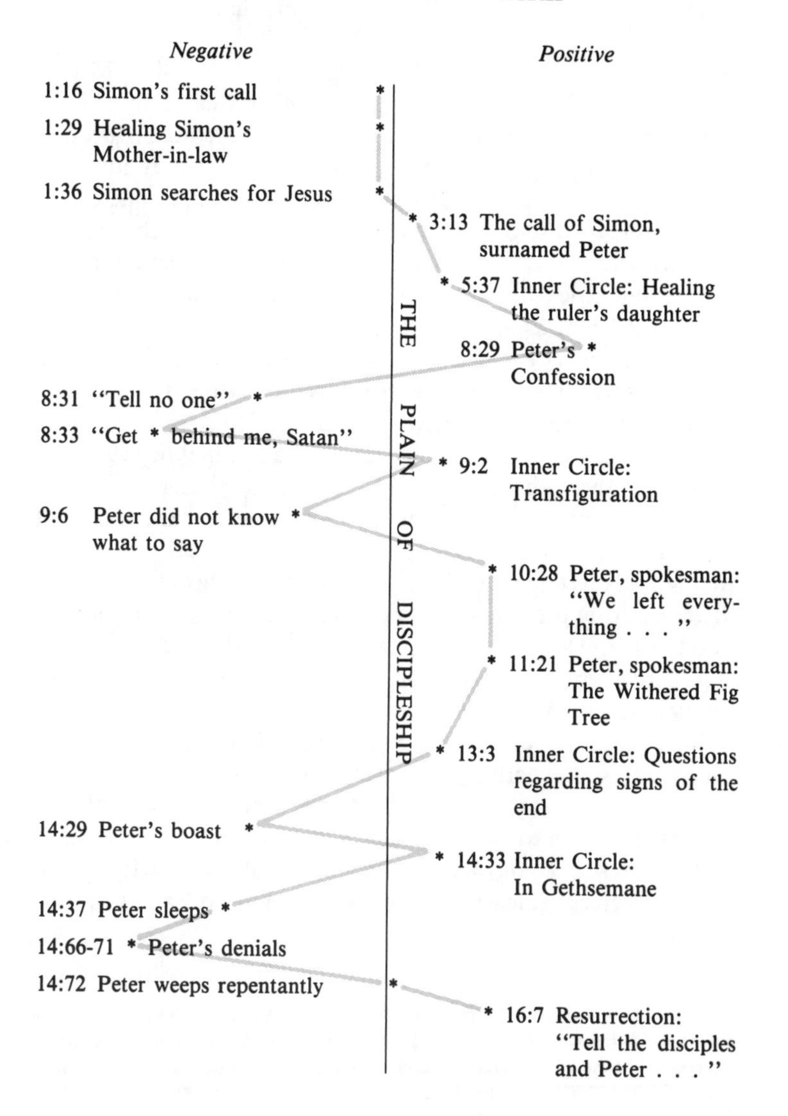

we are able to make a few other general and preliminary observations which may prove to be significant later on.

First, as the Visualization illustrates, references to the first disciple in the Second Gospel are quite evenly distributed. There is no particular concentration of Petrine references as we find in MATTHEW, chapters 14 to 18. On the other hand, since MARK is a much smaller Gospel consisting of only sixteen chapters, the fifteen vignettes involving Peter would seem to accord him proportionately greater prominence. Yet, surprisingly, such is not really the case. Several references simply identify Peter as one of the inner circle of disciples with James and John or as the spokesman for the twelve. These references give him some added exposure, but little real prominence. Comparatively little recognition is accorded him as an individual.

Second, much of the "shock quotient" of MATTHEW is missing in MARK. The roller coaster is less unnerving. True, Peter's confession of Jesus is rejected in Mark 8:30; he is put down as not knowing what to say at the transfiguration in 9:6; and he denies Jesus three times in 14:66-72, but still we seem not to be offended as much as we are by the Petrine negatives in the First Gospel. One reason for our dispassion undoubtedly is the fact that Mark's treatment of Peter here is not generically that much different from that imposed upon the other disciples in the Second Gospel. They fare no better. As part of the "Messianic Secret" programmatic in MARK, the disciples never understand.[5] Similar failures by Peter, therefore, come as no surprise.

Then, too, it is even more disarming to know that in MARK everything will eventually turn out all right for Peter. As Mark 16:7 relates, the messenger at the empty tomb gives special orders to the women to tell the disciples "and Peter" that the resurrected Jesus is going before them into Galilee. Obviously, in MARK, Peter is at least partially reinstated to his leadership role

[5] "Messianic secret" is a term coined by Wilhelm Wrede in a book of the same title (English trans., 1971; German ed., 1901). Much of Wrede's thesis is no longer accepted, but the term has remained in use as a handy way to describe the curious portrayal in MARK whereby the disciples never understand and are forbidden by Jesus to witness about him.

among the disciples in the post-Easter "Church" even after his denials.[6]

It will be interesting to see what Matthew does with these passages and with this MARCAN portrayal.

Peter in Q

Identifying Q materials is somewhat more difficult than was the case with MARK. There is no extant copy of Q available to use for purposes of direct comparison, aside from proposed scholarly reconstructions from texts common to MATTHEW and LUKE.[7] One cannot be absolutely sure, consequently, how the "original" Q actually read in all cases.

The text under study here is Matthew 18:21-22, the last of the five uniquely Matthean Petrine passages in the First Gospel.

On Reconciliation

LUKE 17:3-4	MATTHEW 18:21-22
(Jesus said:) [3]Take heed to yourselves; if your brother sins, rebuke him, and if he repents, forgive him;	
[4]and if he sins against you seven times in the day, and turns to you seven times, and says, 'I repent,' you must forgive him."	[21]Then Peter came up and said to him, "Lord, how often shall my brother sin against me, and I forgive him? As many as seven times?" [22]Jesus said to him, "I do not say to you seven times, but seventy times seven."

There can be little doubt but that this passage in MATTHEW shares a Q origin with Luke 17:3-4. Note the common references

[6]Eduard Schweizer, *The Good News According to Mark* (1970) 372, says this reference to Peter constitutes a second, or renewed call to discipleship. Cf. the similar reinstatements of Peter in Luke 24:34, John 21:15-17, 1 Corinthians 15:5.

[7]Unfortunately, for American readers, much of the early work on Q was done in German. Cf. Dieter Lührmann, *Die Redaktion der Logienquelle*, WMANT 33 (1969), Siegfried Schulz, *Q—Die Spruchquelle der Evangelisten* (1972). In English: Kloppenborg, *Formation* (1987). Cf. chap. 3, p. 39, n. 3, above.

to "brother," "sinning against," "seven times," and "forgiving," where the same, or cognate, Greek terms are used.[8]

What divergences do exist can in almost every case be accounted for in terms of Matthew's own editing. The opening "then," in Matthew 18:21 is found ninety times in the First Gospel, in most situations replacing MARK's *kai* ("and") parataxis linking one tradition with the next. The addition of "Peter" is clearly Matthean since the first evangelist inserts the name in at least four other places, as we have already observed, and because personal references are extremely rare elsewhere in Q as we know it.[9] It must be admitted, however, that replacing Jesus with Peter as the spokesperson here is an exceptionally daring bit of editorial license. "Came," or more correctly "coming," or "approaching," using the Greek present participle, *proselthwn,* is also a typical Matthean convention, appearing thirty-eight times. Finally, there is the vocative address "Lord" which Matthew employs on thirty occasions while Mark has it only twice.[10]

We are confronted with a reverse problem, however, when we observe that Matthew has no reference to "repenting" *metanoiein,* in Matthew 18:22 as does Luke 17:3, 4. Did Matthew omit the concept, or did Luke add it to the original Q source? We cannot be sure. The verb is found in both Q and in LUCAN redactional contexts.[11] Matthew, of course, reproduces it, too, in traditional settings,[12] but, interestingly, he nowhere adds it, or in any way indicates that repenting is of particular importance to him as a demand before community membership may be granted. As Robert Gundry has observed, the emphasis here is on the need of the sinned against brother to forgive rather than on the need

[8]Cf. Brown, et al., *Peter in the New Testament* (1973) 78. W. C. Allen, *Gospel According to S. Matthew* (1907) 199.

[9]Q seems to have included references to John the Baptist (Matt 11:2/Luke 7:18), to the centurion (Matt 8:5/Luke 7:2), and to a demoniac (Matt 12:22/Luke 11:14), but not to any individual disciple.

[10]See *Kurie* in Luz, *Matthew 1-7* (1989) 61.

[11]Cf. Matthew 11:21/Luke 10:13; Luke 13:3,5, 15:7, and many instances in Acts.

[12]Cf. Matthew 3:2/Mark 1:4, 15. Matthew does add the noun cognate "repentance" in 3:11, but this is still in a traditional context. But note that Matthew 3:2 does not have "for the forgiveness of sins" as does Mark 1:4.

of the sinning brother to repent.[13] Matthew seems to want it that way as the succeeding parable of the Unmerciful Servant, 18: 23-35, makes clear. Verse 35 reads: "So also my heavenly Father will do to every one of you, if you do not forgive your brother from your heart." Matthew apparently views repentance as an important aspect of the sanctified life, but not as a prerequisite for forgiveness. Forgiveness is to be unconditional, total, and unilateral.

This observation may help us understand the next problem: Where did Matthew find the familiar "seventy times seven," or perhaps more accurately, the "seventy-seven times" (NRSV) saying of 18:22c? There is no precedent with which to compare it, either in Q, MARK or MATTHEW. The reference in Genesis 4:24 where Lamech is quoted as saying: "If Cain is avenged sevenfold, truly Lamech seventy-sevenfold," undoubtedly comes closest. In view of what we have just learned about Matthew's special concern for the Christian's need to forgive, I would favor as an answer to the source question here that Matthew added this exaggerated traditional phrase to emphasize the need for unlimited forgiveness, redeeming Lamech's Old Testament confession of unlimited guilt.

Reviewing the passage as a whole, Matthew 18:21-22 is a composite of traditional Q and Old Testament materials extensively redacted by Matthew himself. In terms of our research, these verses are reminiscent of Matthew 15:15-16, as touched upon earlier. There the first evangelist replaced the disciples (Mark 7:17) with Peter as the one who asks Jesus to explain the Parable of the Blind Leading the Blind. Here Matthew goes a step further, exchanging Peter for Jesus as the spokesman in the Q passage found in Luke 17:3-4 about forgiving a sinning brother. We would like to ask: Why?, but "why?" is a redaction-critical question and must await further study in chapter 6. It is hoped that by the time we arrive there some of the smoke now clouding Matthew's portrait of Peter will have been cleared away.

[13]Robert H. Gundry, *Matthew, A Commentary on His Literary and Theological Art* (1982) 370f.

Matthew 14:28-30: Matthean Composition

But three more passages still await our source analysis, and they promise to be significant! These are the three major Petrine insertions found only in MATTHEW: the account of Peter Walking on the Water in 14:28-30, the Commissioning of Peter in 16:17-19, and the curious story of Peter and the Temple Tax in 17:24-27. We shall consider them in the order in which they are found in the First Gospel.

Walking on the Water

MARK 6:45-52	MATTHEW 14:22-33
[45]Immediately he made his disciples get into the boat and go before him to the other side, to Bethsaida, while he dismissed the crowd.	[22]Then he made the disciples get into the boat and go before him to the other side, while he dismissed the crowds.
[46]And after he had taken leave of them, he went up on the mountain to pray.	[23]And after he had dismissed the crowds, he went up on the mountain to pray.
[47]And when evening came, the boat was out on the sea, and he was there alone on the land. [48]And he saw that they were making headway painfully, for the wind was against them.	When evening came, he was there alone, [24]but the boat by this time was many furlongs distant from the land, beaten by the waves; for the wind was against them.
And about the fourth watch of the night, he came to them, walking on the sea. [49]He meant to pass them by, but when they saw him walking on the sea, they thought it was a ghost, and cried out; for they all saw him and were terrified. [50]But immediately he spoke to them and said, "Take heart, it is I; have no fear."	[25]And in the fourth watch of the night, he came to them, walking on the sea. [26]But when the disciples saw him walking on the sea, they were terrified, saying, "It is a Ghost!" And they cried out for fear. [27]But immediately he spoke to them, saying, "Take heart, it is I; have no fear." [28]And Peter answered him, "Lord, if it is you, bid me come to you on the water." [29]He said, "Come." So Peter got out of the boat and walked on the

	water and came to Jesus; [30]but when he saw the wind, he was afraid, and beginning to sink he cried out, "Lord, save me." [31]Jesus immediately reached out his hand and caught him, saying to him, "O man of little faith, why did you doubt?"
[51]And he got into the boat with them and the wind ceased and they were utterly astounded [52]for they did not understand about the loaves, but their hearts were hardened.	[32]And when they got into the boat, the wind ceased. [33]And those in the boat worshipped him saying, "Truly you are the Son of God."

Many commentators on MATTHEW, especially older form-critical ones, consider the Peter Walking on the Water addition an ordinary tradition extant in the New Testament Church which the evangelist dutifully recorded for posterity.[14] I beg to differ.[15] Although the setting on the Sea of Galilee, taken from Mark 6:45-52, may suggest Palestinian provenance, nothing else does. Semitic resonances, such as we shall find so common in the two remaining Petrine passages, Matthew 16:17-19 and 17:24-27, are conspicuously absent here. If the Peter Walking on the Water account had a prior history as a tradition in Matthew's community, the first evangelist has so thoroughly redacted it as to make it his own.

Everything here, in fact, points to original Matthean composition. M. D. Goulder counts seventeen terms and phrases out of

[14]Cf. B. W. Bacon, "The Petrine Supplements of Matthew," *The Expositor,* 8th series, 73 (1917) 10. Eduard Schweizer, *The Good News According to Matthew* (1975) 323f.; H. B. Green, *Matthew* (1975) 141f.

[15]Of course, I am not alone. Cf. M.D. Goulder, *Midrash and Lection in Matthew* (1974) 377–378. H. J. Held, "Matthew as Interpreter of the Miracle Stories," in Bornkamm, Barth, Held, *Tradition and Interpretation in Matthew* (1963) 165–299, esp. 204–206. Georg Braumann, "Der Sinkende Petrus: Matth. 14:28-31," *Theologische Zeitschrift,* 22 (Basel, 1966) 403–414. Brown, Donfried, Reumann, *Peter in the New Testament* (1973) 81, n. 183.

the total of sixty-six Greek words in the four verses, 28-31, that are typical of the first evangelist. The remaining forty-nine, with but one exception, are conventional.[16] We need list only a few Mattheanisms by way of illustration to prove the point that Matthew himself authored these lines. First, in verse 28, there is the designation of Peter which we have already seen editorially inserted also in Matthew 15:15 and 18:21. Then there is the familiar Matthean formula "answering . . . said," translated simply "answered" in the RSV. It is found forty-five times in the First Gospel. Again, there is the address "Lord," in the vocative, as in 18:21. The word "bid," *keleuson,* is found seven times in MATTHEW. The exchange of "water," *hudwr,* in verses 28 and 29, for "sea," *thalassa,* in verse 25, as taken over from MARK, repeats an identical Matthean replacement in the story of the Gadarene Demoniacs in Matthew 8:32d/Mark 5:13c. "Immediately," spelled *euthews,* is another typical Matthean alteration of the MARCAN *euthus.* "Little-faith," *oligopiste,* is also a term which Matthew likes to use to describe the disciples (6:30, 8:26, 16:8), replacing Mark's favorite derogatory remark that they did not understand. This is the only instance, however, where Matthew attributes "little-faith" to an individual.

The accompanying accusatory question, "Why did you doubt?" employs a verb, *distazw,* which is less familiar, but perhaps all the more interesting. It is found only one other time in this Gospel, also as a redactional insertion. I refer to that curious comment in Matthew 28:17 where Matthew tells his readers that when the disciples met the resurrected Jesus in Galilee "they worshipped him, but some doubted." Apparently, the same kind of Petrine instability persisted among other disciples even after the resurrection.

Robert Gundry agrees that Matthew 14:28-31 is Matthean composition, but he tries to show that the evangelist based his art on Old Testament "walking on water" episodes.[17] However, it is not necessary to go even that far afield. Many of the forty-nine conventional terms are clearly taken from the contextual story of Jesus

[16] M. D. Goulder, *Midrash and Lection in Matthew* (1974) 377f.

[17] Gundry, *Matthew*, 300.

Walking Upon the Sea in Matthew 14:22-27/Mark 6:45-52. Note the correspondences: "wind," "walking," "fear," "cried out," and "immediately." Surely, Matthew designed his Petrine vignette in verses 28-31 to mirror the parent MARCAN account related in verses 22-27.

The one possibly problematic term, referred to earlier, is the Greek word *epelabeto,* translated "caught" in verse 31a. This is the only time it appears in the First Gospel, suggesting that it may not be a true Matthean word. In view of the preponderance of evidence in support of the Matthean authorship of this brief story as previously noted, however, it is undoubtedly safe to call this one minor irregularity "the exception that proves the rule." After long analysis, H. J. Held agrees: "This all points to the fact that the insertion really does stem from the hand of Matthew."[18]

This has been a rewarding study. The discoveries that this Peter Walking on the Water episode is the first of Matthew's special Petrine materials, and that the evangelist wrote it himself, suggest that it may play a more determinative role in Matthew's design for Peter in the First Gospel than previously considered. But more on this later.

Matthew 16:17-19: Jewish Christian Tradition

The Confession at Ceasarea Philippi

MARK 8:27-30	MATTHEW 16:13-20
[27]And Jesus went on with his disciples, to the villages of Caesarea Philippi; and on the way he asked his disciples, "Who do men say that I am?" [28]And they told him, "John the Baptist; and others say, Elijah; and others one of the prophets."	[13]Now when Jesus came in the district of Caesarea Philippi, he asked his disciples, "Who do men say that the Son of Man is?" [14]And they said, "Some say John the Baptist, others say Elijah; and others Jeremiah or one of the prophets."
[29]And he asked them, "But who do you say that I am?"	[15]He said to them, "But who do you say that I am?"

[18]Held, "Miracle Stories," in *Tradition and Interpretation* (1963) 205.

MARK 8:27-30	MATTHEW 16:13-20
Peter answered him, "You are the Christ."	[16]Simon Peter replied, "You are the Christ, the Son of the living God."
	[17]And Jesus answered him, "Blessed are you, Simon Bar-Jonah! For flesh and blood has not revealed this to you, but my father who is in heaven. [18]And I tell you, you are Peter, and on this rock I will build my church, and the powers of death shall not prevail against it. [19]I will give you the keys of the kingdom of heaven, and whatever you bind on earth shall be bound in heaven, and whatever you loose on earth shall be loosed in heaven."
[30]Then he strictly charged the disciples to tell no one that he was the Christ.	[20]And he charged them to tell no one about him.

When we turn to this pivotal Petrine passage in MATTHEW, 16:17-19, we find an entirely different literary ambiance. Aside from the typically Matthean linking phrases, literally "Jesus answering said to him" in verse 17 and "I say to you" introducing verse 18, everything else is consistently Semitic although written in translation Greek. First there is the blessing formula: "Blessed are you . . . . " Makarisms, or beatitudes, like this are found also in classical Greek literature, but Robert Guelich, in his study of the Sermon on the Mount, sees the Old Testament as the closer matrix for this New Testament example. He counts forty-five occurrences of the form in the Old Testament, mostly in the Psalms and Wisdom literature.[19] "Simon Bar-Jonah" is a direct transliteration of the Aramaic. It indirectly, but perhaps intentionally, relates Peter to Jonah, the reluctant prophet of the Old Testa-

[19]Robert A. Guelich, *The Sermon on the Mount* (1982) 63, but cf. 62–67 for a more complete study.

ment.[20] "Flesh and blood," "gates of death," and "bind . . . loose" are also all translations of common Hebraic phrases. And let's not forget the Aramaic *Keepha* . . . *keepha* combination that lies behind the Peter . . . rock association in verse 18, as Cardinal Bellarmine has taught us.

Vögtle, Strecker, and Gundry, all of whom we have met before, have tried to salvage some significant involvement of Matthew himself in this passage by claiming as typical of the first evangelist the threefold use of "heaven," (literally the Greek plural *ouranoi,* "heavens") in verse 19abc, especially the favorite designation "Kingdom of Heaven."[21] Matthew certainly is capable of using "heavens" in the plural as a carryover from the Hebrew collective plural *ha shamayim.* Closer examination, however, reveals that such use is preferred only in traditional contexts and liturgical formulations, while in redactional settings, such as Matthew 6:10, 18:18 and 28:18, the singular *ouranos* suits Matthew better. The presence of "heaven" in a plural form here, then, supports, rather than detracts from the view that this passage, Matthew 16:17-19, is a translated Aramaic, Jewish Christian tradition and not Matthean composition.

Confirming this conclusion further is the number of *hapax legomena,* "once used words," in this relatively short passage. The Greek terms translated "Bar-Jonah," "flesh and blood," "gates of death," "prevail," and "keys" are found nowhere else in MATTHEW. "Church," *eccleesia,* is used again in the Church-disciplinary rubric of Matthew 18:17 but nowhere else in the four Gospels. An editor is surely capable of using an occasional new term in the course of his or her presentation, but when the new vocabulary is as concentrated as it is here, the chances are good that a "foreign" author, or origin, is involved.

[20]Oscar Cullmann argues that "Bar-Jonah" could imply "terrorist." O. Cullmann, *Peter, Disciple-Apostle-Martyr* (1962) 23. The suggestion has not caught on.

[21]*Basileia twn ouranwn* is found thirty-two times, only in MATTHEW. Cf. Luz, *Matthew 1–7* (1989) 56. However, "Kingdom of God" also appears four times, two of which may be redactional, Matthew 21:31 and 43. Cf. Moulton and Geden, *Concordance to the New Testament*, 4th ed. (1963) 141f. Heinrich Zimmerman, 'Die Innere Struktur der Kirche und das Petrusamt nach Mt 18," in *Catholica*, 30 (1976) 168–183, also notes Matthew's own preference for *ouranos* in the singular when used in close conjunction with "earth."

Finally, there are two or three grammatical and philological irregularities here which impact on the question of authorship. "Revealed" in the Greek text of Matthew 16:17 has no direct object. "This" has been added by the RSV editors to render the English translation intelligible. Similarly, the referrent of the feminine reflexive pronoun "it," *autees,* at the close of verse 18, is uncertain. As it stands, it corresponds in gender and number both with "rock" and "church." Which is it? The noted Dutch scholar and Churchman Eduard Schillebeeckx, as quoted by Stock,[22] would like to focus on "my church"—so much so that he is willing to concede that "properly speaking Matthew 16:18-19 is not concerned with the primacy of Peter" at all, but with Jesus' own concern for his Church. As tempting to most Protestants as this perspective may be, it cannot stand here. The focus throughout this passage is consistently upon Peter. The operative personal pronouns and verbs are all second-person singular. All this argues for "rock," *keepha,* as the intended referrent of *autees* in verse 18. If we might risk a sense translation of the original Aramaic tradition it would probably read: "You are Rock, and upon this same rock, I will build my church, and the gates of sheol shall not prevail against you as that rock."

A third discrepancy is the mixed metaphor of keys "binding and loosing" in verse 19 instead of the more appropriate "opening and shutting." Could we have here a combination of two originally discrete traditions?

The point is probably not worth arguing. What we really want to know is: If Matthew had composed these lines, would he not have sensed these inconsistencies and corrected them? We would certainly think so. Such irregularities result much more frequently from either a too literal translation or an out-of-context quotation.

If, then, we can agree that Matthew 16:17-19 had its source in Jewish-Christian tradition, we still need to ask when and under what circumstances did it develop? These are form-critical questions and several form critics have attempted to answer them. Rudolph Bultmann, you will recall, considered it a genuine post-Easter statement of Jesus from within the Jerusalem Christian

[22]Augustine Stock, "Is Matthew's Presentation of Peter Ironic?" *Biblical Theology Bulletin*, 17 (1987) 67.

community.[23] Matthew had simply anachronistically located it in the period of Jesus' Galilean ministry. In Matthew, Bultmann further conjectured, the tradition served as a "legend of faith."[24]

The statement of one of Bultmann's students, Günther Bornkamm, however, is more historically and theologically responsible. He writes, and I agree:

> All of this [data] militates against the view that the origin of the logion in its present form is to be sought in the earliest Jerusalem community, where all of this, particularly this position of Peter, is historically hardly conceivable. This saying presupposes the resurrection, the delayed parousia, the hellenistic concept of the ecclesia and its energetic correction in the direction of a renewed assertion of the obligatory nature of the commandments. But all this means that Mt. 16:18f. reflects the entrance of Jewish Christian tradition into Hellenistic Christianity and that it manifests an outspoken critical tendency towards all charismatic movements, which are here already presupposed.[25]

By "charismatic movements" Bornkamm had in mind those early Christian groups which attempted to live and function under the direct guidance of God, the indwelling Christ and/or the Holy Spirit. The first twelve chapters of Acts, especially, witness to this kind of spiritual orientation. Acts 8:15-16, for example, records that Peter and John "came down and prayed for them (at Samaria) that they might receive the Holy Spirit; for it had not yet fallen on any of them." Generally speaking, such charismatic ecclesiology is more characteristic of Paul's genuine letters, discounting the deutero-Pauline Pastoral Epistles.

In opposition to such free movements, however, other ecclesial forces favored greater organization and structure to give iden-

[23]Rudolf Bultmann, "Die Frage nach dem messianischen Bewusstsein Jesu und das Petrus-Bekenntnis," *Zeitschrift für die Neutestamentliche Wissenschaft*, 19 (1919–1920) 165–174.

[24]Rudolf Bultmann, *History of the Synoptic Tradition* (1963) 257–258.

[25]Günther Bornkamm, "The Risen Lord and the Earthly Jesus, Matthew 28:16-20," *The Future of Our Religious Past, Essays in Honour of Rudolf Bultmann* (1978) 220.

tity, discipline, and stability to the nascent Church. At work was the sociological necessity to institutionalize the new Christian idea if it was to survive. One way in which this concern expressed itself was in the identification of like-minded individuals and groups with chosen faith-heroes, such as Peter or Paul, or James, the Lord's brother in Jerusalem. It was a natural carryover from Judaism with its Levites, Priests, and High Priests rankings. The process of authority selection and identification began early as we have already seen in Corinth (1 Cor 1:12-13), and it continued for centuries. If Ignatius was a (younger) contemporary of Matthew, it is entirely possible that his efforts to establish a hierarchical (in its etymological definition as a "leadership of priests") polity for the Antiochan Christian community had already begun.

It is, then, a distinct possibility, if not probability, as Bornkamm has said, that the Matthew 16:17-19 tradition had its origin, or at least its popularity, within the Jewish Christian segment of Matthew's community committed to Peter as its figurehead patriarch. The blessing bestowed upon the first disciple in verse 17, the association of his name with his function implying his foreordained destiny in verse 18, and the delegation of sweeping powers and privileges pertaining thereto in verse 19 all add up to an eloquent accolade in praise of Peter.

In terms of ancient Greek and Roman rhetoric this type of salute is called an encomium.[26] Aristotle in the fourth century B.C.E. already employed and analyzed the form. He saw it as a subcategory of "epideictic," i.e., demonstrative, oratory meant to be performed in public as a eulogy, a panegyric, an aretalogy, or in some instances, as an apology. Before long, however, encomia were being recorded and began to appear more frequently in ancient literature. Eventually, encomia were put to practical use in the courts and "town halls" of the more democratic Greek

[26]Cf. Donald Lemen Clark, *Rhetoric in Greco-Roman Education* (1957) esp. 194–198. George Kennedy, *The Art of Persuasion in Greece* (1963). Stanley F. Bonner, *Education in Ancient Rome* (1977). Philip L. Shuler, *A Genre for the Gospels* (1982) esp. 45–57, and Charles Sears Baldwin, *Medieval Rhetoric* (1989) 30–33. Burton L. Mack, *Rhetoric and the New Testament* (1990) 47f. I found the first and last mentioned the most helpful. The Greek word *'εγκώμιον* is thought to have been derived from the cheers and chants of the adoring crowds (*κῶμος*) for their athletic or military champions.

and Roman cities. If a citizen was to take his place as a civic leader in his community or nation, he had to know how to persuade, convince, and promote his favorite cause or candidate. As a result, by the time of MATTHEW's composition in the first century C.E., the study of rhetoric was the central focus of Roman education.

Quintilian (35–96 C.E.), a direct contemporary of Matthew, if our dates are correct, was the outstanding educator and rhetorician of that day.[27] He also enjoyed the significant friendship of all the emperors from Galba to Domitian (69–96 C.E.). His influence, accordingly, was felt everywhere within the Roman Empire. Rhetorical forms, including the encomium, consequently, must have been at the height of their popularity just at Matthew's time and place in the provincial capital city of first century C.E. Roman Syria.

According to Quintilian, and Roman educators who followed him, there were more than thirty different techniques and areas of emphasis which comprise an encomium.[28] Basic were amplification and comparison focusing on the family, ancestry, birthplace, education, and wealth of the person to be praised. It was also appropriate to allude to oracles, omens, fortunate coincidences, and other divine endowments. Exaggeration was permissible and expected. While encomia could be, and were, composed in honor of such mundane objects as ants and bees, others were designed to praise the gods or godly men (aretalogies).[29]

It is obvious that Matthew 16:17-19 fits many of these categories and certainly functions here as an encomium in praise of Peter. "Bar-Jonah," verse 17, voices his ancestry identifying him with the celebrated reluctant prophet of ancient Israel. "Revealed . . ." indicates his association with the divine. The "Peter . . . rock" combination in verse 18 is one of those fortunate plays-

[27]Cf. Shuler, *Genre* (1982) and James J. Murphy, *Quintilian on the Teaching of Speaking and Writing* (1987).

[28]Theon, an early second century C.E. successor to Quintilian, actually lists thirty-six. Cf. Shuler, *Genre* (1982) 55f.

[29]Some of the better-known encomia reviewed by Shuler, *Genre* (1982) 58–87, include one in honor of Helen of Troy by Isocrates, Philo's "De vita Mosis," and Lucian's "Life of Demonax."

on-words which bespeak Peter's sturdy, foundational importance. And the "keys . . . binding . . . loosing . . . in heaven and on earth" metaphor in verse 19 signifies the dimensions of his divine commission.

Of course, typical Greek encomia were much longer. Matthew 16:17-19, by comparison, is more reminiscent of one of Quintilian's shorter school exercises. It may be, however, that this passage consists of a series of brief excerpts as the Matthean introductory phrases opening verses 17 and 18 seem to signal.

In terms of the relevant considerations of form, function, content, time, and location, then, it seems appropriate to conclude that Matthew 16:17-19 constitutes a Hellenistic Jewish Christian adaptation of a first-century C.E. encomium dedicated to the honor of Peter as a kind of mythopoeic patriarch or spiritual leader of at least part of Matthew's Antiochan community.

Matthew 17:24-27: Jewish Christian Tradition

The Temple Tax

MATTHEW 17:24-27

[24]When they came to Capernaum, the collectors of the half-shekel tax went up to Peter and said, "Does not your teacher pay the tax?" [25]He said, "Yes." And when he came home, Jesus spoke to him first, saying, "What do you think, Simon? From whom do kings of the earth take toll or tribute? From their sons or from others?" [26]And when he said, "From others," Jesus said to him, "Then the sons are free. [27]However, not to give offense to them, go to the sea and cast a hook, and take the first fish that comes up, and when you open its mouth you will find a shekel; take that and give it to them for me and for yourself.

Turning now to the third and final Petrine passage unique to MATTHEW, the curious account of Peter and the Temple Tax, we experience a strong sense of *deja vu.* Here again is the Semitic "Simon", verse 25, the Aramaisms: "half-shekel," *"did-*

raxma,"[30] and "kings of the earth," (cf. Psalm 2:2), also a concentration of *hapax legomena:* "half-shekel," "spoke . . . first," *proephthasen,* "toll," "others," "free," "hook," "shekel," and finally a pervasive congratulatory attitude toward Peter. In verse 25 he speaks for Jesus, the only time this occurs in any of the Gospels. In verse 26 he correctly answers Jesus' question, and in the end he is more closely identified with Jesus in the phrase "for me and for yourself," verse 27, than any other disciple ever was.

True, there is also more evidence of possible Matthean redaction in this passage than in 16:17-19. "Went up," *proserxomai,* is employed redactionally by the first evangelist about fifty times, according to Luz's listing.[31] "What do you think?" is found six times, only in MATTHEW, and "offend," *skandalizomai,* is used nineteen times in the First Gospel, five of those times in its verb or cognate noun forms in the nearby succeeding three verses, 18:6-9. It does seem evident, then, that Matthew did edit this account slightly—and we have yet to discover why—but certainly not enough to alter its basic character as a Jewish Christian tradition.

There is a final complication. Grammatical and syntactical checks hint that verses 24-26 and verse 27 were originally two separate vignettes. Form-critically speaking, they represent two entirely different classifications. The first is a pronouncement story, the second, an unfinished miracle story—the only one of its kind in the entire Bible.[32] Again, the first consists of a series of sentences beginning with participial phrases, followed by clauses with

[30]A *didraxmon* (singular) is half of a *stateer,* verse 17. The use of these coins is significant for locating MATTHEW's composition in Antioch because they were minted in the nearby Syrian cities of Tyre and Damascus. This "Tyrian stater" was the only coin which could pay the temple tax for two persons. The King James Version of the Bible translated it "penny," giving rise to the Roman Catholic term "Peter's Pence" as the name for the annual offering for the support of the Vatican. Cf. J. Duncan M. Derrett, "Peter's Penny: Fresh Light on Matthew XVII 24–27," *Novum Testamentum*, 6 (1963) 1–15.

[31]Luz, *Matthew 1–7*, 67.

[32]William G. Thompson, *Matthew's Advice to a Divided Community, Mt. 17:22-18:35,* Analecta Biblica (1970) 50, complains that this is also "the only incident in which Jesus uses his extraordinary power and knowledge for his own advantage." Brown, Donfried and Reumann, *Peter in the New Testament* (1973) agree.

aorist verbs, and followed once more by direct speech in the present tense. Verse 27, on the other hand, is characterized by what C.F.D. Moule has identified as a typical Hellenistic hypotaxis,[33] i.e., a purpose clause in the aorist subjunctive, followed by four sets of aorist participles, three of which have aorist imperatives and one a future indicative: "you will find. . . . " The rhythm is poetic, but out of step with the preceding narrative. The only glue which holds these two disparate forms together is a common adulatory interest in Peter. Whatever their separate derivations, then, this much seems certain: Matthew 17:24-27 is a composite tradition with a strong Jewish Christian flavor, especially in verses 24-26, designed to the greater glory of the first disciple. In other words, all indications are that Matthew 17:24-27 constitutes a second slice of a larger Petrine encomium which probably also included Matthew 16:17-19.

With that, our cursory source analysis of all the Peter passages in MATTHEW is complete. What we found, in summary, is that of the total of fifteen pericopes, eleven are based on MARK; one is derived from Q; two are encomiastic traditions which Matthew likely took from his community; and one—significantly, the first one unique to MATTHEW—is from the evangelist's own pen.

The time has arrived to sharpen the focus, redaction-critically.

[33]C.F.D. Moule, *An Idiom Book of New Testament Greek* (1963) 172f.

4

Redaction Criticism: Matthean Omissions

Winston Churchill is credited with the oxymoron: "Democracy is the worst form of government that ever worked." The same could undoubtedly be claimed for redaction criticism as an exegetical method for biblical understanding. It is geared to try to read the evangelist's mind—always a precarious task—in matters sociological and theological based on the redactor's choice of words, selection or deletion of traditional material, addition of original compositions, and the location of it all in the finished text. Because of this methodological orientation and commitment many scholars like to complain, with E. P. Sanders and Margaret Davies, about "the intentional fallacy" whereby redaction criticism "treats all texts as if they were a covert form of autobiography."[1]

It is true that there is a natural temptation to succumb to the tendency to read more into a text than is really there. Nevertheless, redaction criticism works! It both deepens and broadens the horizons of biblical understanding. Much can be learned about an author's convictions, personality, and situation from the editorial conventions he or she employs. In our specific area of concern, for example, essentially all the truly reliable exegetical contributions to the study of the role of Peter in MATTHEW to date, as we saw in chapter 2, have been made by redaction critics

[1]E. P. Sanders and Margaret Davies, *Studying the Synoptic Gospels* (1989) 223.

with a little help from their friends, source and form critics. So, unless we wish to abandon much of the progress made thus far, there is no alternative but to use this exegetical tool. In opposition, then, to Joachim Jeremias who saw the Petrine issue in Matthew so intractable that it would guarantee the failure of redaction criticism,[2] I see this method, with all its potential pitfalls, as our best hope. Let the evidence speak for itself.

Redaction criticism in the Synoptic Gospels is made easier by the widely accepted Two-Source Hypothesis which proposes that MATTHEW and LUKE, while working independently, used MARK and Q as their basic sources. But why would Matthew decide to rewrite MARK in the first place? Surely, from his addition of the birth narratives in MATTHEW chapters 1 and 2, it is safe to conclude at the minimum that he felt MARK was biographically incomplete. Again, from his incorporation of five major sermons we may confidently assume that Matthew was of the opinion that MARK needed more instructional material even though he, i.e., Matthew, was patently uncomfortable with Mark's frequent identification of Jesus as *didaskalos,* "teacher."[3] Matthew permits only the uninformed (8:19, 19:16), the Scribes and Pharisees (12:38, 22:15), and the Sadducees (22:24, 36), to address Jesus in this manner.[4]

The specific question facing us, however, is: What did the first evangelist have in mind for Peter in view of the five MARCAN

[2]Joachim Jeremias, *New Testament Theology, I* (1971) 307, n. 1. The full statement of what is for me Jeremias' critical challenge, given in this footnote, reads: "The answer to the question why Matthew on the one hand is the only one to report Peter's overwhelming praise in Matthew 16:17-19 and yet on the other deletes *kai tw Petrw* (Mark 16.7) and introduces the story of Peter's wavering faith (Matt 14:28-33) is that this unconcerned juxtaposition of conflicting traditions is almost a characteristic of his: cf. also 6.17f. with 9.15; 8.12 with 13.38; 9.13b with 10.41b; 10.5f. with 28.18f.; 12.8 with 24.20; 16.6 with 23.3a. This may be one of the fundamental reasons why the redaction-critical analysis of the first gospel cannot achieve success."

[3]Moulton and Geden, *A Concordance to the Greek Testament* (1897, repr. 1970) 209, lists twelve occurences of *didaskalos* referring to Jesus in MARK.

[4]Note also the general prohibition in Matthew 23:8: "But you are not to be called rabbi, for you have one teacher, and you are all brethren." In Matthew 26:18, however, Matthew repeats Jesus' reference to himself as *ho didaskalos,* "the Teacher," as taken over from Mark 14:14.

Petrine passages that he omitted, the five he added, and the ten he reproduced but edited? (Cf. Figures 1 and 2, pp. 25 and 41, above.)

We begin slowly in our pursuit of an answer to this question in this chapter with an analysis of the five Petrine references that Matthew deleted, or at least failed to transfer, from MARK to his own Gospel. As noted earlier, these include (1) the account of Simon and the disciples seeking Jesus in Galilee [Mark 1:35-39]; (2) The Healing of Jairus' Daughter [Mark 5:21-24a, 35-43]; (3) The Withered Fig Tree [Mark 11:12-14, 20-23]; (4) the question of the destruction of the temple [Mark 13:3-4]; and (5) the announcement of Jesus' post-resurrection journey to Galilee [Mark 16:7].

Actually, in three of the five cases, Matthew retains the basic accounts, leaving out only the identifications of Peter and a few of the other disciples. Obviously, neither considerations regarding the general content of these three pericopes nor space limitations were involved in Matthew's editorial decision, but for some still undetermined reason, he simply chose not to associate Peter with the events recorded.

Arguments based on silence from omitted references like these are notoriously fragile, but an examination of them may, nevertheless, at least suggest clues for further investigation in the chapters to follow. Let us observe the patterns and commonalities that emerge from a general comparison of these passages and then see if we can detect their impact relative to Peter upon the final redaction of the First Gospel.

1. The first observation to be made is the surprising fact that in none of the original MARCAN passages involved is Peter viewed negatively. He is never corrected or rebuked. Rather, he is given modest prominence in that he is listed first among the inner circle of disciples in two pericopes (Mark 5:37 and 13:3), serves as the spokesman for all the disciples in another (Mark 11:21), and in Mark 16:7 is actually singled out and accorded special mention when the messenger at the empty tomb advises the women: "Go and tell the disciples 'and Peter' that he (Jesus) is going before you to Galilee." If Matthew's editorial intent was to show Peter as the rock on which the Church was to be built

why would he dismiss these lateral, positive references to Peter in the material taken over from MARK? Such omissions suggest at the very least that Matthew was not determined at all costs to promote Peter by granting him favorable exposure at every opportunity in the First Gospel.

2. None of the omitted segments, if they had been transposed into the First Gospel, would normally have fallen within chapters 14 to 18 where the first evangelist has concentrated his own five Petrine additions.

If Matthew had included the MARCAN reference to Simon and the disciples seeking Jesus (Mark 1:35-39) in his account of Jesus' early Galilean ministry, it would undoubtedly have appeared in conjunction with Matthew 4:23: "And he went about all of Galilee teaching in their synagogues and preaching the gospel of the kingdom . . . " For convenience sake, we might identify this location as within MATTHEW's Book I, chapters 3 to 7. Or, if he had transferred this vignette in direct sequence it would have been placed shortly after the account of Jesus' healing Peter's mother-in-law in Matthew 8:14-17, i.e., in MATTHEW's Book II, chapters 8 to 10.

The next pericope, The Healing of Jairus' Daughter (Mark 5:21-24a, 35-43), falls into the latter category as well. Matthew actually repeats the narrative in 9:18-26 as part of his list of miracle stories. However, he completely omits MARK's reference to Peter and the inner circle of disciples.

Similarly, the episode of The Withered Fig Tree in Mark 11:12-14, 20-26, is recounted in Matthew 21:18-22, in MATTHEW's Book V, chapters 19–25, except for the fact that the first evangelist has the disciples replace Peter as the ones who question Jesus about the tree's sudden demise.

Mark 13:3, where Peter, James, and John ask Jesus about the time when the prophesied destruction of the temple would occur, is likewise found in MATTHEW's Book V (24:3-8), minus the reference to any disciples by name.

Finally, MARK's post-Easter announcement concerning the disciples "and Peter" given to the women at the empty tomb (Mark 16:7) is repeated in Matthew's reconstruction of the same scene in his resurrection account, Matthew 28:1-10, but again only the specification of Peter as the one to whom the message was to be relayed is noticeably absent.

By way of contrast MARK's threefold identification of Peter in passages which do fall within MATTHEW's Book IV (Peter's Confession [Mark 8:27-30/Matt 16:13-16]; the Satan-Saying [Mark 8:31-33/Matt 16:21-23]; and the story of the transfiguration [Mark 9:2-8/Matt 17:1-8]) are all repeated relatively intact.

Curiously, there are no Petrine references at all in Matthew's Book III, chapters 11–13:52.

The net effect of Matthew's omission of the five Petrine references, then, is to drastically reduce Peter's exposure in the First Gospel outside of Book IV. Only seven references to him now remain in these twenty-three chapters. Simultaneously, and in contrast, Peter's visibility in Matthew 14–18 has been tremendously increased. Peter now appears eight times in these five chapters alone, three carry-over accounts from MARK, plus the five additions of Matthew's own. This is a fascinating editorial phenomenon . . . and too obvious to have been accidental. Why this concentration? What is so special about Book IV? What does Peter have in common with it? It is still too soon to ask (cf. chapter 6). It is enough just to keep these data in mind.

3. In three of the five omitted MARCAN designations of Peter, the first disciple plays no individual role. He is present but says or does nothing notable. In a fourth instance, at the empty tomb, he isn't even physically present, although he receives special recognition by way of the messenger's announcement. Could this inactivity have been a factor in Matthew's decision to delete these references?

Before we get too comfortable with our answer to that semi-rhetorical question we had better look at the one case where Matthew red-pencils "Peter" even though he did play an active part in Mark's portrayal. In the story of The Withered Fig Tree (Mark 11:12-14, 20-26 and Matt 21:18-22), Mark has Peter exclaim: "Master, look! The fig tree which you cursed has withered." Matthew by contrast has the disciples ask: "How did the fig tree wither at once?" There are only two places in the First Gospel where this kind of exchange between Peter and the disciples in general occurs, here, and in reverse order, in Matthew 15:15 and Mark

7:17, the question of What Defiles a Man. What could have prompted this kind of editorial Peter/disciples flip-flop? The sample is too small to base a judgment on these incidences alone, but perhaps the next observation will suggest a more credible explanation.

4. To one degree or another, four of the five passages under consideration have some connection with the temple, with Israel, and with the old Jewish order in general. The first passage omitted has to do with Jesus' early Galilean mission; in the second, Jairus, according to MARK, is a ruler of a synagogue. Next, the two-part MARCAN Withered Fig Tree account brackets the story of the cleansing of the temple (Mark 11:15-19). Also, as many redaction critical exegetes have sensed, the fig tree is a metaphor for Israel. The withering of the tree, accordingly, presages the destruction of the temple and the demise of old order Judaism. Finally, the same theme characterizes the explicit question about the time for the destruction of the temple in Mark 13:3. The evidence forces us to ask: Was Matthew shielding Peter from associations with old order concerns? Is this why Peter was removed from the story of The Withered Fig Tree and replaced by the disciples? It is certainly another possibility worth watching.

5. Two of these five passages under review involve Mark's inner circle of disciples construct—Mark 5:37 and Matthew 9:18ff., in the healing of Jairus' daughter account, and in Mark 13:3 and Matthew 24:3ff., relative to the impending destruction of the temple. Matthew deletes both occurences. Mark employs the familiar trio of Peter, James, and John, and sometimes Andrew, five times in his Gospel.[5] He portrays them as witnesses to Jesus' private miracles and personal epiphanies, such as at the transfiguration, and as inside confidants to his special apocalyptic revelations, Mark 13:3-37. The observation here that Matthew omits these two instances of this MARCAN convention suggests that he is not really committed to this inner circle idea or cares to carry over its functions into his Gospel.[6] The inner circle concept is

[5]Cf. Mark 1:16-20, 5:37, 9:2, 13:3, and 14:33. Mark also speaks of James and John in 10:35, and of John alone in 9:38f.

[6]Matthew's omission of the names of the inner circle, and their replacement simply with "disciples" in 24:3 could also have been prompted by Matthew's con-

simply not essential to his understanding of the disciples generally. However, its deletion clearly reduces Peter's prominence to a considerable degree in the First Gospel. This is another perspective we will have to file in our mental data bank because of its potential implications for the special design of Peter's role in MATTHEW.

6. It is exegetically impossible to leave this study without another look at Matthew's deletion of "and Peter" in Mark 16:7 and Matthew 28:7. In my opinion it is extraordinarily significant. Its omission by Matthew was enough to make Jeremias throw up his hands in despair at the first evangelist's "unconcerned juxtaposition of conflicting traditions."[7] What this omission says, redaction-critically, is that Matthew had a ready-made opportunity to include Peter in the crucial post-Easter story of the embryonic development of the Christian movement, but consciously and intentionally passed up the chance. The result is that without this reference the last glimpse MATTHEW's readers have of Peter is the pathetic scene of the great disciple remorsefully sobbing outside the high priest's judgment hall.[8] Equally important, it means that Peter plays no individual part at all in the resurrection or in the disciples' response to the resurrection in Matthew's portrayal. Rather, at the close of the First Gospel, Peter is left, like an old soldier, to fade away and become absorbed in the faceless company of "the eleven" (Matt 28:16). This is so contradictory to Peter's prominence elsewhere, especially in Matthew 14–18, and it is so unusual when compared with all other New Testament traditions included in the other Gospels, Acts, and Paul's letters, that it renders us extremely uncomfortable. What impression of Peter could the evangelist have possibly wanted to leave with his readers?

sistent practice of having Jesus address his sermons primarily to the disciples as a group. Cf. Matt 5:1-2, 10:1. 13:10; 18:1, (23:1), 24:3.

[7]Cf. p. 60, n. 2, above.

[8]The comments of R.E.O. White are insightful and supportive: "After describing in detail the denial of Jesus by Peter . . . Matthew is the only gospel writer who states, curtly, 'he went out, and wept bitterly' and never mentions Peter again. . . . Matthew's readers could scarcely miss the significance of that!" R.E.O. White, *The Mind of Matthew* (1979) 152f.

This review of the five MATTHEAN omissions of MARCAN Petrine passages leaves us with very ambivalent feelings and more questions than answers. In general, we have observed that these deletions have reduced Peter's exposure in much of the First Gospel, with the exception of Matthew's Book IV, prompting a tentative conclusion that Matthew was not interested in Peter's prominence for its, or his, own sake. At the same time, we have detected a couple of Matthean redactional tendencies which appear to shape Peter's role in very specific ways. Peter tends not to relate to "old order" issues, and amazingly has no part in the MATTHEAN resurrection and post-resurrection scenes.

Obviously, Matthew was a very capable editor, able to nuance his portrayal of Peter in accordance with some predetermined, but still undisclosed purpose.

We definitely need more enlightenment.

5

Marcan Petrine Passages in Matthew

Be forewarned: The problem of Peter in MATTHEW will become even more convoluted as we now research Matthew's redaction of those Petrine passages "copied" from MARK. Yet, here and there a new insight, a contributing factor, and a fascinating possibility will surface to make the effort exciting and worthwhile.

It has been my observation that one of the principal weaknesses of virtually all studies of the role of Peter in MATTHEW to date has been that these transplanted Petrine pericopes have been considered marginal, especially when compared to the five uniquely Matthean additions, and therefore have been exempted from rigorous analysis. This failure to critically examine Matthew's editorial activity in these passages, however slight, has led to such facile conclusions as that expressed by Brown, Donfried, and Reumann that ". . . in the two Gospels [i.e., in the materials common to MATTHEW and MARK] there is no significantly different treatment of Peter . . . ."[1] We shall see about that. If we do not wish to jump uncritically to such ready-made dogmatic answers we had better do our exegetical homework on these pericopes as well.

There are ten MARCAN Petrine passages recounted in MATTHEW. The list is worth repeating:[2]

[1]Brown, Donfried, Reumann, eds., *Peter in the New Testament* (1973) 76.

[2]Cf. chap. 3, p. 40, above.

1. The Call to Become Fishers of Men (Mark 1:16-20/Matt 4:18-22)
2. Healing Peter's Mother-in-law (Mark 1:29-31/Matt 8:14-17)
3. The List of the Twelve Disciples (Mark 3:14-19/Matt 10:2-4)
4. Peter's Confession at Caesarea Philippi (Mark 8:27-30/ Matt 16:13-16)
5. The Satan-Saying (Mark 8:31-33/Matt 16:21-23)
6. The Transfiguration (Mark 9:2-8/Matt 17:1-8)
7. Peter Asks about Rewards (Mark 10:28-31/Matt 19:27-30)
8. Peter's Boast (Mark 14:26-31/Matt 26:30-35)
9. Asleep in Gethsemane (Mark 14:32-41/Matt 26:36-46)
10. Peter's Denials (Mark 14:66-72/Matt 26:69-75)

Thoroughness requires that these pericopes be analyzed individually and in the order in which they are found. Numbers 4 and 5, however, will form the context for the special material in Matthew 16:17-19. A detailed investigation of these two passages, therefore, is better left to chapter 6. The same is true for an eleventh passage common to MATTHEW and MARK, Mark 7:17/Matthew 15:15, where, however, only Matthew inserts an interlocutory role for Peter.

1. The Call to Become Fishers of Men

MARK 1:16-20

[16]And passing along by the Sea of Galilee, he saw Simon and Andrew the brother of Simon casting a net into the sea; for they were fishermen. [17]And Jesus said to them, "Follow me, and I will make you become fishers of men." [18]And immediately they left their nets and followed him. [19]And going on a little farther, he saw James the son of Zebedee and John his brother, in the boat with Zebedee their father, mending their nets. [20]And im-

MATTHEW 4:18-22

[18]As he walked by the Sea of Galilee, he saw two brothers, Simon who is called Peter and Andrew his brother, casting a net into the sea; for they were fishermen. [19]And he said to them, "Follow me and I will make you fishers of men." [20]Immediately they left their nets and followed him. [21]And going on from there he saw two other brothers, James the son of Zebedee and John his brother, in the boat with Zebedee their father,

mediately he called them, and they left their father Zebedee in the boat with the hired servants, and followed him.

mending their nets, and he called them. [22]Immediately they left the boat and their father, and followed him.

The similarity between the MATTHEAN and MARCAN renditions of this account is obvious. Matthew makes a few stylistic improvements, balancing the "brothers" relationship between Peter and Andrew vs. James and John, and slightly elevating the readers' view of Zebedee, the father of James and John, by omitting any reference to "hired servants" as his associates (cf. Mark 1:20b).

The only Matthean editorial comment that interests us, however, is the identifying phrase "who is called Peter" *ton legomenon Petron,* in Matthew 4:18b. It calls attention to two very different perspectives in the first two Gospels as far as the names used for the first disciple are concerned.

In Mark, the given name of the first fisherman whom Jesus called to follow him was "Simon," a transliteration of the Aramaic "Simeon." Accordingly, it was also "Simon's" house where "Simon's" mother-in-law was healed (Mark 1:29 and 30), just as it was "Simon" who pursued Jesus at the outset of the Galilean mission (Mark 1:36). The name "Peter" does not appear in the Second Gospel until 3:16, and then in a rather curious fashion. Mark employs the verb *epititheemi,* 'to lay, put, place, or bestow." A literal translation of the sentence, then, might read: "He (Jesus) imposed on Simon a name, Rock." In other words, from now on, "Peter," or Rock, was to be Simon's official name as a designated disciple.[3] After that, "Peter" is used consistently nineteen more times in the Second Gospel, with only one exception. In Mark 14:37, "Simon" momentarily resurfaces apparently to avoid redundancy.

Curiously, there is no hint given in MARK as to why Jesus conferred the name "Peter" on Simon. Certainly, Peter is never

[3]The RSV translation "surnamed" may be acceptable, but it lacks the force of the verb *epititheemi.* A. Loisy, *L'Evangile selon Marc* (1912) 413, differentiates between the names this way: "le pecheur Simon . . . l'Apotre Pierre," i.e., "the fisherman Simon . . . the Apostle Peter."

shown to be rock-like, foundational, or even very dependable anywhere in the Second Gospel. Of course, neither are any of the other disciples.

In MATTHEW, the situation is different. Simon is identified as "Peter" right from the start. It is "Peter's" house and mother-in-law in 8:14. "Simon," in fact, never appears without some kind of explanation that "Peter" is meant. Of course, "Simon" does show up again in the official listing of the twelve, as taken from MARK, in Matthew 10:2ff., and in connection with the Jewish Christian tradition represented by Matthew 16:17-19. In the former, Matthew abandons Mark's notion of "imposing" the nickname "Peter" on Simon. As in Matthew 4:18, Simon is simply "called" Peter, *ho legomenos Petros,* in 10:2.[4] In the latter, the "Peter . . . rock" combination in Matthew 16:18 strongly implies that Peter was called by that name because of his function as the foundation-stone of Christ's Church.[5] Elsewhere in the First Gospel, however, Peter is portrayed as no more rock-solid than in MARK. As far as Matthew, himself, is concerned, "Peter" was simply a Greek name identifying the first disciple, to go with his transliterated Aramaic given name, "Simon." In fact, the prevalence and persistence of "Peter" in the First Gospel, suggests that in the Hellenistic diaspora setting in which Matthew was writing, "Peter" was the name by which the first disciple was known generally, if not exclusively.

There is a lateral observation of some significance. Matthew's attitude here toward the name "Simon" parallels his use, or disuse, of other Aramaic terms inherited from MARK. He omits the

[4]The fact that Matthew deletes the MARCAN verb *epititheemi* in Matthew 10:2/Mark 3:16 argues against John P. Meier, *Matthew* (1980) 34, where he writes: "Unlike Mk, Mt. mentions Simon's title of Peter (Rock) at the call, thus pointing to Matthew 16:18." This is a case of the "Matthew 16:17-19 syndrome" in action. There is no hint in either Matthew 4:18 or 10:2 that Matthew thought of "Peter" as a title. As a matter of fact, the only clearly redactional "titles" for Peter in MATTHEW are *oligopiste,* "little-faith," in 14:31 and *skandalon,* "stumblingblock," in 16:23.

[5]Just because Matthew quotes this traditional passage does not necessarily mean that he affirms it. The automatic assumption that Matthew does affirm it simply because he includes it is the logical non-sequitur that lies at the heart of the "Matthew 16:17-19 syndrome."

Greek transliteration of the Aramaic *talitha koum,* "little girl, I say to you, arise" (Mark 5:41) in Matthew 9:25. He does the same with *korban,* "given to God" (Mark 7:11) in Matthew 15:5. *Ephphatha* from Mark 7:34 and *Abba* from Mark 14:36 are not repeated in Matthew 15:30 and 26:39, respectively. In Matthew 27:46, the first evangelist corrects MARK's Aramaic *Eloi, Eloi,* "My God, my God!" (Mark 15:34), making it correspond with the opening words of the Hebrew text of Psalm 22:1, *Eli, Eli. . . .* And in the transfiguration text (Mark 9:5b/Matt 17:4b) Matthew also exchanges the Greek *Kurie,* "Lord," for MARK's Aramaic *rabbi,* "teacher."[6]

Matthew's retention of Golgotha (Matt 27:30) and rabbi (Matt 23:7-8, 26:25) indicates that he is familiar with Semitic terms and knows how to use them. Yet, it remains true that in most cases he prefers to delete them. This relative aversion to Aramaic words suggests something about Matthew's own linguistic orientation and, undoubtedly, also about the ethnic and cultural mix of his readership.

Further, a recognition of this editorial preference and practice is added confirmation of our early source-critical conclusion that Matthew 16:17-19, with its Aramaic reference to "Simon Bar-Jonah," *et al.,* was indeed a Jewish Christian tradition, representing second-party sentiments, and not Matthean redactional composition.

Thus, while the Matthew 4:18f. pericope has been of some lateral value in our study, as it stands, it serves simply as an appropriate, balanced introduction of Peter, Andrew, James, and John as potential disciples in the First Gospel. No Petrine preoccupation or profile is as yet visible.

[6]Robert H. Gundry, *Matthew. A Commentary on His Literary and Theological Art* (1982) 332, in an effort to show that Bar-Jonah in 16:17 could be Matthean redaction notes that on three occasions the first evangelist adds "rabbi" (Matt 23:7, 8 and 26:25). However, it must be noted that in the first two instances, Matthew is condemning the use of the term within the Christian community, and in the latter, he has placed the word on the tongue of Judas, the betrayer, feigning innocence at the last supper. Clearly, Matthew knows the Aramaic terms, but sees no benefit in burdening his Greek-speaking readership with them. Matthew employs Aramaic terms when quoting traditional statements as in Matthew 16:17-19 and 17:24-27 and when referring to Semitic personal names or locations.

2. The Healing of Peter's Mother-in-law

MARK 1:29-31	MATTHEW 8:14-15
[29]And immediately he left the synagogue, and entered the house of Simon and Andrew, with James and John.	[14]And when Jesus entered Peter's house,
[30]Now Simon's mother-in-law lay sick with a fever, and immediately they told him of her.	he saw his mother-in-law lying sick with fever;
[31]And he came and took her by the hand and lifted her up, and the fever left her; and she served them.	[15]and he touched her hand and the fever left her, and she rose and served him.

Neither the MARCAN nor the MATTHEAN renditions of the Healing of Peter's mother-in-law is technically a Petrine passage. Simon, or Peter, is present in name only. It is his house and his mother-in-law which are involved with Jesus in this episode. Still, once again, there are editorial nuances present that attract our curiosity.

While Matthew obviously relocated this pericope to include it in his list of ten miracle stories in chapters 8 and 9,[7] and has abbreviated it "to the bone," his deletions all add up to one fascinating phenomenon: a reduction in the cast to include only Jesus and Peter's mother-in-law. The names of Andrew, James, and John are totally erased. Of the four called to be fishers-of-men in Matthew 4:18-20, only Peter's name remains, even though he is personally also left out of sight in the wings.

What is significant about this observation is that this passage begins an editorial tendency that will obtain throughout the First Gospel. The focus remains on Peter while the other disciples fade more and more into the background.

Aside from the list of the twelve disciples in Matthew 10:2ff., seven are never heard from again in the First Gospel. Of the five remaining instances "Matthew" appears only once as the replace-

[7]For more detailed studies of Matthew's construction of these two chapters, see Wm. G. Thompson, "Reflections on the Composition of Mt. 8:1–9:34," *The Catholic Biblical Quarterly* 33 (1971) 368–387; Also Jack Dean Kingsbury, "Observations on the 'Miracle Chapters' of Matthew 8–9," *Catholic Biblical Quarterly* 40 (1978) 559–573.

ment for MARK's "Levi" in Mark 2:14/Matthew 9:9, but says nothing. Two others, the brothers, James and John appear together with Peter in Matthew 1:22 and 17:1, but, while present, in neither story do James and John play any active role. As detected in the previous chapter, the inner-circle idea was omitted from Matthew's retelling of the Healing of Jairus' Daughter account as well as from the pericope which asked about the appointed time for the destruction of the temple. Now, we see they are removed from the Healing of Peter's Mother-in-law miracle story as well.

In the remaining MARCAN passages which involved James and John, the first evangelist is at his cleverest in shielding them from the readers' view. In Matthew's version of the story of Jesus at Prayer in the Garden of Gethsemane (Mark14:33/Matt 26:37), James and John lose what little individual identity they have left when Matthew reduces them simply to "the sons of Zebedee." And in his retelling of the Mark 10:35-45/Matthew 20:20-28 account of James' and John's question to Jesus about what honored positions they might have in the Kingdom of God, Matthew has their mother make the request for them. Even if the evangelist's reason was to protect the two disciples from being responsible for such a self-aggrandizing petition, their replacement by "Mrs. Zebedee" nevertheless has the effect of pushing them one step closer to oblivion. It leaves them without one speaking role in the entire drama of the First Gospel.

Even in the transfiguration story (Mark 9:2-8/Matt 17:1-8), where Matthew does retain the inner-circle construct, the focus is directed more intently upon Peter. He speaks in the future first-person singular instead of the first-person plural as in MARK, saying: "If you wish, I will build, *poieesw,* three booths here. . . ."

Finally, there is the further illuminating fact that Matthew eliminates the Mark 9:38-41 episode in which John, acting alone without his brother, asks Jesus about the man who was casting out demons in Jesus' name. The absence of this account means that only Judas Iscariot compares at all with Peter in the First Gospel. They are the only two disciples who are specifically named and fill speaking roles. Judas, of course, did so when he betrayed Jesus in Matthew 26:14-16 and 25 and when he committed suicide in 27:3-10. Ironically, Judas' contrition as expressed only in

MATTHEW (27:4a) is more explicit than Peter's after his denials (26:75c). Other than these few instances, Peter is the only one who speaks or acts independently in the first Gospel, thanks to Matthew's careful redaction.

What is the import of this editorial focus on Peter? In 95 percent of the First Gospel, Peter stands alone. As for the other disciples, for the most part, they act *en masse.* Peter is listed among them, and occasionally speaks for them. Yet, he is in a class by himself. It is plain that Peter was of particular interest to Matthew—almost an obsession—but what the precise nature of that predisposition was is a thorny question which at this point remains beyond reach.

3. The List of the Twelve Disciples

MARK 3:14-19

[14]And he appointed twelve to be with him, and to be sent out to preach [15]and have authority to cast out demons; [16]Simon whom he surnamed Peter; [17]James the son of Zebedee and John the brother of James, whom he surnamed Boanerges, that is, sons of thunder; [18]Andrew, and Philip, and Bartholomew, and Matthew, and Thomas, and James the son of Alphaeus, and Thaddeus, and Simon the Cananaean, and Judas Iscariot who betrayed him.

MATTHEW 10:2-4

[2]The names of the twelve apostles are these: first Simon, who is called Peter, and Andrew his brother; James the son of Zebedee and John his brother.
[3]Philip and Bartholomew, Thomas and Matthew, the tax collector, James the son of Alphaeus, and Thaddeus, [4]Simon the Cananaean, and Judas Iscariot, who betrayed him.

Matthew's list of the twelve disciples is certainly more poetic than was the case in his MARCAN source. He presents them neatly in pairs, supplying additional identifying phrases for those whom the reader has met before (Matthew), or will again (Judas), and those lesser known apostles whose given names are the same as those more familiar disciples, specifically James and Simon.[8] Style was a concern of the first evangelist. He is a "scribe trained. . . . " (Matt 13:52).

The one item here of particular interest to us is Matthew's insertion of the single word "first," *prwtos,* before "Simon called Peter" in 10:2. MARK didn't have it. What compelled Matthew to add it? I suppose we could conclude with Kingsbury, Schweizer, and Strecker that the evangelist just felt a need to make explicit what was obvious, that Peter is listed first whenever he is found in the company of other disciples.[9] However, there is certainly more to it than mere numerical priority. When "first" is made explicit, leading off a list of supposed peers, it quite naturally also conveys the notion of priority in terms of responsibility and/or privilege. There is some "pride of place," if you will. R.V.G. Tasker, in his commentary, opines that "first" automatically implies "foremost."[10] Otherwise it would be redundant.[11] At the very least, its presence here suggests that Peter is a *primus inter pares,* a "first among equals" within the company of the twelve disciples.[12]

However, this is not the last word about being "first" in Matthew's Gospel. The concept appears again in several locations.

[8]This is the observation of Joachim Jeremias, *New Testament Theology, I* (1971) 232. Gundry, *Matthew* (1982) 182f. adds the thought that Matthew liked the "brother" concept because of its metaphorical connotation denoting Christian fellowship. Gundry also suggests that Matthew may have paired the disciples because he had earlier omitted the MARCAN missionary command to go out "two by two" (Mark 6:7).

[9]This is the focus of Jack Dean Kingsbury, "The Figure of Peter in Matthew's Gospel as a Theological Problem," *Journal of Biblical Literature,* 98, 1 (March 1979) 69–76. Eduard Schweizer, *The Good News According to Matthew* (1975) 237, avers that "first" in Matthew 10:2 does not refer "to some special primacy." Georg Strecker, *Der Weg der Gerechtigkeit* (1971) 204, n. 1, says that "first" in MATTHEW is hardly anything more than a "concretizing" of the MARCAN text.

[10]R.V.G. Tasker, *The Gosepl According to St. Matthew. Tyndale New Testament Commentaries* (1961) 106.

[11]Cf. W. F. Albright and C. S. Mann, *Matthew, The Anchor Bible* (1971) 117.

[12]I personally do not like the phrase, "first among equals." It is too politically pliable, allowing everyone to place the emphasis where he or she chooses. Of course, that is also why it is appropriate at this early stage in our rehearsal of the research when we are still not sure what Matthew has in mind for Peter.

The impact of these passages may have something to say about the way the insertion here is to be understood.

In Matthew 19:30, in another MARCAN Petrine passage to be analyzed later, Jesus concludes a series of eschatolological promises to Peter and to the disciples with the warning, "But many that are first will be last, and the last first." Then, as if that were not enough, Matthew adds from his own sources the Parable of the Laborers in the Vineyard (20:1-16) which closes with the same emphatic reminder: "So the last will be first, and the first last."[13] Finally, as if to make the point unmistakably clear, there is a third statement in the next paragraph, Matthew 20:27: "Whoever would be first among you must be your slave." This trilogy, showing the hand of Matthean redaction throughout, surely evinces a special Matthean concern: Neither priority, nor prominence necessarily translate into preeminence in the Kingdom of Heaven, or in Matthew's concept of the Church.

There is no explicit connection, of course, between "first" in 10:2 and "the first shall be last" in 19:30 and 20:16, 27, and we would probably ignore the mere appearance of such an association if it were not for the fact that Matthew's portrayal of Peter in the First Gospel so closely adheres to this suggested design. By virtue of Peter's denials of Jesus and his absence from Matthew's resurrection accounts, he who was once "first" in terms of his call, prominence, and general visibility, for all practical purposes, ends up last, nameless and out of sight in the post-Passion accounts.

Once again, we quote Augustine Stock, quoting Van Iersel: "Matthew's gospel presents a broad picture of Peter that can be summed up as 'good beginning—poor ending.' "[14] That is the lesson we learn from Matthew 10:2-4, and particularly Matthew's insertion of "first." What the evangelist gives he can also take away.[15]

[13]The shift in sequence form first-last-last-first in Matthew 19:30 to last-first-first-last in 20:16 seems more curious than significant. In the second instance, the sequence of the Laborers in the Vineyard parable is reflected. Matthew is not encouraging tardiness or sloth.

[14]Stock, "Ironic?" (1987) 68.

[15]The fact that, to my knowledge, no other published exegete has taken the "first . . . first-last" combination seriously has often made me wonder if I were "reach-

4. The Transfiguration

MARK 9:2-8	MATTHEW 17:1-8
[2]And after six days Jesus took with him Peter and James and John, and led them up a high mountain apart by themselves; and he was transfigured before them, [3]and his garments became glistening, intensely white, as no fuller on earth could bleach them.	[1]And after six days Jesus took with him Peter and James and John his brother, and led them up a high mountain apart. [2]And he was transfigured before them, and his face shone like the sun, and his garments became white as light.
[4]And there appeared to them Elijah with Moses; and they were talking to Jesus.	[3]And behold, there appeared to them Moses and Elijah, talking with him.
[5]And Peter said to Jesus, "Master, it is well that we are here; let us make three booths, one for you and one for Moses and one for Elijah."	[4]And Peter said to Jesus, "Lord, it is well that we are here; if you wish, I will make three booths here, one for you and one for Moses and one for Elijah."
[6]For he did not know what to say, for they were exceedingly afraid.	
[7]And a cloud overshadowed them, and a voice came out of the cloud, "This is my beloved Son; listen to him."	[5]He was still speaking, when lo, a bright cloud overshadowed them, and a voice from the cloud said, "This is my beloved Son, with whom I am well pleased; listen to him."
	[6]When the disciples heard this, they fell on their faces, and were filled with awe.
	[7]But Jesus came and touched them, saying, "Rise, and have no fear."
[8]And suddenly looking around they no longer saw anyone with them but Jesus only.	[8]And when they lifted up their eyes, they saw no one but Jesus only.

ing" for significance here. Yet, in view of Matthew's recognized penchant for inclusios and careful paralleling of terms elsewhere I concluded that the widely separated references to "first" in 10:2 and 19:30 etc., nevertheless had to be seen in relationship one to the other.

Just when it seems that we may be detecting some pattern in Matthew's treatment of Peter, we come to this "throw-back" account, as far as the first disciple is concerned. The Transfiguration according to Matthew appears to be an old Jewish Christian tradition[16] that exalts Jesus Christologically,[17] retains the inner circle of disciples idea, and improves the portrait of Peter. It is the kind of pericope that seems to support all the old traditional views inherent in the Matthew 16:17-19 syndrome.

MARK'S version of the Transfiguration still shows some of the rough edges of originality. There is the redundant emphasis on Jesus' privacy, *kat' idian monous,* "by himself alone" (9:2). Sounding very much like an Oxydol commercial, MARK recorded graphically that Jesus' garments "became glistening, intensely white as no fuller (bleacher, launderer) on earth could bleach them." Jesus' guests, curiously, were "Elijah *with* Moses" (9:4). This awkward construction suggests that perhaps the account originally had to do only with Elijah as the eschatological forerunner of the Messiah (Mal 3:1 and 4:5).[18] Peter naturally acted as spokesman for the inner circle in MARK, making the all too human suggestion that they build three shrines for the three

[16]Among the better studies of this pericope are those by Ernst Lohmeyer, "Die Verklärung Jesus nach dem Markus-Evangelium," *Zeitschrift für die neutestamentliche Wissenschaft* 21, 3 (1922) 185–215; G. H. Boobyer, *St. Mark and the Transfiguration Story* (1942); Harald Riesenfeld, *Jésus Transfiguré* (1947); Howard Clark Kee, "The Transfiguration in Mark: Epiphany or Apocalyptic Vision," *Understanding the Sacred Text,* ed. John Reumann (1972) 137–152.

[17]Boobyer, *St. Mark and the Transfiguration Story* (1942) 27–47; Riesenfeld, *Transfiguré* (1947) 304f.; and Kee, "The Transfiguration in Mark" (1972) 149, argue that the theological orientation and focus of the transfiguration is eschatological. Much of the terminology is apocalyptic: "mountain," "cloud." There are also eschatological overtones in the Matthean context, especially in Matthew 17:9-10 (cf. also Luke 9:31). However, Matthew's redaction with its enhanced Mosaic motif reminiscent of Deuteronomy 18:15 and the expanded response of the disciples to the heavenly announcement of Jesus' divine Sonship add up to make this account in the First Gospel a Christological epiphany, a Christophany. For more on the Mosaic themes in the Matthean Transfiguration story, see O. Lamar Cope, "Matthew, A Scribe Trained for the Kingdom of Heaven," *The Catholic Biblical Quarterly,* Monograph Series 5 (1976) 99–102.

[18]Schweizer, *The Good News According to Matthew* (1975) 349, sees the "Elijah with Moses" order, plus the singular verb, as evidence that the "episode was originally an appearance of Elijah, to which Moses was added later. . . . "

heavenly guests. That impractical idea was met with the denunciation in Mark 9:6, suggesting that Peter didn't know what he was talking about. The disciples' fear had deluded their minds. Then came the climax to the story. A voice from out of the clouds identified Jesus as God's beloved Son and encouraged all to listen to him.

Matthew retains nearly 90 percent of MARK's words, but rearranges and edits the material in very subtle, significant ways. The redundant *monous,* "alone" is removed in Matthew 17:1. Jesus' clothing now becomes a more celestial "white as the light," and Matthew adds "his face shone like the sun," emphasizing the Mosaic motif (cf. Exod 34:29). Moses is now also listed before Elijah in correct chronological order. Peter's prominence is slightly increased by the fact that in Matthew 17:4 he politely asks "if you wish," and then speaks only for himself in the future first person singular, "I will build. . . . " The vacuousness of this proposal is still signaled by Jesus cutting Peter off in mid-sentence, but, note, the negative comment, so typical of Mark's Messianic Secret approach, indicating that Peter did not realize what he had said, has been deleted. The slate of Peter's sins of misspeak has been wiped clean. Now, in the middle of the pericope instead of at the end as in MARK, the voice from heaven identifies Jesus as the Son of God, adding "with whom I am well pleased," reminiscent of Jesus' baptism (Matt 3:17). It is at this point, after the *Bath Qol,* the voice from heaven, that the disciples, are overwhelmed with awe and fear. Matthew redactionally adds two entire verses (Matt 17:6-7) of his own composition to describe the disciples' plight and Jesus' response. Jesus "touches" them and reassures them with the admonition: "Rise and have no fear." With that the curtain descends on this marvelous story.

But what a reversal from all the negatives with regard to Peter that we had uncovered in previous accounts! Were we mistaken? Does this discredit our redactional-critical approach?

No, for two reasons.

First, if we will follow the same practice as we did with *prwtos* in the previous review of Matthew 10:2, we will find that Matthew's deletion of Mark 9:5 about Peter not knowing what he was saying is duplicated with regard to all of the disciples in Gethsemane in Matthew 26:43 vs. Mark 14:40c. There, in MARK, the disciples did not know how to answer Jesus' remonstrance when he found them asleep. Matthew, thus, parallels Peter and the disciples. He is not only concerned to redress the image of Peter. He seeks to do the same for the other disciples as well. We will have to remain equally sensitive to this editorial detail as our research continues.

Second, it is necessary to remember that this Transfiguration account is located within Matthew's Book IV where his five Petrine insertions are also found. A quick glance at several of them indicates that Matthew's redaction of this passage is remarkably consistent with what we find there. Christology is the basic theme. The story of Jesus and Peter walking on the water concludes with the disciples in the boat confessing, by virtue of Matthew's redaction: "Truly, you are the Son of God" (cf. Matt 14:33 vs. Mark 6:52). Similarly, Matthew 16:16 has Peter acknowledging Jesus as "the Christ, the Son of the Living God." Even the question about "sons of the kingdom" in the Temple Tax episode (17:24-27), reflects a Christological interest. Now here in the Transfiguration Story the voice from heaven similarly identifies Jesus as "my beloved Son" (Matt 17:5). Peter is always portrayed as seen in relation to Jesus.

In each pericope a kind of comparison, or contrast, situation between Jesus and Peter or Jesus and the disciples is also set up, with a "good beginning—poor ending." In Matthew 14:28-31, Peter walks on the water in the same way that Jesus walked on the sea, but then he sinks and requires divine rescue. Jesus extends his hand and lifts the soggy disciple above the waves. In the Caesarea Philippi presentation, Peter correctly confesses Jesus to be the Christ, but then very shortly thereafter again self-destructs by attempting to obstruct Jesus' mission to "go to Jerusalem and suffer many things from the elders and chief priests and scribes, and be killed, and on the third day be raised" (16:21-23). Jesus has to rebuke him in the strongest terms as Satan to restore him to his senses. The situation in the Temple Tax episode is not as clear, but even there Peter is closely identified with Jesus in Matthew 17:24-27, only to require redactional correction a few verses later in the question about how often should a person forgive a sinning brother (Matt 18:21-22).

Now, we find that Matthew has redactionally designed the same kind of situation in his rendition of the Transfiguration by adding verses 6 and 7. After the disciples, i.e., Peter, James, and John, had heard the *bath qol,* in verse 5, they are struck down with awe and fear. They could not stand in the presence of the Son of God. Jesus has to come himself to "touch" them (*haptw,* the same word used for healing diseases, cf. 8:3, 15, 9:29, 20:34) and to call them back to reality with the tender rebuke: "Rise and have no fear," verse 7. The scene is reminiscent of Peter in 14:31.

Matthew's use of comparison and/or contrast, then, is another editorial technique that bears watching. He seems to like it, but what does he intend to accomplish with it?

Our study of the transfiguration pericope has shown us that there is design and consistency in Matthew's editorial practice. To what ultimate end, however, remains to be seen.

5. Peter Asks about Rewards

MARK 10:28-31	MATTHEW 19:27-30
[28]Peter began to say to him, "Lo, we have left everything and followed you."	[27]Then Peter said in reply, "Lo, we have left everything and followed you. What then shall we have?"
[29]Jesus said, "Truly I say to you,	[28]Jesus said to them, "Truly, I say to you, in the new world when the Son of Man shall sit on his glorious throne, you who have followed me will also sit on twelve thrones, judging the twelve tribes of Israel.
there is no one who has left house or brothers or sisters or mother or father or children or lands, for my sake and for the gospel, [30]who will not receive a hundredfold now in this time, houses and brothers and sisters and mothers and children and lands, with persecutions, and	[29]And everyone who has left houses or brothers or sisters or father or mother or children or lands, for my name's sake, will receive a hundredfold,

MARK 10:28-31	MATTHEW 19:27-30
in the age to come eternal life. [31]But many that are first will be last, and the last first."	and inherit eternal life. [30]But many that are first will be last, and the last first."

This Petrine conversation is a sub-section of, or sequel to, the story of "The Rich Young Ruler" (Mark 10:17-31/Matt 19:16-30/ Luke 18:18-30). It appears in MATTHEW's Book V. Jesus had just finished decrying the distractive power of riches. "It is easier for a camel to go through the eye of a needle than for a rich man to enter the Kingdom of God" (Mark 10:25/Matt 19:24). Peter now enters into the dialogue in his capacity as spokesman for the disciples. According to MARK, Peter states a simple fact, whatever its implication may have been: "Lo, we have left everything and followed you" (Mark 10:28). Matthew, on the other hand, makes explicit the implication left implicit in the MARCAN version of the question, interjecting a note of self-centeredness: "What then shall we have?" (Matt 19:27). According to MARK, Jesus' reply promised a long list of rewards to be enjoyed "now in this time . . . and in the age to come eternal life" (Mark 10:29-30). Matthew, significantly, drops all references to the present time in favor of the future order, *paliggenesia,*[19] "when the Son of man shall sit on his glorious throne." No rewards in terms of possessions, powers, or privileges are to be anticipated in this life, not even "with persecutions" as Mark's obtrusive comment suggests in Mark 10:30. Rather, as a general principle, "the first will be last and the last first" (Matt 19:30).

[19]Literally "rebirth" or "regeneration." Siegfied Schultz, *Q, Die Spruchquelle der Evangelisten* (1972) 331, identifies the term as coming from Q. Cf. Luke 18:29. The word is found only twice in the New Testament, here and in Titus 3:5. In extra-canonical literature it has appeared in Philo and Josephus. Its origin, however, is believed to have been in Stoic philosophy. The popular contemporary idea of a convert being "born again" is a later derived meaning (Tit 3:5). The familiar King James Version rendering of John 3:3: " . . . except a man be born again . . . " translates *anwthen,* "from above," as in the NRSV. The RSV has "anew." *paliggenesia* is not used here. Cf. W. C. Allen, *A Critical and Exegetical Commentary on the Gospel According to S. Matthew* (1907) 212; T. W. Manson, *The Sayings of Jesus* (1957) 216f.; F. C. Fenton, *The Gospel of Matthew* (1963) 316f.; H. Benedict Green, *The Gospel According to Matthew* (1975) 172f.; Gundry, *Matthew* (1982) 398f.

This statement is consistent in tone and direction with another found only in Matthew 23:8-11:

> But you are not to be called rabbi, for you have one teacher and you are all brethren. And call no man your father on earth, for you have one Father, who is in heaven. Neither be called masters, for you have one master, the Christ. He who is greatest among you shall be your servant; whoever exalts himself shall be humbled, and whoever humbles himself will be exalted.

Matthew is a champion of the cherished Christian principle of "delayed gratification." On earth, and in time, he countenances no social or ecclesial stratification within the Christian community. All rewards are to be realized only in the world to come. No one, therefore, should covet them in the present.

In view of the accolades heaped upon Peter about his authority "on earth and in heaven" in connection with his confession of Jesus at Caesarea Philippi (16:17-19), and in conjunction with the Temple Tax question (17:24-27), these redactionally inserted, first-last, anti-status comments sound a curious note of discord.

6. Peter's Boast

MARK 14:26-31

[26]And when they had sung a hymn, they went out to the Mount of Olives. [27]And Jesus said to them, "You will all fall away; for it is written, 'I will strike the shepherd, and the sheep will be scattered.' [28]But after I am raised up, I will go before you to Galilee."

[29]Peter said to him, "Even though they all fall away, I will not." [30]And Jesus said to him, "Truly, I say to you, this very night, before the cock crows twice, you will deny

MATTHEW 26:30-35

[30]And when they had sung a hymn, they went out to the Mount of Olives. [31]The Jesus said to them, "You will all fall away because of me this night; for it is written, 'I will strike the shepherd, and the sheep of the flock will be scattered.' [32]But after I am raised up, I will go before you to Galilee."

[33]Peter declared to him, "Though they all fall away because of you, I will never fall away." [34]Jesus said to him, "Truly, I say to you, this very night, before the cock crows,

MARK 14:26-31	MATTHEW 26:30-35
me three times." [31]But he said vehemently, "If I must die with you, I will not deny you."	you will deny me three times." [35]Peter said to him, "Even if I must die with you, I will not deny you."
And they all said the same.	And so said all the disciples.

Only a superficial comparison of the Matthean version of this "Peter's Boast" pericope with its MARCAN source will reveal their almost verbatim concurrence.[20] There is little sign of redactional activity on the part of the first evangelist, and what there is, at least on the surface, manifests no particular design or tendency.

Matthew omits "twice" in 26:34 (cf. Mark 14:30). We might see this as a way that Matthew was intending to increase Peter's guilt, speeding up his denials, as it were. However, such an interpretation, while logical enough, would undoubtedly prove spurious. When the denial scene as presented in MARK is reviewed, it indicates that all of Peter's denials occur before MARK mentions any cockcrow (14:72),[21] even though that very early morning hour when the events related occurred may have been known as the second cockcrow. It is more likely, therefore, that Matthew is simply correcting this prediction to fit the facts as he received them.

On the other hand, Matthew's omission of "vehemently," *ekperissws,* in Matthew 26:35 vs. Mark 14:31, could suggest that Matthew wished to soften Peter's boast, and his responsibility for it, to some degree. Perhaps. But again there are small telltale signs to the contrary. In verse 33, compared to Mark 14:29, Matthew adds a second "fall away," *skandalistheesomai,* and strengthens MARK's "I will not," with a simple *ouk,* to "I will never. . . ." *oudepote.* It is counter-productive to quibble over such tradeoffs.

From my perspective, the real significance of this pericope lies in Matthew's use of the verb translated "to fall away," *skandalizw.* Although common also in MARK where it is found eight times, Matthew employs the verb nineteen times and its noun cog-

[20]Matthew keeps sixty-three of MARK's ninety words.

[21]The addition of "Then the cock crowed" at Mark 14:68c in the NRSV is text-critically unfounded in my estimation.

nate an additional five times.[22] Such frequent occurrence suggests that for the first evangelist "falling away," "offending," or acting as a "stumblingblock" or "scandal" to others was a very serious problem, no doubt one which prevailed within his own community.

Of particular interest in this study are the previous occurrences of this concept in Matthew 16:23, 17:27, and 18:6-9. In the first instance, and in a key sentence found only in MATTHEW, Jesus follows up his Satan-saying by directly denouncing Peter as a *skandalon,* i.e., "a hindrance" or a "stumblingblock."[23] In Matthew 17:27, Peter is again associated with the danger of misleading the tax collectors as Jesus cautions him to pay the tax in order "not to give offence," *skandaliswmen.* Finally, in 18:6-9, as part of MATTHEW's sermon on the Church, Jesus discusses in graphic detail the gravity of offending, *skandalisee,* the "little ones," or of permitting a hand or an eye to cause one to sin, *skandalizei.* In the redacted addition, verse 7, Jesus even voices the explicit warning: " . . . woe to the man by whom the temptation, *skandalon,* comes." Peter, then, in Matthew's portrayal, should have been well aware of his vulnerability and propensity for "scandalizing." This fact makes his boast here in 26:33, just before his denials, all the more self-incriminating. He knew it, he disclaimed it, and yet he did it!

This brief pericope of Peter's Boast which Matthew repeats almost as he found it in MARK may appear disarmingly unremarkable on the surface, but in view of earlier redactional emphases made elsewhere in the First Gospel, it now assumes a rather crucial position in Matthew's Petrine picture after all.

7. Asleep in Gethsemane

MARK 14:32-42

[32]And they went to a place which was called Gethsemane; and he said

MATTHEW 26:36-46

[36]Then Jesus went with them to a place called Gethsemane, and he

[22]Cf. Luz, *Matthew 1-7* (1989) 68.

[23]Happily, the NRSV has returned to the translation "stumbling block," replacing the too weak "hindrance" in the RSV.

MARK 14:32-42

to his disciples, "Sit here, while I pray. [33]And he took with him Peter and James and John, and began to be greatly distressed and troubled. [34]And he said to them, "My soul is very sorrowful, even to death: remain here, and watch." [35]And going a little farther, he fell on the ground and prayed that, if it were possible, the hour might pass from him. [36]And he said, "Abba, Father, all things are possible to thee; remove this cup from me; yet not what I will, but what thou wilt."

[37]And he came and found them sleeping, and he said to Peter, "Simon, are you sleeping? Could you not watch one hour? [38]Watch and pray that you may not enter into temptation; the spirit indeed is willing, but the flesh is weak."

[39]And again he went away and prayed saying the same words.

[40]And again he came and found them sleeping, for their eyes were very heavy; and they did not know what to answer him.

[41]And he came the third time, and said to them, "Are you still sleeping and taking your rest? It is enough; the hour has come; the Son of Man is betrayed into the hands of sinners. [42]Rise, let us be going; see, my betrayer is at hand."

MATTHEW 26:36-46

said to his disciples, "Sit here, while I go yonder and pray." [37]And taking with him Peter and the two sons of Zebedee, he began to be sorrowful and troubled. [38]Then he said to them, "My soul is very sorrowful, even to death; remain here, and watch with me." [39]And going a little farther, he fell on his face and prayed,

My Father, if it be possible, let this cup pass from me; nevertheless, not as I will, but as thou wilt."

[40]And he came to the disciples and found them sleeping; and he said to Peter, "So you could not watch with me one hour? [41]Watch and pray that you may not enter into temptation; the spirit indeed is willing, but the flesh is weak."

[42]Again, for the second time he went away and prayed, "My Father, if this cannot pass unless I drink it, thy will be done."

[43]And again he came and found them sleeping, for their eyes were heavy.

So leaving them again, he went away and prayed for the third time, saying the same words.

[45]Then he came to the disciples and said to them, "Are you still sleeping and taking your rest? Behold, the hour is at hand, and the Son of Man is betrayed into the hands of sinners. [46]Rise, let us be going; see, my betrayer is at hand."

This poignant pericope of Jesus suffering in Gethsemane falls hard on the heels of the one just reviewed. The only difference between the two is that this one truly is unremarkable from a redaction-critical point of view. What points of interest there are have already been noted in previous analyses. Matthew typically reduces the inner circle to Peter and the "sons of Zebedee" instead of naming James and John in verse 37. In verse 40, he omits the Aramaic "Simon" (cf. Mark 14:37) and in verse 43 he similarly deletes the MARCAN comment that "the disciples did not know what to answer" Jesus, reminding us of Matthew's parallel erasure of Peter's supposed dumbfoundedness in Mark's Transfiguration account (Mark 9:6).

Other than that, we might say that the greatest contribution of this Petrine reference is that it serves as the quiet before the storm.

8. Peter's Denials[24]

MARK 14:53-72	MATTHEW 26:57-75
[53]And they led Jesus to the high priest; and all the chief priests and the elders and the scribes were assembled. [54]And Peter had followed him at a distance, right into the courtyard of the high preist; and he was sitting with the guards, and warming himself at the fire. [66]And as Peter was below in the courtyard, one of the maids of the high priest came; [67]and seeing Peter warming himself, she looked at	[57]Then those who had seized Jesus led him to Caiaphas the high priest, where the scribes and the elders had gathered. [58]But Peter followed him at a distance, as far as the couryard of the high priest, and going inside he sat with the guards to see the end. [69]Now Peter was sitting outside in the couryard. And a maid came up to him, and said,

[24]For more extended analyses of the Peter's Denials accounts see Günter Klein, "Die Verleugnung des Petrus. Eine traditionsgeschichtliche Untersuchung," *Zeitschrift für Theologie und Kirche,* 58, 3 (February 1962) 285–328; Eta Linnemann, "Die Verleugnung des Petrus," *Zeitschrift für Theologie und Kirche,* 63 (1966) 1–32; Rudolf Pesch, "Die Verleugnung des Petrus. Eine Studie zu Mk 14, 54. 66–72" (Mark 14, 26–31) (1974) 42–62; Donald P. Senior, *The Passion Narrative According to Matthew: A Redactional Study* (1975) 192–209.

MARK 14:53-72	MATTHEW 26:57-75
him, and said, "You also were with the Nazarene, Jesus." [68]But he denied it, saying, "I neither know nor understand what you mean." And he went out into the gateway. [69]And the maid saw him, and began again to say to the bystanders, "This man is one of them." [70]But again he denied it. And after a little while again the bystanders said to Peter, "Certainly you are one of them; for you are a Galilean." [71]But he began to invoke a curse on himself and to swear, "I do not know this man of whom you speak." [72]And immediately the cock crowed a second time. And Peter remembered how Jesus had said to him, "Before the cock crows twice, you will deny me three times." And he broke down and wept.	"You also were with Jesus the Galilean." [70]But he denied it before them all, saying "I do not know what you mean." [71]And when he went out to the porch, another maid saw him, and she said, to the bystanders, "This man was with Jesus of Nazareth." [72]And again he denied it with an oath, "I do not know the man." [73]After a little while the bystanders came up and said to Peter, "Certainly you are also one of them, for your accent betrays you." [74]Then he began to invoke a curse on himself and to swear, "I do not know the man." And immediately the cock crowed. [75]And Peter remembered the saying of Jesus, "Before the cock crows, you will deny me three times." And he went out and wept bitterly.

Like Matthew's transpositions of the Peter's Boast and Asleep in Gethsemane accounts, this one recounting Peter's denials may at first appear equally unimaginative when viewed redaction-critically. But as we have learned to our peril, first impressions in MATTHEW can be deceiving. The evidence here is cumulative, subtle, and very explosive!

The description of events in MATTHEW begins on a fatalistic note. Matthew 26:58 concludes: "Peter . . . sat with the guards to see the end," replacing Mark's " . . . he was sitting with the guards, and warming himself at the fire" (Mark 14:54). Apparently, Matthew would have his readers believe that Peter was not very optimistic about Jesus' chances from the start, a sure sign of weak faith. Peter had feet of clay.

In verse 69, the first evangelist omits Mark's identification of the maid as one employed by the high priest. In MATTHEW, she was just a maid without any association with power, about as unthreatening as anyone could be.[25] Nevertheless, when she suggests that he, Peter, was also seen with Jesus, Peter feigns ignorance and denies "before them all." This is an important Matthean addition. Peter's guilt is public.

In verse 71, a second maid confronts Peter—not the same maid as in MARK (14:69). This time, Peter's denial is punctuated with an oath and is made more Christologically explicit. He does not know the "man," Jesus of Nazareth. In Mark 14:70a there had been no oath and the subject matter of Peter's denial had been more impersonal. "He denied 'it,' " that is, what the maid had said about his also having been in the company of the Nazarene.

Matthew's account of the third denial (Matt 26:74) is almost identical to that of MARK which was certainly denigrating enough (Mark 14:71). Peter "began to invoke a curse on himself and to swear, 'I do not know the man.' " What, if any, significance is to be attached to Matthew's exchange of compound verbs translated "to invoke a curse," *katathematizein,* for Mark's *anathematizein,* is difficult to say.[26] However, it should be noted that both are active infinitives and usually require an object. However, there is none here. The RSV translators cautiously assume, therefore, that Peter invoked a curse "on himself." But the verbs are not reflexive. As several scholars have suggested, the implication here could just as well be that Peter cursed Jesus as a way of dramatizing his disdain for the accused.[27] That would be the ultimate blasphemy. Either way, this is not a pretty scene!

[25]*paidiskee,* "maid" in the RSV, is a diminutive of *pais* and literally means "little girl" or "young female slave."

[26]F. W. Beare, *The Gospel According to Matthew* (1981) 524, says Matthew's alteration involves no change in meaning. However, Eduard Schweizer, *The Good News According to Matthew* (1975) 500, demurs: "If anything, Matthew places even more stress on the curse."

[27]In favor of this perspective are Helmut Merkel, "Peter's Curse," *The Trial of Jesus* (1970) 66–71; Gundry, *Matthew* (1982) 551. Disagreeing are Allen, *Matthew* (1907) 286; Albright and Mann, *Matthew* (1971) 337; Beare, *Matthew* (1981) 524. Uncertain is Meier, *Matthew* (1980) 335: "most probably on himself, though possibly on Jesus." In his *The Vision of Matthew. Christ, Church and Morality in the First Gospel* (1979) 194, n. 231, Meier admits that if the curse was intended for Jesus, it "would bring the crescendo of curses to a terrifyng conclusion." - If intransitive here, it is the only such use of *katathematizein* found anywhere.

In summary, then, not only has Matthew portrayed Peter as denying before two harmless accusers, as in MARK, but before three, and in fact, "before them all." And not only did Matthew have Peter resort to cursing and swearing on one occasion, as in MARK, but on two.

What is doubly devastating, however, is the discovery that MATTHEW had redactionally added explicit anticipatory prohibitions against both denying and swearing. In 10:33 Matthew employed a passage, generally recognized as coming from Q, which says expressly: "Whoever denies me before men, I also will deny before my Father who is in heaven." Yet, here, thanks to Matthew's redaction, Peter denied "before them all!" Similarly, in Matthew 5:34, in a saying of Jesus which may also be traditional, but is found only in the First Gospel, Jesus says: "Do not swear at all, either by heaven . . . or by the earth . . . or by Jerusalem. . . . Let what you say be simply 'Yes' or 'No'; anything more than this comes from evil." Judged by these standards in the First Gospel, Peter's denials, as edited by the first evangelist, locate him as tripping dangerously along the precipice of divine rejection.[28] The crescendo of Petrine self-incrimination has reached its climax.

More subtle, but equally significant, Matthew now deigns to leave Peter permanently mired in this personal and spiritual morass. The denials scene concludes with Peter haunted by his guilt retreating from the courtyard of the high priest, weeping bitterly as he goes (Matt 26:75c). And that is the dreary conclusion to the story of Peter in MATTHEW! He is never mentioned by name again. There is no attempt at any explicit rehabilitation.[29] How the mighty has fallen!

We are again haunted by that omnipresent question: Why? Mat-

[28]Gundry, *Matthew* (1982) 548f., concludes: "Peter is forfeiting his salvation." But this must be an overstatement. Matthew continues to speak of the "eleven." If Judas is the one who is missing, Matthew must have intended Peter to be retained in the company of the eleven disciples. His role has been drastically diminished, but not excluded.

[29] By way of contrast, see Mark 16:7; Luke 24:34; John 21: 15-19; Acts 1-12; 1 Corinthians 15:5. In short, MATTHEW stands virtually alone in neglecting this familiar aspect of early Church tradition. This fact itself should be enough to arouse suspicion as to Matthew's perspective and intention.

thew's step-by-step intensification of Peter's plight here seems so unnecessary. In comparison with the presentation in MARK, which was already demeaning enough, Matthew's redaction appears uncompromisingly vindictive. What editorial purpose could have prompted such a sad climax to what began as such a promising story about fishermen becoming fishers-of-men?

As we close this review of the eight MARCAN Petrine accounts reprised in MATTHEW, we feel much like "the Man from La Mancha" who didn't know where he was going, but was sure he was making progress. We have learned to recognize more and more of Matthew's conventions, preferences, concerns, and themes. We have detected more indications of redactional consistency which give rise to hope for a solution to the enigmas that remain. But the keys to understanding Matthew's basic editorial practice and theological purpose continue to elude us. Curiosity compels us onward.

6

Petrine References Unique to Matthew

The spotlight now swings to center stage, to the five decisive Petrine references found only in the First Gospel. These are truly unique passages, especially the three larger pericopes, 14:28-31, 16:17-19, and 17:24-27. Nowhere else, in any of the Gospels, is any other disciple described in the trappings of deity as is Peter in Matthew 14:29, walking on water. Nowhere else is any other disciple the recipient of such inordinate praise, power, and privilege as is Peter in 16:17-19. And nowhere else is anyone identified with Jesus in such personal terms—not even his mother and brothers—as is Peter in the Temple Tax account (Matt 17:24-27) where Jesus tells him to use one coin to pay the tax "for me and for yourself."

The other two references, Matthew 15:15 and 18:21, are less spectacular. Their uniqueness lies in the fact that the First Gospel alone introduces Peter as the one who asks significant questions which had been expressed either by the disciples generally or by Jesus himself in the originating MARK and Q source materials.

If anything in this First Gospel is going to reveal the evangelist's intentions, perspectives, and techniques, we might think these passages would do it. After all, Matthew himself selected them, or even composed them, and carefully located them in the scenario of his Gospel where they would best accomplish his editorial purposes. They appear to promise just what redaction-critics are looking for. Unfortunately, practically every exegete from Bacon on has taken the bait,[1] meeting with only limited success. Researching these five passages exclusively, or giving them disproportionate attention, inevitably results in skewed analyses of the problem of Peter in MATTHEW. These five insertions, on balance, are clearly weighted in Peter's favor with Matthew 16:17-19 especially tipping the scale. As already noted, however, Peter's role elsewhere in the First Gospel is not all that complimentary. A holistic approach, therefore, is required if Matthew's editorial plan and consistency are to be recognized and appreciated.[2] That is why in this study we elected to begin slowly with a source-critical review of all of the Petrine passages in MATTHEW, followed by an investigation of the first evangelist's omissions of MARCAN Petrine references, and continuing with an examination of his redaction of all the Petrine pericopes transposed from the Second Gospel. By following this gradual procedure, we have tried to develop a broad framework—a trajectory, if you will—within which these five major Petrine references will hopefully now prove more productive, either confirming previous tentative conclusions or exposing what is spurious among earlier suggested options.

Excursus: MATTHEW'S Book IV

Before plunging into the texts themselves, however, there is still one other brief digression that should be made to complete our understanding of the setting for these special passages. From the very beginning we have noted the tantalizing fact that all five of

[1]Foremost among the studies focusing almost exclusively on the five uniquely MATTHEAN Petrine passages are B. W. Bacon, "The Petrine Supplements of Matthew," *The Expositor,* 8th series, 73 (1917) 1-23; Georg Strecker, *Der Weg der Gerechtigkeit* (1971) 196-206; eds. Raymond Brown, Carl Donfried, and John Reumann, *Peter in the New Testament* (1973) 75-107. Numerous other scholars have studied only one or another of the Petrine passages individually. Jack D. Kingsbury, "The Figure of Peter in Matthew's Gospel as a Theological Problem," *Journal of Biblical Literature,* 98, 1 (March 1979), makes a broad assessment of all Petrine passages in MATTHEW, but, in my view, fails to carefully distinguish between what is, and what is not, of redactional importance.

[2]The descending Matthean Petrine trajectory, from the positive addition of "first" in 10:2 to the negative deletion of Peter from Mark 16:7, is very important for providing perspective for interpretation.

these uniquely Matthean Petrine references are clustered within chapters 14–18, one in each chapter, of what has been traditionally recognized as MATTHEW's Book IV. We need to look at these five chapters now to discover the general thematic matrix of these five Petrine passages.[3]

Prior to Matthew 13:52 the first evangelist had redacted freely and copiously, adding, subtracting, and rearranging materials at will, but now as he reaches chapter 6 in his primary source, the Gospel of MARK, he suddenly becomes very restrained.[4] From this point to the end of the First Gospel, Matthew follows MARK with rare consistency. This means, however, that whatever editorial additions, omissions, or alterations do appear naturally assume potentially greater significance as reflecting a higher degree of uniqueness and redactional intentionality, whatever the bent of that intentionality may be.

MATTHEW's Book IV falls within this category. It encompasses the materials covered in Mark 6:1 to 9:50. In doing so, MATTHEW's Gospel straddles the two halves of MARK. According to the most common outline of the Second Gospel, Mark 1:1 to 8:30 presents a series of Christological glimpses of Jesus as teacher and miracle worker climaxing with Peter's good but still incomplete confession: "You are the Christ" (Mark 8:29).[5] Then, in Mark 8:31, MARK's passion history begins with Jesus' first of three uniform announcements (8:31, 9:31, and 10:33f.)

[3]For more detailed analyses of MATTHEW's Book IV, see John P. Meier, *The Vision of Matthew* (1979) 94–135; Also Hubert Frankemölle, *Jahwebund und Kirche Christi* (1974); B. W. Bacon, *Studies in Matthew* (1930) 218; and J. C. Fenton, *Saint Matthew* (1963) 235, note and discuss this sudden shift in Matthean editorial practice.

[4]The precise location where Matthew began to follow MARK more closely is still debated. Luz, *Matthew 1–7* (1989) 37, says Matthew 12:1/Mark 2:23. Because of the obvious Matthean construction of the Parables Discourse in Matthew 13:1-52, however, the consistency between MARK and MATTHEW is more visible in the narrative section beginning with Matthew 13:53.

[5]There is some indecision among MARCAN scholars whether Mark 8:27-33 climaxes the first half of MARK or initiates the second half. The determination apparently depends upon whether a geographical or a Christological outline is proposed. Cf. Willi Marxsen, *Mark the Evangelist* (1969) 70–73; Vincent Taylor, *The Gospel According to St. Mark,* 2nd ed. (1966) 107–111, 373; Eduard Schweizer, *The Good News According to Mark* (1970) 8–10.

of his impending arrest, conviction, and death. The underlying theme remains Christological throughout. Mark's passion story simply adds the emphasis that a true understanding of Christology, like the true practice of discipleship, necessarily involves suffering.[6]

Matthew now adopts this MARCAN material almost as is. With the help of a few omissions and a few more additions, however, he successfully reshapes a new unit of his own.

First, he omits two healing miracle stories (Mark 7:32-36 and 8:22-26)[7] which were either anticipated in his miracle chapters, Matthew 8:1–9:34, or subsumed in brief summaries such as Matthew 15:29-31. As mentioned earlier, the first evangelist also leaves out the account of the disciple John asking about "the strange exorcist" (Mark 9:38-41). Finally, he erases the brief digression about the Pharisees' practice of ritually washing everything before eating after their return from the market (Mark 7:3-4).

The impact of these omissions on Matthew's presentation is subtle. Jesus' prominence as a miracle-worker is slightly reduced in this section. On the other hand, the subtraction of John and the story of The Strange Exorcist, of course, makes the five additions of Peter all the more exceptional and noteworthy.[8] Peter, as an individual, remains unchallenged in the spotlight. The deletion of the discussion about the Pharisees' extensive ritual cleansing is undoubtedly due to the circumstance that Matthew was writing for a readership which was in large measure culturally Jewish in character. For them, a description of such traditional prac-

[6]Cf. Mark 8:34-35, 15:39.

[7]These are the Healing of the Deaf Man with a Speech Impediment and the Healing of the Blind Man from Bethsaida, respectively. Both involve the use of spit. Was Matthew too fastidious to use them? See also Matthew 12:22ff. where Jesus heals a man who was both blind and dumb. Did Matthew combine the two MARCAN stories into one? Cf. Jack Dean Kingsbury, "Observations on the 'Miracle Chapters' of Matthew 8–9," *The Catholic Biblical Quarterly,* 40, 4 (October 1978) 559–573.

[8]Another contributory reason for the omission of Mark 9:38-41 may be its focus on an outsider. MATTHEW's Sermon deals only with inside, i.e., Church, issues. Cf. J. D. Kingsbury, "The Verb AKOLOUTHEIN ('To Follow') as an Index of Matthew's View of His Community," *Journal of Biblical Literature,* 91, 1 (1978) 56–73.

tices was not necessary. It is vital to note, however, that Matthew did not hesitate to redactionally articulate the corresponding Christian view on ritual purification in Matthew 15:20: " . . . to eat with unwashed hands does not defile a man."

Compared to these omissions from MARK, Matthew's additions and intercalations are more significant and contributory to the new tone of this Book IV. There are three types of insertions: (1) those which involve Peter, and are already familiar to us; (2) several dominical sayings mostly from Q (cf. Matt 18:7/Luke 17:1; Matt 18:12-13/Luke 15:3-5; Matt 18:16-17, 19-20; Matt 18:21-22/ Luke 17:3-4; and Matt 18:23-35) which help to form the sermonic discourse in Matthew 18; and finally (3) an assortment of smaller passages about the disciples' relationship with the wider Jewish community, the Gentiles, and each other (cf. Matt 15:14/Luke 6:39; Matt 15:20, 16:3-4, 11-12). These insertions, taken together, give this section a pronounced didactic thrust focusing on the issue of proper relationships within as well as outside the circle of the disciples. In other words, in MATTHEW, ecclesiological, i.e., churchly, concerns are made to share the spotlight with the Christological emphasis inherited from MARK.

The concluding and climactic sermon in Matthew 18 is undoubtedly as determinative of the overall character of this Book IV as are the Petrine references.[9] It is addressed to the disciples (v. 1), as are all of Matthew's sermons. Its subject matter is varied and yet uniform, concerning life together within the Christian community.

Verses 1b-6 treat the reprehensible inclination of the disciples toward status-seeking in the Kingdom of Heaven. No one individual should aspire to dominate over the others. Rather, humility and child-like trust are required.

Verses 7-9 discuss the danger of scandalizing, *skandalizw,* i.e., causing others to sin. As we learned earlier, this must have been a serious community problem, deserving of the most certain and

[9]For exegetical studies of Matthew 18, see Wilhelm Pesch, "Die sogenannte Gemeindeordnung Mt 18," *Biblische Zeitschrift,* Neue Folge 7 (1963) 220–235; Wm. G. Thompson, *Matthew's Advice to a Divided Community, Mt. 17:22–18:35* (1970); Wolfgang Trilling, *Hausordnung Gottes Eine Auslegung von Matthäus 18* (1960); Georg Strecker, *Weg* (1971); James Martin, "The Church in Matthew," *Interpretating the Gospels,* ed. James Luther Mays (1981) 97–114.

severe punishment of the perpetrator: "It would be better for him to have a great millstone fastened round his neck and to be drowned in the depth of the sea."

The "little ones," *mikroi,* become the focus of verses 10-14. According to Matthew 10:42, "little ones" are also included among the disciples. They are not literally youths, but spiritual children, recent converts, novices, or weak and vulnerable members of the community.[10] Matthew is concerned that they be accepted and integrated. Accordingly, his version of the Q Parable of the Lost Sheep (Matt 18:12-14) does not deal with the subject of repentance as does the LUCAN rendition in 15:3-7, but with seeking the straying "little ones" to avoid back-door losses.[11]

With Matthew 18:15 the first evangelist turns our attention to another aspect of discipleship, the erring "brother," *adelphos.* The rest of the sermon discusses this subject outlining the proper three-step procedure for disciplining the sinning brother (vv. 15-18),[12] the need for prayer and communion with Christ (vv. 19-20), and above all, as the Parable of the Unforgiving Servant is made to illustrate, the absolute requirement that forgiveness be unlimited and sincere (vv. 21-35).

[10]J. D. Kingsbury, "Miracle Chapters," *Catholic Biblical Quarterly* (1978) 566, refers to the little ones as "no-accounts" in Matthew's community. Eduard Schweizer, "Observations of the Law and Charismatic Activity in Matthew," *New Testament Studies,* 16, 3 (1970) 222, describes them as "ascetic, charismatic, anti-official." H. B. Green, *The Gospel According to Matthew* (1975) 158, is more negative. Basing his views on Matthew 5:19, he sees them as relaxers of the Commandments, perhaps Gentile converts. Robert H. Gundry, *Matthew* (1982) 362, says "the masses." Thompson, *Advice* (1970) 119, denies any distinction between little ones and the disciples generally. The term is found also in the "Gospel of Thomas," 46, in *Synopsis Quattuor Evangeliorum,* ed. Kurt Aland (1963, 1985) 523.

[11]The classic study of this parable is that of Joachim Jeremias, *The Parables of Jesus* (1954) 38–40.

[12]The relationship of Matthew 18:15-17 to verse 18 is debated by various scholars. Thompson, *Advice* (1970) 179, says 18:15-17 is a pre-Matthean tradition. Gundry, *Matthew* (1982) 368, argues for Matthean composition. Trilling, *Hausordnung* (1960) 47, says verse 18 is integral to verses 15-17. The switch from singular to plural verbs in verse 18, however, argues for separate derivation. My position is that in 18:18 Matthew reproduced 16:19b distributing Peter's proposed authority to all disciples.

Significantly, it is in Matthew 18:17 that we find two of three explicit uses of "church," *ecclesia,* in the Gospels. The other occurrence is found just two chapters earlier in the critical "You are Peter" passage (16:18). The exclusive appearance in the Gospels of all three uses of "church" within the narrow confines of this MATTHEAN Book IV, relating events purportedly still within the public ministry of Jesus who otherwise spoke only of the Kingdom of God/Heaven, is clear evidence that Matthew was working, somewhat anachronistically, with later traditions developed, or at least, extant within his own community. "Church" here also gives the entire section a definite ecclesiological ambiance and Peter who is mentioned so prominently, a particular ecclesiastical aura.

It was the careful analyses of the various themes in this Book IV that led Gerhard Barth to conclude that the first evangelist while ostensibly writing about Jesus' disciples really had the Christians of his own community in mind;[13] that convinced Paul Hoffmann that Matthew's concept of the Church was that of a *Bruderschaft,* an unstratified "brotherhood";[14] and that prompted Wm. G. Thompson to characterize this Book IV, and especially its concluding discourse, as "Matthew's Advice to a Divided Community."[15]

Additionally, it was such snide, personal comments about "their" synagogues in Matthew 13:54 and the emotional depiction of the Pharisees as "blind guides" in 15:14 that suggested

[13]Gerhard Barth, "Matthew's Understanding of the Law," in *Tradition and Interpretation in Matthew* (1963) 111, says "Matthew . . . writes the situation of the Church into the life of the disciples." Jeremias, *Parables* (1954) 40, identifies the disciples with community leaders, i.e., the clergy. In agreement are H. Frankemölle, "Amtskritik im Matthäus-Evangelium?" *Biblica,* 54 (1973) 247–262, esp. 259. J. P. Meier, *Vision* (1979) 127–135, says "would-be leaders." R. Gundry, *Matthew* (1982) 362, believes "antinomian leaders." I see "disciples" used as a general designation of community members, i.e., Christians. "Brothers," and "little ones" are sub-categories.

[14]Paul Hoffmann, "Der Petrus-Primat im Matthäus-Evangelium," *Neues Testament und Kirche* (1974) 94–114.

[15]Thompson, *Advice* (1970). W. B. Bacon, *Studies* (1930) 297, entitles the section: "Concerning Church Administration." H. B. Green, *Matthew* (1975) 138, sees "The Church Foreshadowed" in Matthew 13:53–18:35.

to Krister Stendahl that Matthew must have been writing with a synagogue immediately "across the street" in mind.[16]

The net effect of the redactional alterations throughout this Book IV is that Matthew's new unit is manifestly more concerned than was MARK about community issues, internal and external—i.e., with ecclesiology[17]—rather than with Christology alone as in MARK. This is true even though two redactional Christological confessions are found in this section and continue to play an important part.

Peter's role has also become clearer. He is associated almost exclusively with Jesus or with matters internal to the community of the disciples, confirming the tendency detected already in our earlier comparison of Matthew 21:18-22 with Matthew 15:15. It is apparent from this observation that in this ecclesiological Book IV, as well as in subsequent sections of this First Gospel, Matthew is portraying Peter as a potential ecclesial, if not ecclesiastical, figure, as can be seen especially in 16:17-19. Redactionally speaking, Peter's shaky role as the foundation stone of the Church is of the essense of this Book IV. Clearly, however, the evangelist is not concerned with the Peter of history, but with the Peter of tradition exhibiting potentially larger-than-life ecclesiological contours within Matthew's own community.

END EXCURSUS

Perhaps now, with this overall view of the context in Matthew's Book IV in mind, we are better equipped to deal responsibly with the anomalies found in the special Petrine material in the First Gospel.

[16]Krister Stendahl, *The School of St. Matthew* (CWK Gleerup, Lund, n.d.) xi.

[17]J. P. Meier's characterization of the Church in MATTHEW as a *proleptic parousia* seems most apropos. An institution is not envisioned but a spiritual community of eschatological proportions is. Cf. Meier, *Vision* (1979) 215, n. 270. For additional reading on the concept of Church in MATTHEW, see David Stanley, "Kingdom to Church" in *Theological Studies,* 16 (1955) 1–29; Olaf Linton, *Das Problem der Urkirche in der Neuerren Forschung* (1932) esp. 132–138; Frankemölle, *Yahwebund* (1974) 41–56.

1. Peter Walking on the Water

MARK 6:45-52

[45]Immediately he made his disciples get into the boat and go before him to the other side, to Bethsaida, while he dismissed the crowd. [46]And after he had taken leave of them, he went up on the mountain to pray. [47]And when evening came, the boat was out on the sea, and he was alone on the land. [48]And he saw that they were making headway painfully, for the wind was against them. And about the fourth watch of the night he came to them, walking on the sea. He meant to pass by them, [49]but when they saw him walking on the sea, they thought it was a ghost, and cried out; [50]for they all saw him and were terrified. But immediately he spoke to them and said, "Take heart, it is I; have no fear."

[51]And he got into the boat with them and the wind ceased. And they were utterly astounded, [52]for

MATTHEW 14:22-33

[22]Then he made the disciples get into the boat and go before him to the other side, while he dismissed the crowds. [23]And after he had dismissed the crowds, he went up on the mountain by himself to pray. When evening came, he was there alone, [24]but the boat by this time was many furlongs distant from the land, beaten by the waves; for the wind was against them. [25]And in the fourth watch of the night he came to them, walking on the sea.

[26]But when the disciples saw him walking on the sea, they were terrified, saying, "It is a ghost!" And they cried out for fear.

[27]But immediately he spoke to them, saying, "Take heart, it is I; have no fear."

[28]And Peter answered him, "Lord, if it is you, bid me come to you on the water." [29]He said, "Come." So Peter got out of the boat and walked on the water and came to Jesus; [30]but when he saw the wind, he was afraid, and beginning to sink he cried out, "Lord, save me." [31]Jesus immediately reached out his hand and caught him, saying to him, "O man of little faith, why did you doubt?"

[32]And when they got into the boat, the wind ceased. [33]And those in the boat worshipped him, saying,

they did not understand about the loaves, but their hearts were hardened.	"Truly you are the Son of God."

Matthew's critical insertion here of verses 28-31 recounting the story of Peter Walking on the Water would come as something of a shock to a first-time reader of the First Gospel. Because of the two earlier deletions of materials taken from MARK, 1:36 and 5:37, Peter's visibility in the first thirteen chapters of MATTHEW had been limited and not at all exceptional. He had not spoken or acted independently anywhere. Only the word "first" in Matthew 10:2 hinted of potential greatness. But now, suddenly, here is Peter asking Jesus for permission to walk on water in the middle of a raging storm, and doing so, just as Jesus had done before him. Peter's brush with divinity, however, is embarrassingly short-lived. He sees the wind (sic) and overcome with fear sinks beneath the waves. Desperate, he cries for help: "Lord, *Kurie,* save me." Jesus rescues him, but with the rebuke: "Little-faith, why did you doubt?" With that, the two board the boat together. The wind ceases, and everyone in the boat worships Jesus, confessing: "Truly you are the Son of God."

What a remarkable shift from the cryptic conclusion in Mark 6:51-52: "And they were utterly astounded, for they did not understand about the loaves, but their hearts were hardened!"

What is to be made of this spectacular Peter Walking Upon the Water story-within-a-story and its redacted conclusion?[18] There has been a natural inclination among commentators to accentuate the positive in an effort to make the portrait of Peter here correspond with the portrayal in the dominant Matthew

[18]Scholarly studies of varying quality include Georg Braumann, "Der Sinkende Petrus: Matth. 14:28-31," *Theologische Zeitschrift,* 22 (Basel, 1966) 403–414; H. Van Der Loos, *The Miracles of Jesus, Supplements to Novum Testamentum* (1968) 650–669; Gilles Gaide, "Jésus et Pierre Marchent sur les Eaux, Mt 14,22-23," (sic) *Assemblées du Seigneur: Catechese dés dimanches et dés fêtes,* 50 (1974) 23–31; J. Duncan M. Derrett, "Why and How Jesus Walked on the Sea," *Novum Testamentum,* XXIII, 4 (1981) 330–348; B. W. Bacon, "Supplements" (1917) 8–11; Heinz J. Held, "Matthew as Interpreter of Miracle Stories," in Bornkamm, Barth, Held, *Tradition and Interpretation in Matthew* (1963) 204–206, 272; Strecker, *Weg* (1971) 198–199; J. D. Kingsbury, *Matthew: Structure, Christology, Kingdom* (1975) 66f.; Brown, et al., *Peter in the New Testament* (1973) 80–83.

16:17-19 passage.[19] Accordingly, it is emphasized that Peter did indeed successfully walk on water, *peripateesen* (aorist), just as Jesus had, and that even when he began to sink he did not lose faith, addressing Jesus as *Kurie,* "Lord." These observations are exegetically sound as far as they go.

Less commendable is the occasional effort to see "little-faith" as a Matthean improvement on Mark's persistent and insistent description of the disciples as "know-nothings," almost to the point of making "little-faith" a compliment.[20] The effort is obviously forced. Matthew apparently found the noun *oligopiste,* "little-faith," in the Q logion on anxiety in the Sermon on the Mount/Plain, Matthew 6:30/Luke 12:28, and thought it appropriate. He consequently applies it redactionally to the disciples on three other occasions, Matthew 8:26, 16:8, and 17:20. The text under review, Matthew 14:31, marks the only time, however, that the term is used to refer to an individual. "Little-faith," then, is Matthew's alternate assessment of the disciple's spiritual condition, but not a word of commendation or rehabilitation. It still denotes weakness and constitutes a rebuke, though not a rejection.

This fact is reinforced by the added reprimand: "Why did you doubt?" in verse 31. The verb "to doubt," *distazo,* is rare, found only in MATTHEW in the New Testament.[21] But the fact that

[19]E.g., Bruce M. Metzger, *A Textual Commentary on the Greek New Testament* (1971) 38, explains that the reason why the editorial committee for *The Greek New Testament* decided to place the poorly supported word *isxuron,* "strong" in brackets in the third ed. of *The Greek New Testament* was because "a majority was inclined to regard its presence as intrinsically required in order to explain Peter's increasing fear." This is an extreme case of the "Matthew 16:17-19 syndrome" blinding scholars in the face of superior text-critical evidence to the contrary. Compounding the error, the NRSV has now incorporated "strong" into the text of the new English translation. Hear also Brown et al., *Peter in the New Testament* (1973) 83: " . . . it is important for Matthew's community to know that Jesus saves Peter when he begins to sink, because, as Matthew will narrate later, Peter is the rock on which the church is to be built." This is another gratuitous dogmatic assertion posing as exegetical evidence.

[20]The fact that Matthew adds "little-faith" in 17:20 where MARK had no negative comment about the disciples indicates that the first evangelist did not use the term simply to improve MARK's description of the Twelve. He saw it as appropriate in its own right.

[21]Schweizer defines *distazw* etymologically as "going in two directions at once." Cf. Schweizer, *Matthew* (1975) 321.

it appears twice in the First Gospel, and on both occasions under rather strained redactional circumstances, makes its appearance all the more fascinating. The second location is in that curious comment in Matthew 28:17 where Matthew records that the disciples in Galilee worshipped the resurrected Jesus, "but some doubted!" Who or what was he referring to? Exegetically speaking, we can only surmise that Matthew wished to imply that even after the resurrection, in the early Church—yes, in his own Antiochan community—there were still some who shared Peter-like doubts. The sample is small and the locations of the word distant from one another, but if this faint allusion is correct, it would constitute further evidence that Matthew is not really concerned with the Peter of history but with the mythopoeic Peter who lives on in the religious fervor of his champions within Matthew's contemporary society and congregation.

This account of Peter Walking on the Water, as already noted in chapter 3 outlining source-critical evidence, is a piece of Matthew's own composition inserted here as a type of mirror reflection of the MARCAN story of Jesus Walking Upon the Sea (6:45-52). It serves also as Matthew's introduction to the "new" Peter who is to be further personified and evaluated elsewhere in Book IV. Peter is here compared, both positively and negatively, with Jesus. He is also paralleled with the other disciples as possessed of little-faith and doubt—all recognized Matthean editorial artifices we have seen before.

But Matthew isn't finished yet. He now daringly reverses Mark's conclusion to the Jesus Walking on the Sea account. According to Matthew 14:32, those in the boat (Bornkamm says we are to read "church")[22] now prostrate themselves, *prosekuneesan,* before Jesus and say: "Truly you are the Son of God." It is another case, with Matthew 16:16, where Peter is, at least indirectly, associated with marvelous Christological confessions of Jesus. It sets up also another example of Peter/disciples parallelization. What is equally unmistakable, and perhaps more disconcerting, however, is the fact that this confession by the disciples here in Matthew 14:33 necessarily detracts to a major extent from Peter's

[22]Cf. Günther Bornkamm, "The Stilling of the Storm in Matthew," *Tradition and Interpretation* (1963) 52–57.

own celebrated acknowledgment of Jesus as "the Christ, the Son of the Living God," later on in 16:16. His creedal statement there is then neither first, nor unique—roles it enjoyed even in MARK's rendition. The Notre Dame theologian John L. McKenzie, in his *Jerome Biblical Commentary* discussion of this passage says Matthew 14:33 "not only anticipates 16:16, but comes near to making 16:16-18 meaningless."[23] If that is truly the case, it will put a whole new light on our later study of the third Petrine insertion, Matthew 16:17-19.

For most casual readers of MATTHEW, the combined accounts of Jesus and Peter Walking on the Water is an entertaining devotional story. For us, however, viewing it redaction-critically, it has assumed much greater import as a window upon Matthew's contrast/comparison approach to portraying Peter in relation to Jesus and to the other disciples in the First Gospel.

2. Peter Requests an Explanation

MARK 7:14-23

[14]And he called the people to him again, and said to them, "Hear me, all of you, and understand: [14]there is nothing outside a man which by going into him can defile him; but the things which come out of a man are what defile him."

MATTHEW 15:10-20

[10]And he called the people to him and said to them, "Hear and understand:

[11]not what goes into the mouth defiles a man, but what comes out of the mouth, this defiles a man." [12]Then the disciples came and said to him, "Do you know that the Pharisees were offended when they heard this saying?" [13]He answered, "Every plant which my heavenly Father has not planted will be rooted up. [14]Let them alone; they are blind guides. And if a blind

[23]John L. McKenzie, "The Gospel According to Matthew," *The Jerome Biblical Commentary* (1968) 89. Schweizer, *Matthew* (1975) 321, also says: "This confession in fact depreciates the confession of Peter in 16:16."

[17]And when he had entered the house, and left the people, his disciples asked him about the parable. [18]And he said to them, "Then are you also without understanding? Do you not see that whatever goes into a man from outside cannot defile him [19]since it enters, not his heart but his stomach, and so passes on?" (Thus he declared all foods clean.) [20]And he said, "What comes out of a man is what defiles a man. [21]For from within, out of the heart of man, come evil thoughts, fornication, theft, murder, adultery, [22]coveting, wickedness, deceit, licentiousness, envy, slander, pride, foolishness. [23]All these evil things come from within, and they defile a man."

man leads a blind man, both will fall into a pit."
[15]But *Peter* said to him, "Explain the parable to us." [16]And he said, "Are you also still without understanding? [17]Do you not see that whatever goes into the mouth

passes into the stomach, and so passes on?
[18]But what comes out of the mouth proceeds from the heart, and this defiles a man. [19]For out of the heart come evil thoughts, murder, adultery, fornication, theft, false witness, slander.

[20]These are what defile a man; but to eat with unwashed hands does not defile a man."

B. W. Bacon categorized this reference to Peter in Matthew 15:15 among Matthew's "slighter editorial touches" and then immediately moved on to consider more "ample phenomena."[24] That was a mistake, and one all too common.

It is true that Matthew does little more than interject the name of the first disciple into this MARCAN passage. He even retains MARK's second-person-plural verbs and pronouns in Jesus' reply to Peter's request: "Are you (pl.) also still without understanding?" Peter is thus cast in the role of spokesman for the disciples, a role that is likewise more typical of MARK than of MATTHEW. But sometimes retaining a single fragment from an earlier source while eradicating all other related references renders that one vestige all the more exceptional and redactionally significant. That is what has happened here.

[24]Bacon, *Studies* (1930) 224. G. D. Kilpatrick, *The Origins of the Gospel According to St. Matthew* (1946) 38, dedicates one paragraph to this text. Strecker, *Weg* (1971) 203, has two brief sentences.

As commentators often like to point out, Matthew deletes or reinterprets every instance where MARK employed the verb *sunieni,* "to understand," in a negative sense referring to the disciples,[25] thereby suggesting that Matthew considerably elevates the role of the Twelve in the First Gospel. What they fail to indicate, however, is that on one occasion Matthew does retain the MARCAN negative *asunetos,* "senseless, without understanding," and does nothing to relieve the acrimony of the indictment. Our passage, Matthew 15:16, is that one exception! Isn't it at least a little curious that at the very place where Matthew interjects Peter he and the other disciples are subjected to one of the most severe criticisms Matthew, following MARK, has to offer? One need not be super-suspicious to consider the possibility that the first evangelist intentionally "set up" Peter by introducing him here just in time to knock him down again.[26]

Perhaps we should not be surprised. In the previous Petrine pericope, Peter was designated a little-faith and a doubter. Now all the disciples, but Peter in particular, are also seen as without understanding. It is a programmatic of correction and criticism of Peter that will persist unabated throughout the rest of the First Gospel, except, of course, for those brief, intoxicating moments in the Jewish Christian traditions incorporated into MATTHEW at 16:17-19 and 17:24-27 which uncharacteristically paint an infinitely more positive picture of the first disciple.

In fact, Matthew even makes the situation here worse than it was in MARK by strengthening MARK's initial *houtws,* "thus" or "so," replacing it with the exclamation *akmeen,* "still!" or

[25]Cf. Mark 6:52/Matt 14:33, Mark 8:17/Matt 16:9, Mark 8:21/Matt 16:11-12, Mark 9:32/Matt 17:23. Also Michael H. Crosby, *House of Disciples* (1988) 58; David E. Orton, *The Understanding Scribe* (1989) 143f. Even Ulrich Luz, "Die Jünger im Matthäusevangelium," *Zeitschrift für die Neutestamentliche Wissenschaft und die Kunde der alteren Kirche* 62, 3/4 (1971) 148, English trans., 102, says "the disciples lack of understanding in Mark is the only unflattering aspect of the Markan picture of the disciples that Matthew has consistently improved."

[26]Contra J. P. Meier, *Vision* (1979) 102. Meier suggests that Peter was introduced in 15:15 as a contrast to the Pharisees whom Jesus had just described as plants which the heavenly Father had not planted. Peter, on the other hand, was a true planting of God, a seeing guide, able to transmit the correct teaching. Meier admits, however, that Jesus' "without understanding" criticism here seems unnecessarily harsh.

"yet!" Jesus literally declares: " 'Still,' you (pl.) are also (or 'even') without understanding!"[27] In other words, Peter, and by implication, the disciples were worse off than the Pharisees who did understand, at least enough to be offended (cf. v. 12).

Matthew obviously isn't interested in whitewashing the MARCAN depiction of the disciples, as is sometimes assumed. Rather, the evidence continues to accumulate that Matthew describes the disciples in all their complexity and vulnerability to match the real-life Christians of his own community, with Peter individually—and together with all that he represents in the First Gospel—suffering the most abuse of all.

Matthew's distinctive perspective of Peter is also indirectly highlighted by his inclusion of the earlier redactionally inserted verses 12b-14 where the disciples are made to ask about the Pharisees' response to Jesus' dismissal of their purification rites: "Do you know that the Pharisees were offended when they heard this saying?" We are moved to ask: If the evangelist had decided to add a new question in verse 12 why didn't he there also employ a new questioner, like Peter, instead of engineering this exchange of interlocutors? The answer, as we have observed before, undoubtedly is that Peter, as redactionally described, is only involved with issues concerning the new order, i.e., with the Church, while external problems, such as relations with the Pharisees, are left to the disciples generally. Remember the reverse switch, exhibiting the same characteristics, in the story of The Withered Fig Tree (Mark 11:21/Matt 21:20)?

Matthew is a remarkably clever, careful, and consistent editor. Even the simple, single insertion of Peter's name in this pericope has succeeded in adding another dimension to our understanding of the role of Peter in MATTHEW. Peter, the acclaimed churchman, still does not understand the rudiments of the Christian dietary ethic and requires Jesus' further instruction. Remembering how Matthew redacted the account of Peter's Denials to Peter's further detriment, the editorial artifice employed here

[27]Does "still" refer back to 13:51 or 15:10? Perhaps both. I do not understand Orton's comment that *"akmeen . . . and the emphatic position of kai"* means that Jesus' rebuke really applies to the Pharisees rather than to the disciples. Cf. Orton, *Understanding Scribe* (1989) 143f.

which functions to jeopardize Peter's good name by inserting it into such a vulnerable context should no longer surprise us.

3. Peter's Confession at Caesarea Philippi

MARK 8:27-33	MATTHEW 16:13-23
[27]And Jesus went on with his disciples, to the villages of Caesarea Philippi; and on the way he asked his disciples, "Who do men say that I am?" [28]And they told him, "John the Baptist; and others say, Elijah; and others one of the prophets." [29]And he asked them, "But who do you say that I am?" Peter answered him, "You are the Christ."	[13]Now when Jesus came into the district of Caesarea Philippi, he asked his disciples, "Who do men say that the Son of Man is?" [14]And they said, "Some say John the Baptist, others say Elijah, and others Jeremiah or one of the prophets." [15]He said to them, "But who do you say that I am?" [16]Simon Peter replied, "You are the Christ, the Son of the living God."
	[17]And Jesus answered him, "Blessed are you, Simon Bar-Jonah! For flesh and blood has not revealed this to you, but my Father who is in heaven. [18]And I tell you, you are Peter, and on this rock I will build my church, and the powers of death shall not prevail against it. [19]I will give you the keys of the kingdom of heaven, and whatever you bind on earth shall be bound in heaven, and whatever you loose on earth shall be loosed in heaven."
[30]And he charged them to tell no one about him.	[20]Then he strictly charged the disciples to tell no one that he was the Christ.
[31]And he began to teach them that the Son of Man must suffer many things, and be rejected by the elders and the chief priests and the scribes, and be	[21]From that time Jesus began to show his disciples that he must go to Jerusalem and suffer many

killed, and after three days rise again. [32]And he said this plainly. And Peter took him, and began to rebuke him. [33]But turning and seeing his disciples, he rebuked Peter, and said, "Get behind me, Satan! For you are not on the side of God, but of men."

things from the elders and chief priests and scribes, and be killed, and on the third day be raised. [22]And Peter took him and began to rebuke him, saying, "God forbid, Lord! This shall never happen to you." [23]But he turned and said to Peter, "Get behind me, Satan! You are a hindrance to me; for you are not on the side of God, but of men."

We have finally arrived at the "grandfather" of all Petrine passages, the Petrine pericope *kat' exsoxeen,* "par excellance," the home of the "Matthew 16:17-19 syndrome," and the standard by which the Petrine portrait in the First Gospel has been interpreted for the past eighteen centuries. It is doubtful whether any passage in the entire Bible has been more often quoted, more thoroughly scrutinized or more vociferously argued than Matthew 16:13-19. And the end is not yet. We are moved to ask: Is it deserving of all the attention it has attracted, of the trust that has been invested in it, and of all the structures, theological and architectural, which have been built upon it?[28]

The placement of the material unique to MATTHEW in its context here certainly displays the evangelist's editorial virtuosity. The bracketing accounts of Peter's Confession, 16:13-16, and the First Passion Prediction, 16:21-23, are actually transplants from Mark 8:27-29 and 31-33, respectively, which we had left untouched in our analysis of the transferred Petrine material in chapter 4. Matthew now weds these two pericopes to form a new unit by inserting the Jewish Christian encomiastic tradition, Matthew 16:17-19, between them.[29] Specifically, he does so in two ways. In verse 16

[28]Krister Stendahl, "Matthew" *Peake's Commentary on the Bible* (1962) 787, calls Matthew 16:17-19 a "majestic passage;" Frankemölle, *Amtskritik* (1973) 248, labels it "ein prismatisch gebündelter Kristallisationspunkt." For a comparatively brief review of the principal studies focusing on this text see Joseph A. Burgess, *A History of the Exegesis of Matthew 16:17-19 from 1781 to 1965* (1976).

[29]That Matthew 16:17-19 was not an original part of the Caesarea Philippi story which Mark happened to omit is seen in the theological shift from Christology

he adds the unusual Aramaic name 'Simon'' to tie the preceding confession together with the subsequent beatitude addressed to "Simon Bar-Jonah" in verse 17, making the identification unmistakable. Secondly, he employs a resounding series of "you are's" using the second-person-singular of the verb *eimi*[30] to link all three sections with a dramatic countermanding thematic reversal:

16:16: "You are the Christ. . . . "
16:17: "Blessed are you. . . . "
16:18: "You are Peter. . . . " and
16:23: "You are a stumblingblock!"

A concerned first-century reader could hardly have missed the linkage or the irony.

Recognizing all ten verses of Matthew 16:13-23 as a unit changes completely the dynamics of the 16:17-19 insertion. Peter is now seen as once more working up to an awful let-down. It is Peter walking on the water . . . and sinking all over again. He who was a little-faith and a doubter in Matthew 14:31, and without understanding in 15:16, is here labeled a Satan and a stumblingblock. It is another case of a comparison/contrast between Jesus, the Christ, and Peter, the disciple and traditional "patron saint" of some in Matthew's community, with the same predictable results.

Obviously, this perspective is radically different from almost every other interpretation ever proposed for Matthew 16:13-23 or the role of Peter in MATTHEW. The normal practice, car-

in 16:16, to ecclesiology in 16:17-19, and back to Christology in Matthew 16:20. Our proposal that Matthew 16:13-23 is a new unit in MATTHEW argues against the position of Kingsbury, *Matthew* (1975) 7ff., who finds a major break evidenced by *apo tote eerxsato* introducing verse 21. Cf. also 4:17. However, H. Frankemölle, *Jahwebund* (1974) 344, n. 35, identifies this phrase as a "LXX Floskel," i.e., a "Septuagintal flourish." We have adopted the five-book schematic for Matthew rather than a theological outline. Kingsbury's divisions would place MATTHEW's special Petrine materials in two separate parts of the First Gospel.

[30]This is an observation of Brown et al., *Peter in the New Testament* (1973) 93f. There was a similar, though less obvious, linkage pattern in the Walking on the Water account, Matthew 14:27-33: *egw eimi* in 14:27; *ei su ei* in 14:28; *theou uios ei* in 14:33.

ried over from MARK and from form-critical convention, has been to treat Peter's confession and commendation in 16:13-20 as one pericope and the subsequent Satan-saying account in 16:21-23 as an entirely different and unrelated section. This bifurcation allows the positive aspect of Peter's portrait to stand uncontested.[31] In fact, the acclaim accorded Peter in 16:17-19 is then seen as so powerful it practically buries all its competition, i.e., all contrary depictions of Peter. However, as we have seen hinted in the "first/first-last" combination of 10:2 and 19:30 et al., suggested in the Transfiguration story, and most vividly demonstrated in the Peter Walking on the Water pericope, Matthew likes to employ a comparison/contrast technique by which Jesus ultimately emerges victorious leaving all rivals stunned by their own weakness and ineptitude. We should have been able to see it coming also in this unit, Matthew 16:13-23.

There is additional supportive evidence. Although Matthew does his typical masterful job of editing Jesus' initial question to the disciples in 16:13 so that the "Son of man" dimension is already present in the question, thereby making Peter's answer Christologically complete by its recognition of Jesus as the "Son of God" (16:16), it is nevertheless undeniable that the similar prior confession uttered by all the disciples in 14:33 detracts measurably from the uniqueness of Peter's confession here. Everything he said was by now common knowledge to Matthew's readers.[32]

[31]Several scholars have been tremendously imaginative and industrious in researching the possible nuances incorporated in the Matthew 16:17-19 tradition. J. Massingberd Ford, "Thou Art 'Abraham' and Upon this Rock . . . ," *Heythorp Journal* 6 (1975) 289-301, researches rabbinic and pseudepigraphic literature to show how prevalent an Abraham/rock association was. In Matthew 16:18, then, Peter is portrayed as a new Abraham. Joachim Jeremias, "kleis," *Theological Dictionary of the New Testament* III, 744-753, notes that "keys" in rabbinic traditions are used to open the seventh heaven and the 40,000 gates of the last hell. Schweizer, *Matthew* (1975) 345, recalls that in Isaiah 8:14-16 God is designated a "stone of offense." The implication is that Peter may be in good company in 16:23 where Jesus says "You are a *skandalon,* i.e., an 'offense,' unto me." Many commentators prefer two other Isaiah passages, such as 22:20-22 and 28:14-16, for phrases about keys and rocks which may have formed some of the inspiration or background for ideas in Matthew 16:17-19, thereby making sense of Peter's exceptional role in it. The intellectual strain required, however, is all too evident.

[32]Meier, *Vision* (1979) 100, admits the general redundancy of Matthew 16:16, but insists that Peter's confession is "fuller and more solemn." Schweizer, *Mat-*

Just as this case of anticipatory reportage had deflected much of the impact of Matthew 16:16, so does the redistribution to all the disciples of the authority to bind and loose in Matthew 18:18 detract from the privileges given initially to Peter alone in Matthew 16:19. Matthew makes the association unmistakable by employing the very same words in 18:18 as in 16:19, allowing only his typical use of "heaven," in the singular in 18:18, to betray his own compositional hand.[33]

Finally, a few comments about Matthew's redaction of the First Passion Prediction, or Satan-saying, portion of this literary complex (Matt 16:21-23). One Matthean characteristic is already familiar to us. That is Matthew's focus upon Peter by removing Mark's curious asides, "And he said this plainly," in Mark 8:32a, and "But turning and seeing his disciples," in Mark 8:33. These comments suggest that Mark intended Jesus' rebuke of Peter to be shared, at least to some degree, by all within hearing distance. In Matthew's version, however, there is no such suggestion. Jesus' rebuke "Get behind me, Satan. . . . " is aimed at Peter, and at Peter alone. This passage, then, functions as a direct counterbalance to Matthew 16:17-18.

Even more conclusive is Matthew's key insertion in verse 23c: "You are a hindrance unto me," *skandalon ei emou.* As an added Matthean comment, it rivals in intensity the prior Satan-saying itself, taken over from MARK. As previously noted, the RSV translation of *skandalon* as "hindrance" is notoriously weak and has

thew (1975) 340, however, argues that "Son of man" in Matthew does not convey a distinctive connotation as it does in Mark, but is just a more ambiguous alternate term for "Son of God." Brown et al., *Peter in the New Testament* (1973) 87, acknowledge that Peter's confession is no longer the turning point in the gospel narrative as it was in MARK.

[33]Contra Hoffmann, "Petrus-Primat" (1974) 99–102, and Ernst Käsemann, "Die Anfänge Christlicher Theologie," *Exegetische Versuche und Besinnungen,* Band 2 (1964) 104, who are of the opinion that Matthew 18:18 is the original traditional piece which Matthew used to compose 16:19. In either case, Strecker, *Weg* (1971) 206, makes the point: "Der Wandel von 16:19 zu 18:18 lasst eine tatsachliche Elimination der Sonderstellung des Petrus," i.e., the change from 16:19 to 18:18 amounts to an actual elimination of Peter's special position. Günter Klein, "Die Verleugnung des Petrus," *Zeitschrift für Theologie und Kirche* 58, Jahrgang 1961, Heft 3 (1962) 326, speaks of a "Nivellierung Petri," "a levelling of Peter" in Matthew 18:18.

thankfully been improved in the NRSV with "stumbling block," but as a matter of fact, neither do the Greek phrase justice. Here the noun *skandalon* holds the initial, emphatic position. Perhaps the best sense translation of the passage would be to use the English derivative of the Greek word and translate the sentence as an exclamation: "A scandal you are to me!"[34] The problem of scandalizing, offending, or causing others to sin, as we have seen elsewhere (Matt 26:33) is a particular concern of Matthew. Here he makes Peter the personification and prime example of that general problem in his community.

The closing sentence, ". . . for you are not on the side of God, but of men," *twn anthrwpwn* (Matt 16:23), now also serves as a condemning inclusio with the opening question in Matthew 16:13: "Who do men, *hoi anthrwpoi,* say that the Son of man is?" Despite his fine words in 16:16, then, Peter's ultimate understanding of Jesus' messiahship showed no essential improvement over that of persons outside the community of faith.

Far from adding this Jewish Christian fragment of a traditional Petrine encomium in Matthew 16:17-19 with the intention of elevating Peter's prominence to preeminence in the First Gospel, we now see that Matthew's redaction, contextually considered, actually functions in large measure to deflate it. These verses were never intended to be taken literally, in isolation, as the final, focal word about Peter in MATTHEW, but only as modified by

[34]Peter F. Ellis, *Matthew, His Mind and His Message* (1974) 67, n. 89, correctly points out that Matthew reduced *epetimeesen* in Mark 8:33 to a simple *eipen* in Matthew 16:23. Ellis' implication, however, that Jesus, according to Matthew, did not intend the Satan-saying to be taken so seriously is countermanded by Jesus' very emphatic addition of *skandalon ei emou.* The same argument applies to Ernst Haenchen, "Die Komposition von Mk vii 27—ix 1 und Par," *Novum Testamentum* 6 (July 1963) 109, who thinks Matthew may have inserted Matthew 16:17-19 to counteract the MARCAN Satan-saying tradition in Matthew 16:22-23. David Wallace, "An Exegesis of Matthew 16:13-20," *Foundations,* V, 3 (1962) 220, tries to distinguish between Peter personally and his confession. According to him, Jesus' rebuke applied only to the inadequacy of Peter's confession, as in MARK. Kilpatrick, *Origins* (1946) 74f., suggests that Matthew may have put the words into direct speech to give them a more respectful tone. I would think direct speech would do just the opposite. It is amazing how many hoops the "Matthew 16:17-19 syndrome" forces responsible scholars to jump through in order to enable Peter to retain his high station in the face of all the evidence to the contrary in the First Gospel.

what has preceded and by what follows. As Burton Scott Easton wrote already in the 1920s, Matthew 16:17-19 "stands in the New Testament as an almost isolated fragment, not merely out of touch with the main current of the tradition but in conflict with it."[35] As was said before, what the evangelist gives he can also take away, and when it comes to Peter he usually does.[36]

4. Peter and the Temple Tax

> MATTHEW 17:24-27
> [24]When they came to Capernaum, the collectors of the half-shekel tax went up to Peter and said, "Does not your teacher pay the tax?"[25] He said, "Yes." And when he came home, Jesus spoke to him first, saying, "What do you think, Simon? From whom do kings of the earth take toll or tribute? From their sons or from others?" [26]And when he said, "From others," Jesus said to him, "Then the sons are free. [27]However, not to give offense to them, go to the sea and cast a hook, and take the first fish that comes up, and when you open its mouth you will find a shekel; take that and give it to them for me and for yourself."

This so-called Temple Tax account with its coin-in-the-fish's-mouth "trailer" appears to be one huge anomaly. One's initial reaction in confronting it exegetically is to ask: What was Matthew thinking when he literally jammed this piece into his text? A. H. McNeile, as far back as 1915, concluded: "In its present form this narrative cannot be rationalized."[37] In the 1960s, G.

[35]Burton Scott Easton, "Critical Note: St. Matthew 16:17-19," *Anglican Theological Review* 4 (1921–1922) 157.

[36]Agreeing with this position, although perhaps more hesitantly, are two Roman Catholic scholars: Augustine Stock, "Is Matthew's Presentation of Peter Ironic?" *Biblical Theology Bulletin,* 17 (1987). Stock is often more uncomplimentary toward Peter than is my perspective in this book. Also Hubert Frankemölle, "Amtskritik im Matthäus-Evangelium?" *Biblica,* 54 (1973) 247–262. He senses a possible criticism of clericalism in MATTHEW consistent with his view that the disciples, and esp. Peter, represent the clergy in the First Gospel.

[37]Alan Hugh McNeile, *The Gospel According to St. Matthew* (1915) 259.

M. Lee opined: "The story of the coin in the fish's mouth has done more perhaps than anything else to discredit St. Matthew's Gospel as an historical document."[38] Howard Clark Kee was still in agreement with Lee in 1971 when he wrote: "It is an understatement to say that this story, perhaps more than any other of the Synoptic miracles, stretches the credulity of modern man."[39] The best witness to its intractability, however, may be seen in the common perspective of H. A. Homeau and Myron S. Augsburger, both of whom have suggested that a sense of humor may be the only suitable tool for deciphering this narrative's import in the First Gospel.[40]

Its problems are truly legion. Its form is mixed, half pronouncement and half miracle story. As far as miracle stories go, it is the only one in the New Testament where we are not told of its actual successful conclusion. The pericope's vocabulary is troubled, with several Aramaic vestiges ("Simon," "sons of the kingdom," and an assumed temple ambiance), coupled with a long list of *hapax legomena,* mixed with a few Mattheanisms, and all tied together by some very uncharacteristically tortured Greek, e.g., *eipontes de,* in verse 26a, literally "but speaking," but translated expansively in the RSV as "and when he said."[41]

Location is another problem. Why is this pericope placed at this critical juncture, at the conclusion of the narrative section of MATTHEW's Book IV and at the very beginning of the ecclesiological discourse in chapter 18?[42]

[38]G. M. Lee, "Studies in Texts: Matthew 17:24-27," *Theology* LXVIII, 543 (August 1965) 380.

[39]Howard Clark Kee, "The Gospel According to Matthew," *The Interpreter's One Volume Commentary of the Bible* (1971) 631.

[40]H. A. Homeau, "On Fishing for Staters," *The Expository Times,* 85, 11 (1974) 341f. Myron S. Augsburger, *Matthew* (1982) 213.

[41]Thompson, *Advice* (1970) 57, says: "This is the only passage in the New Testament in which this construction introduces direct discourse." C.F.D. Moule, *An Idiom Book of New Testament Greek* (1963) 172f., also notes that the hypotactic style of Matthew 17:27 is "far from typical of this writer."

[42]Cf. Brown, et al., *Peter in the New Testament* (1973) 101; Thompson, *Advice* (1970) 21; and J. P. Meier, *Matthew* (1980) 196. All credit geographic considerations. W. D. Davies, *The Setting of the Sermon on the Mount* (1966) 391, sees a significant alteration in "the hands of men" in the Matthew 17:22 passion

Even theologically the account is suspect. It is the only instance in the New Testament where Jesus is portrayed as using his supernatural powers for a basically selfish reason, to get around paying the tax out of his own pocket.[43]

Finally, there could also be a particular challenge here to our growing thesis that Matthew was redactionally stereotyping Peter as an internal, Church figure. If Matthew is indeed portraying Peter in this account as dealing with collectors of the Jewish temple tax, our theory requires serious alteration.

On three previous occasions, in our discussions of the source-critical evidence in chapter 3 and in our examinations of the Transfiguration and Peter's Boast accounts (Matt 17:1-9 and 26:33-35), we anticipated some aspects of this knotty problem and even dared to make several tentative suggestions: (1) In view of the number of Aramaisms, *hapax legomena,* and several stylistic elements very uncharacteristic of Matthew, this must be a pre-Matthean, Jewish Christian tradition; (2) The facts that Peter is portrayed in this tradition as fulfilling the unusual role as spokesman for Jesus in verse 25 and as an exceptionally close companion of Jesus in the verse 27 comment "for me and for yourself," this pericope must constitute a fragment of an encomium dedicated to the greater praise of Peter, very much in line with the previous Matthew 16:17-19 insertion;[44] (3) Internal as well as external evidence suggests that "Peter" and the concept of giving offense, *skandaliswmen,* in verses 24 and 27, respectively, are the only recognizable redactional emphases in this narrative and, therefore, were undoubtedly determinative for its inclusion here.[45] If these sug-

prediction. The other predictions in Matthew 16:21 and 20:17-19 had "elders, chief priests and scribes." Davies opines that Matthew 17:22, therefore, referred to Roman authorities instead of Jewish ones. Matthew 17:24-27, then, refers back to 17:22-23 and is a warning not to offend Rome by refusing to pay taxes. Cf. also Paul S. Minear, *Matthew, the Teacher's Gospel* (1982) 99f., and Bornkamm, "End Expectation and Church in Matthew," *Tradition and Interpretation* (1963) 19f., for somewhat similar views.

[43]Thompson, *Advice* (1970) 50 and Brown et. al., *Peter in the New Testament* (1973) 102, express this concern.

[44]Davies, *Setting* (1966) 391, also believes that Matthew 17:24-27 and Matthew 16:17-19 come from the same stratum of tradition.

[45]John P. Meier, *Vision* (1979) 125, agrees. In his *Matthew* (1980) 198, Meier writes: " . . . Mt. retains the pericope not for its specific lesson but because it

gestions are correct, and I am inclined to believe they are, this seemingly strange pericope would actually function in a comparably normal capacity as a text, or pretext, for the discussions in the sermon to follow.[46]

There is evidence that such is indeed the case. For example, the danger of giving offense, or causing others to sin, in 17:27, is again picked up shortly thereafter in 18:6-9.[47] Similarly, the prominence of Peter in 17:24-27 is demonstrated once more in 18:21, in the question placed on Peter's lips of how often one should forgive a sinning brother.

Furthermore, in view of the identification of Peter as the personification of "scandal" in our previous analysis of 16:23c, we are tempted to wonder if Matthew may even have had the first disciple in mind when in 18:7c he writes: "Woe to the man by whom the temptation, *skandalon,* comes."

As for Peter's apparently unusual association with representatives of the old Jewish religious order in this account, one can only point to the fact that the story nowhere explicitly identifies the levy mentioned here as a "temple" tax. As a matter of fact, by the time Matthew wrote this Gospel in the 80s or 90s of the first century C.E., the temple was already destroyed.[48] Addition-

both underlines the role of Peter . . . and stresses the obligation of disciples to avoid giving scandal—a theme prominent in chap. 18."

[46]*Ibid.* Once recognized, the connection seems obvious. It must be admitted, however, that the sermon in Matthew 18 is the only one of the five Matthean discourses to begin with such a seemingly abstruse narrative.

[47]J. Duncan M. Derrett, "Peter's Penny: Fresh Light on Matthew XVII 24-27," *Novum Testamentum,* 6 (1963) 1–15, says that priests, and later rabbis, were exempt from the tax "out of regard for the ways of peace." Ed. Herbert Danby, *The Mishnah* (1933) 152, n. 9, translates Shekalim 1, 3, in the *Jerusalem Talmud* as reading "by reason of respect." It was undoubtedly some such phrase, then, which Matthew replaced with "not to give offense" in verse 27, thereby preparing his readers for a discussion of offending and causing others to sin in chap. 18.

[48]It is because of the date of the composition of MATTHEW that several scholars suggest that a later form of tax is meant here than the "temple" tax. Kilpatrick, *Origins* (1946) 42, observes that after the destruction of the temple in 70 C.E., Roman authorities imposed an imperial *fiscus Iudaicus* for the support of the Temple of Jupiter Capitolinus in Rome. Cf. Flavius Josephus "The Wars of the Jews," *Josephus' Complete Works,* part VII, chap. VI, par. 6, trans. William Whiston (1960) 597. Thompson, *Advice* (1970) 68, sees a special tax authorized by the Roman government called the *aurum coronarium* for the support of the

ally there is no mention of either temple or tax in either the immediately prior or subsequent contexts.[49] Therefore, while this tradition could very well have had its origin in pre-destruction Jerusalem, Matthew did not consider it in that context. It was for him a simple story which prominently featured Peter and Jesus and into which he was able to introduce the idea of "giving offense," using the verb *skandalizw.* With all the other evidence previously discovered which identified Peter as associated exclusively with internal, Church concerns, this curious single pericope, even if we adopt a worst-case scenario, could not present a serious challenge to our documented thesis.

It has been a combination of previously observed Matthean conventions elsewhere, mixed with some internal evidence of redaction, that have helped to make sense out of this otherwise abstruce account. The results, however, have been unexpectedly rewarding. Far from being misplaced, we now see the Temple Tax account serving as an introduction to the ecclesiological sermon in chapter 18, casting its long shadow, as it were, on all that follows.

5. Peter Asks about Forgiveness

MATTHEW 18:21-22	LUKE 17:3-4
	[3]"Take heed to yourselves; if your brother sins, rebuke him, and if he repents, forgive him;
[21]Then *Peter* came up and said to him, "How often shall my brother	[4]and if he sins against you seven times in the day, and turns to you

rabbinic school at Jamnia. Richard Cassidy, "Matthew 17:24-27—A Word on Civil Taxes," *Catholic Biblical Quarterly,* 41, 4 (1979) 571–580, observes that in Egypt there was a civil tax of didrachma size. It is also interesting to note that there has been a traditional levy in the Roman Catholic Church called "Peter's Pence" for the support of the Vatican, inspired by this passage.

[49]Contra all those scholars mentioned in note 48, above, who saw "taxes" as the main issue in Matthew 17:24-27. Equally off target from the point of view of this study was B. W. Bacon, "Petrine Supplements" (1917) 19, who thought *eleutheros,* "freedom," was the decisive word. He was followed by numerous commentators, e.g., McKenzie, "Matthew" (1968) 94, and Schweizer, *Matthew* (1975) 357. Thompson, *Advice* (1970) 60, focused on the future tense of *eureeseis,* "you will find," demonstrating Jesus' omniscience. But Jesus' omniscience was never in question.

sin against me, and I forgive him? As many as seven times?" [22]Jesus said to him, "I do not say to you seven times, but seventy times seven."

seven times, and says, 'I repent,' you must forgive him."

If our understanding of Matthew's preferred comparison/contrast approach is correct, then this 18:21 reference to Peter is "the other shoe" to the Temple Tax tradition just reviewed. There we saw Peter on a pedestal, speaking for Jesus, answering Jesus correctly and finally being closely identified with Jesus in the phrase "for me and for yourself."

Now the downside begins. In this extensively redacted passage from Q (Matt 18:21-22/Luke 17:3-4), Matthew reintroduces Peter[50] as interrupting Jesus' sermon with a significant soteriological/ecclesiological question: "Lord, *kurie,* how often shall my brother sin against me, and I forgive him? As many as seven times?" It appeared to be an exceptionally generous offer. The general rubric required that an offended person need forgive his adversary only three times.[51] Peter is thus temporarily placed in a positive light. The inadequacy of his suggestion, however, is soon made manifest when it is seen in comparison with Jesus' own magnanimous perspective of unlimited forgiveness: "I do not say to you seven times, but seventy times seven."[52] In effect,

[50]Thompson, *Advice* (1970) 205, suggests a mechanical editorial convention with Matthew regularly interchanging Peter and the disciples as speakers. Evidence does not support the idea. Kilpatrick, *Origins* (1946) 38, sees Peter connected with legal sayings. But what legal saying is found in the Walking on the Water episode? Schweizer, *Matthew* (1975) 376, sees Peter connected with ecclesiological sayings. That may be too narrow as well. In 16:16 the focus is clearly Christological. Here, in Matthew 18:21-22, the concern is ecclesiological, soteriological, and ethical. The only boundaries which "confine" Peter in MATTHEW are inside concerns for the Church and community. Unfortunately for him, Matthew portrays him as needing help on all counts.

[51]Cf. the three-stage church-disciplinary rubric in Matthew 18:15-17. Cf. *The Babylonian Talmud,* Joma 86b. Also Allen, *Matthew* (1907) 199; F. W. Beare, *The Gospel According to Matthew* (1981) 381. Seven, as suggested by Peter, was the traditional perfect number. Jesus was setting a new and extraordinary standard.

[52]There is text-critical confusion here whether the text should read "seventy times seven" or "seventy-seven." The latter would reverse Lamech's 77-fold venge-

Peter sinks again, falling short of Jesus' expectations. The whole subsequent rehearsal of the Parable of the Unforgiving Servant in 18:23-35 emphasizes how threateningly inadequate only partial and insincere forgiveness really is in the sight of God: "So also my heavenly Father will do to every one of you, if you do not forgive your brother from your heart" (v. 35).

In terms of editorial practice, literary form, and brevity, this Matthew 18:21-22 passage is reminiscent of Matthew 15:15-16 previously reviewed. Both introductions of Peter appear to be almost incidental and individually of little consequence. Yet, they demonstrate redactional consistency on Matthew's part and contribute their share toward quieting any residual enthusiasm for Peter among the readers of the First Gospel.

There is a final observation. Just three verses earlier, in Matthew 18:18, Matthew had redactionally inserted the Jesus-saying redistributing to all the disciples the authority to bind and loose initially given to Peter alone in the traditional statement of Matthew 16:19.[53] Now, in 18:21, Peter is again redactionally introduced as if in defense of his traditional priority and prerogative and makes what appears to be a generous proposal about forgiving, i.e., "loosing" an erring brother. Unfortunately, his offer still does not measure up. Jesus expects unlimited forgiveness. Peter is good, but again not good enough. Viewed in this light, Matthew 18:22 indicates that Peter is ultimately incapable of implementing the privileges bestowed upon him in 16:19.

This passage, 18:21-22, then, is the whole story of Peter in Matthew in a nutshell: good beginning—poor ending, the first becoming last, and a rock dysfunctioning as a stumblingblock. Peter is the epitome of unfulfilled promise.

These five uniquely Matthean Petrine insertions have at times

ance in Genesis 4:24. The former, however, is also an ancient axiom. T. W. Manson, *The Sayings of Jesus* (1957) 212, found it already in the pseudepigraphic *Testament of Benjamin,* chap. 7. Beare, *Matthew* (1981) 381, blames or credits the Vulgate's rendering *septuagies septies* for popularizing the 70 X 7 figure. The NRSV reads "seventy-seven."

[53]It is extremely curious to note that if Matthew really intended Peter to be seen as the chief arbiter of what is to be loosed or bound, forgiven or excluded, according to 16:19, why the evangelist did not find at least one occasion on which to dramatize Peter in this role. Instead we find 18:21-22.

proved to be an exasperating assortment of literary forms, sources, traditions, vocabularies, and grammatical irregularities. Yet, thanks largely to our pre-conditioning as a result of previous examinations of Matthew's redactional practices and preferences, we have been able to detect and confirm a consistency in approach and application which we have identified as a comparison/contrast systematic. Peter is compared and equated with the other disciples and contrasted with Jesus leading to the elevation of Jesus while reflecting the vulnerability of the disciples generally and the disappointing failure on the part of one disciple in particular—the disciple/churchman Peter.

Finally the time has come to try to gather together our conclusions into one comprehensive answer to the problem of Peter in MATTHEW. Hopefully, that answer will also be convincing.

7

Conclusions: Peter in Matthew

The evidence has been ample, varied, and cumulative. We have looked everywhere, probed here and there, and occasionally excavated a promising seam. MATTHEW has been a mine—and a mine-field—of interesting clues to the role Peter is intended to play in the First Gospel.

It may help, by way of a clarifying review, to summarize our discoveries—exegetical, historical, literary, and theological. On the basis of our reading of scholarly authorities and our own analyses of the texts, as detailed in the previous chapters, we have arrived at the following general conclusions:

1. The First Gospel was originally written in Greek, in the vicinity of Antioch, Syria, in the ninth or tenth decades of the first century C.E. It was not an entirely original composition. The Gospel of MARK was its basic model and source. MARK, however, was apparently deemed deficient in some areas. It lacked important biographical information and included surprisingly little actual teaching material. Most importantly, what information it did contain was not in every case designed to be relevant to the prevailing situation in the Antiochan community. MATTHEW, consequently, is a "rewrite" of MARK, restructured into a series of narrative/sermonic sequences, amplified with nativity and Easter stories, Jesus-sayings from Q, Old Testament quotations, and a few new (or at least newer) local traditions, all arranged and edited by the first evangelist to speak to the immediate situation of the Christian community in his own place and time.

The broader applicability of the First Gospel, of course, is seen in its continuing international and ecumenical popularity.

2. "Matthew," the first evangelist, was not the disciple/tax-collector mentioned in Matthew 9:9, but a second- or third-generation diaspora Jewish Christian with a natural Jewish orientation and sensitivity, yet fluent in Greek and most likely formally educated in Greco-Roman schools. We have retained the traditional name for the author in this study only for convenience' sake. This Matthew was obviously well read in the Jewish Scriptures, the Law, and the Prophets, especially in their Greek Septuagintal translation.[1] He apparently saw himself as a concerned professional, a personally involved journalist of religion, or as he said, "a scribe who has been trained for the kingdom of heaven . . . who brings out of his treasure what is new and what is old" (13:52).[2]

3. Antioch[3] at this time was a prosperous and influential cultural, commercial, and political center with an approximately half million population. Rome was the dominant political force of that day under Domitian, its unpopular emperor from 81–96 C.E.[4] Hellenism, however, remained the primary cultural influence in Antioch. *Koine Greek,* a colloquial "street Greek" of mixed dialects colored with many "user-friendly" foreign terms tossed in,

[1]Ulrich Luz, *Matthew 1–7* (1989) 49, says "Matthew is strongly influenced by the Septuagint. . . . The Septuagint influences his language but is not his stylistic norm." Cf. Richard N. Longenecker, *Biblical Exegesis in the Apostolic Period* (1975) 140–152, for a more detailed analysis of Matthew's more eclectic hermeneutical style in dealing with the Hebrew scriptures.

[2]O. Lamar Cope and David E. Orton develop the thesis that Matthew 13:52 is essentially autobiographical. O. Lamar Cope, "Matthew, A Scribe Trained for the Kingdom of Heaven," *The Catholic Biblical Quarterly Monograph Series* (1976); David E. Orton, *The Understanding Scribe; Matthew and the Apocalyptic Ideal* (1989).

[3]Cf. Raymond E. Brown and John P. Meier, *Antioch and Rome: New Testament Cradles of Catholic Christianity* (1983). Robert M. Grant, *Augustus to Constantine* (1970, paperback ed., 1990) 216–220, provides much of the subsequent history of Christianity in Antioch.

[4]Domitian succeeded his brother Titus. He was very anti-senate. There were several attempts on his life, the final successful one with the connivance of his wife, Domitia. Cf. M. Cary and H. H. Scullard, *A History of Rome,* 3rd ed. (1975) 424.

was the *lingua franca.* Economically, the inhabitants were relatively prosperous.[5] The social atmosphere was cosmopolitan. Together with native Greeks and Syrians, freemen and slaves, from around the Mediterranean world, a sizable community of diaspora Jews, some dating back several generations, also lived in the city.[6] This group of Jewish residents had been augmented by a recent influx of refugees who had fled the destruction of Jerusalem by the Romans under Titus in 70 C.E.

There was also a growing Christian community in Antioch consisting of both Jews and Gentiles dating back forty years to the early ministries of Barnabas and Saul/Paul (Acts 11:19-30, 13:1). Besides Matthew, we know only one of these contemporary Antiochan Christians by name. Ignatius,[7] who later became recognized as the first true bishop of Antioch, was undoubtedly already known and respected in the wider Christian community. The Christian congregation, itself, was undoubtedly quite mixed ethnically, generationally, and no doubt also theologically, consisting, according to Michael Crosby, of scattered and assorted house churches.[8]

4. It was an age of extreme religious instability throughout the Roman Empire. Emperor Domitian was actively attempting to rid the capital city of new and foreign religious influences by refur-

[5]Cf. Kilpatrick, *Origins* (1946) 125f.

[6]Cf. Acts 11:19-21.

[7]Cf. William R. Schoedel, *Ignatius of Antioch,* Hermeneia Commentary Series (1985), and Grant, *Augustus to Constantine* (1970) 148–150. There are differences in dates for Ignatius' martyrdom (107 vs. 117 C.E.) and the nature of the problems in Antioch about which Ignatius complains. (Cf. Philadelphians 10.; Smyrnians 11.2; Polycarp 7.1.) Schoedel, *Ignatius,* 10f., believes it had to do with Ignatius' own acceptance as bishop by the people of Antioch. Grant, 149, hypothesizes that the crisis may have been over the selection of Ignatius' successor. If Schoedel is correct, the issue of ecclesiastical leadership about which Matthew is already concerned remained a bone of contention in the Antiochan community for a decade or more.

[8]Michael H. Crosby, *House of Disciples. Church, Economics and Justice in Matthew* (1988) 63, researches *oikos,* "house," in Matthew and notes its sociological connotations. While there is no simple equation between *oikia/oikos* and *eccleesia,* "church," the Church in Matthew is viewed as "the household of true scribes and disciples who perform all that Jesus taught (28:16-20)."

bishing the traditional temples.[9] Still, these multiform religious/mystery cults kept relentlessly moving westward, challenging the dominance of the old Greek and Roman deities, theologies, and moral conventions. Christianity was among them.

Locally, in Antioch, however, the Christian congregation for whom Matthew was writing seems to have had a problem of a specific kind. It was a Church in transition, at the crossroads, rudderless. William Thompson refers to it as a "divided community."[10] There was a problem of integration as the older, experienced "disciples," a few dating back to Barnabas and Paul, had trouble accepting, or even caring about, the inexperienced "little ones" (Matt 18:10-14). Some used their Christian liberty as license and scandalized others (Matt 18:5-9), while simultaneously, the offended found it difficult to forgive (Matt 18:21-35). Specific guidelines for community discipline were a necessity (Matt 18:15-18).

Theologically, the fact of the delayed parousia, that is, the expected return of Christ, had become increasingly troublesome.[11] Spiritual routinization and procrastination were setting in (cf. the Sermon on the Mount, Matt 5–7).

There was disenchantment to a degree. Some Jewish Christians were apparently considering a return to Judaism, or to what was left of Judaism without Jerusalem and the temple, i.e., the schools

[9]Grant, *Augustus to Constantine* (1970) 17, says Domitian restored the Temple of Apollo in Rome at his own expense. Domitian is usually credited as the first emperor after Nero to persecute Christians. Grant, 79, does not deny that there were individual executions, but says the evidence of organized persecution is tenuous. For all his troubles, however, Domitian was one of the few emperors who was never deified by the Roman senate. For a fuller review of the Flavian period, see Bo Reicke, *The New Testament Era,* trans. David Green (1968) 271–314.

[10]William G. Thompson, *Matthew's Advice to a Divided Community, Mt. 17:22–18:35* Analecta Biblica (1970).

[11]There is much debate over the intensity of the perceived problem of the delay in the fulfillment of Jesus' prophecies concerning the coming of the Son of Man (Matt 24–25). Grant, *Augustus to Constantine* (1970) 50, finds little evidence of such concern in first- and second-century literature. However, MATTHEW's fifth discourse, 24–25, on eschatology speaks of preliminary signs, and his Book IV, as we have seen, deals with the institutionalization of the Church, both indications that the parousia was no longer viewed as imminent.

and synagogues of the rabbis[12] (cf. "their" synagogues, Matt 4:23, 12:9, 13:54).

On the positive side, there was the vast harvest of the Gentiles waiting at the edge of the community (Matt 13:24-43). Should it be pursued? How aggressively?

In short, all the tell-tale signs of a third-generation congregation come into view as one reads MATTHEW. Both problems and opportunites, gains and back-door losses, were challenging the status quo in the MATTHEAN community. Some modification of aspirations, expectations, creeds, and practices was necessary.

5. In the prevailing situation, the most pressing and pervasive need, apparently, was for structure and leadership. Leadership was the first question dealt with in Matthew's ecclesiological discourse, Matthew 18:1 (cf. also 20:20-28). Some authority, some institutionalization, some rallying-point, some mark of identification was desperately needed if the Church was to continue, serve, and grow. There were critical decisions to be made, and fast. It was a natural, human, sociological problem. Every movement seeks its monument.

At this early stage in the Christian movement, however, there appear to have been two basic options in terms of polity open to local communities.

The first was the charismatic approach. It looked to the direct intervention, presence, and direction of the divine. We see it reflected in the early chapters of Acts where a replacement for Judas was chosen by lot after prayer (Acts 1:20-26), in the

[12]Cf. Bo Reicke, *The New Testament Era* (1968) 287–289, discusses this movement. Pharisaic scribes, under the chief rabbis Johanan ben Zakkai and Gamaliel II, received permission to restore the Jerusalem Sanhedrin as a faculty of law at the imperial city of Jamnia, located in what we know today as the Gaza Strip. It was also permitted to receive an annual tax of two drachmas. With such imperial assistance, the schools and synagogues presented a formidable alternative and challenge to the struggling Jewish Christian communities. The organization of the synagogues and the early Christian congregations had marked similarities. Gamaliel II was undoubtedly a contemporary of Matthew. The controversial "Eighteen Benedictions" which placed pressure on individuals to decide whether, in effect, they were going to be Jews or Gentiles may be responsible for some of Matthew's vehemence toward the "Scribes and Pharisees," especially in chap. 23. Cf. W.H.C. Frend, *The Early Church* (1965, 1982) 35f.

out-pouring of the Holy Spirit on Pentecost (Acts 2:1-47), and in the visions of Peter at Joppa (Acts 10:9-16). We hear it also in Paul's letters where he exhorts his readers to be "in Christ,"[13] and speaks of Christ as "the head of the body, the church" (Col 1:18).

The second form was the ecclesiastical. It looked to the more visible, tangible, and predictable leadership of persons of faith, whether physically present or living only in esteemed memory. This type we see expressed, for example, in the elevation of James, the Lord's brother, and his extended family to the leadership of the mother Church in Jerusalem.[14] Indirectly, we also sense its presence in Paul's derogatory remarks about "those reputed to be pillars" (Gal 2:9) and "superlative apostles" (2 Cor 12:11).

The first approach was more spiritual, the second supposedly more practical; the first, more dynamic, the second, more stable; the first called for obedience, the second for self-confidence, ability, and ambition.

The choice now confronted the Christian community at Antioch. Both forms are reflected in MATTHEW. The first is articulated in the climactic Great Commission, 28:16-20, where Jesus claims all authority in heaven and on earth and outlines the Church's program for making disciples of all nations by teaching and baptizing in the name and with the authorization of the Triune God. The second polity finds expression in the 16:17-19 passage endorsing Peter as invested with divine insight and authority to bind and loose.

There were undoubtedly other potential candidates for the allegiance of the Antiochan congregation. Barnabas (Acts 11:19-26), Saul/Paul,[15] and Evodius[16] were all at one time or another asso-

[13]The phrase *en Christw* is used approximately ninety times in Paul's letters.

[14]James was martyred in 62 C.E. and was followed by Simon, a cousin of Jesus. A. Harnack, *Kirchenverfassung* (Berlin, 1910) 26, defines the leadership of the Jerusalem congregation after the death of Jesus as a sort of "Caliphate" of Jesus' relatives. For information about James' death, see Reicke, *The New Testament Era* (1968) 215f., also Eusebius, *Ecclesiastical History* (1955) 75 and 99 (Book II, chap. XXIII and Book III, chap. XI).

[15]There is surprisingly little evidence of Pauline influence in Matthew. A basic difference in emphasis exists. Paul's focus in his chief letters was soteriological. Matthew's is Christological. Eusebius, *Ecclesiastical History,* Book III, chap. IV,

ciated with that city and community, but from all the evidence available Peter was the people's choice, at least within the Jewish Christian sector of the congregation. Although Peter was already dead for fifteen or more years, apparently having suffered martyrdom following the Neronian fire of Rome in 64 C.E., his stature had continued to grow. As Ernst Käsemann has surmised, there probably was a *Petrus-Partei,* a Peter Party promoting that heralded disciple as the patron saint and mythopoeic symbol of Antiochan Christianity.[17]

6. It was apparently in the maelstrom of such conflicting issues and partisan views that the evangelist decided to write his Gospel.

As raw materials for his text, as far as Peter was concerned, Matthew had the Petrine pericopes found in MARK plus a few independent traditions of a Jewish Christian provenance extant in his community. This collection of Peter lore was very diverse portraying the first disciple both positively and negatively, ranging from condemnation in the Satan-saying of Mark 8:33 to the encomium of Matthew 16:17-19. The question was: How would Matthew redact this Petrine collage without alienating his partisan readers and still get his own perspective across? Our survey of all the Petrine texts revealed the following editorial techniques.

Redaction-Critical Conclusions

First, Matthew omitted five MARCAN Petrine texts. This immediately suggests that he wasn't interested in providing Peter with all the exposure possible. More telling, however, was the further observation that these five omitted pericopes were among the most positive in their description of Peter in the Second Gospel. They showed Peter actively involved, searching for Jesus in Galilee (Mark 1:35-38), asking Jesus about the withered fig tree (Mark

85, says Luke, the physician and companion of Paul, was also born at Antioch.

[16]Eusebius, *Ecclesiastical History,* Book III, chap. XXII, 104, says Evodius was the first bishop of Antioch. Nothing more is known of him.

[17]Ernst Käsemann, "Die Anfänge Christlicher Theologie," *Exegetische Versuche und Besinnungen,* band 2 (1964) 104.

11:20-25), and receiving a reinstating invitation to rejoin Jesus after the resurrection. Matthew's failure to transfer these texts into his Gospel further hinted that the first evangelist was not at all interested in exalting Peter for his own sake.

The final omission of Mark 16:7 was particularly devastating. It meant that Peter would play no active role whatsoever in Matthew's post-Easter story of the Church. Because this deletion is so obviously intentional, it is clear that Matthew designed this gaping vacuum and wanted it so.

When reviewing the ten pericopes that Matthew did carry over from MARK, in chapter 5, we noted that compared to the texts he had deleted these were among the most negative toward Peter. Here was the account of Peter's inadequate confession of Christ (Mark 8:27-30), the Satan-saying (Mark 8:31-33), Peter's Boast and poor performance in Gethsemane (Mark 14:26-42), and finally the account of Peter's Denials (Mark 14:66-72). Most devastating to Peter's prominence, however, was the fact that Matthew not only repeated these uncomplimentary portrayals but in some instances even made them more demeaning, especially the denials. The "first" (Matt 10:2) had been made last (Matt 26:75).

One pericope, the Story of the Transfiguration, did initially appear to disrupt the pattern. In it Matthew removed a negative comment from Mark 9:6 about Peter "talking through his hat," as it were. Upon closer examination, however, we learned that the evangelist had removed the same criticism from MARK's description of the disciples generally in Mark 14:40b. Obviously, Matthew was meticulously shading all the characters of his Gospel to fit some predetermined model.

After researching the five omitted Petrine texts plus the ten transposed pericopes from MARK, we were left with five additional Petrine passages unique to MATTHEW, all squeezed together with three Marcan Petrine accounts into the tight confines of chapters 14–18, Matthew's Book IV. These passages along with the redacted construct of the discourse on the Church in chapter 18, give this Book IV and the character of Peter a distinctive ecclesiological ambiance. Peter is portrayed as a contender for Church leadership.

Other minor but contributory redactional stratagems as far as

Peter is concerned which had surfaced in the earlier review of the Petrine omissions and transpositions in MATTHEW were also now confirmed. Peter was being highlighted while all other peers among the disciples were being relegated to the shadows. Peter was stylized as concerned only with internal Church issues, while outside interests regarding relations with Judaism and the Gentiles, were delegated to the disciples generally. And finally, we detected, despite apparent convolutions, a decided descending trajectory in Matthew's Petrine portrait. He who had been the first called to discipleship (Matt 4:18-19) was nowhere in sight in the post-resurrection scene.

Specifically, in our review of these crucial five uniquely Matthean Petrine passages, we observed that two of them (15:15 and 18:21-22) were also transplants from older sources, MARK and Q, respectively. Matthew, seemingly displaying some abitrariness, had simply inserted the name of Peter into both. The common effect, however, was totally predictable. In one, Peter was lumped together with the other disciples and criticized by Jesus as "still without understanding." In the other, he was depicted as being deficient in his appreciation of the dimensions of true forgiveness, an embarrassing happenstance for one who had been previously and ostensibly given the power to "bind and loose" on earth and in heaven (Matt 16:19).

Two of the three remaining special passages (16:17-19 and 17:24-27) were now also recognized on the basis of their phraseology and vocabulary as remnants of Jewish Christian tradition. Both were exceptionally complimentary to Peter, reminiscent of ancient encomia. As such, they not only appear to be, but are, when viewed in isolation, out of character with all other Petrine references in MATTHEW, except, perhaps, the word "first" in 10:2. The first evangelist, however, is careful to locate these insertions in contexts which modify their impact. Matthew 16:17-19 is sandwiched between the MARCAN pericopes of Peter's Confession and the Satan-Saying. In a dramatic reversal, the blessed now become the cursed. The Temple Tax account, meanwhile, is placed at the very beginning of the Discourse on Discipleship and the Church. There it serves as kind of text suggesting the related themes of "Peter" and "scandalizing" which are then immediately taken up in the sermon which follows. The reader is reminded of Peter who had been redactionally labeled a scandal, *skandalon,* in Matthew 16:23, when Jesus is heard to warn in Matthew 18:7: "Woe to the man by whom the temptation, *skandalon,* comes."

In Matthew 18:18, similarly, all the privileges to bind and loose bestowed upon Peter in that encomiastic tradition of Matthew 16:19 are redistributed to all the disciples. And summarily, in Matthew 18:21-22, Peter is prominently displayed by way of Matthean redaction as one who lacks a proper forgiving disposition and commitment.

The one remaining special Petrine text in MATTHEW, 14:28-33, dramatizing Peter walking upon the stormy waters of the Sea of Galilee, is undoubtedly the most revealing of all. Our diagnosis in chapter 3 discovered that it displayed all the evidences of original Matthean composition. That fact gave it added significance. Furthermore, the circumstance that Matthew had placed it at the very beginning of his list of special Petrine references also suggested its role as a paradigm for the presentation of Peter to follow.

Nestled here between the beginning and end of the MARCAN story of Jesus Walking Upon the Sea (6:47-52), the Matthean account is a story-within-a-story in which the experience and expertise of Jesus and Peter are contrasted. Peter momentarily succeeds and compares well with Jesus, but then fails and sinks. Jesus' victory is proclaimed by all in the boat: "Truly you are the Son of God." Peter is triply defeated. Not only did he fail to walk on water for any length of time; he was also reprimanded as a "little-faith" and a "doubter." Finally, the confession of those in the boat also served to detract from Peter's own very similar confession at Caesarea Philippi in Matthew 16:16.

The net effect of all this research was the general discovery that Matthew was simultaneously engaged in two fundamental editorial enterprises. He was comparing and identifying Peter with the disciples while contrasting him with Jesus, both to the denigration of the first disciple.

The careful manner with which Matthew compared, or equated, Peter with the other disciples is illustrated in figure 3, page 132. He used identical, or near identical, terms to describe both parties. Both were labeled little-faiths, doubters, without understand-

Visualization of Matthew's Redactional Parallelization of Peter and the Disciples

Thematic Characteristic	Location in the Tradition	Traditional Ascription	Redactional Location	Redactional Ascription
1. *ὀλιγόπιστος* "little-faith"	Q Matt 6:30/Luke 12:28	Disciples	Matt 14:31c	Peter
2. *διστάζειν* to doubt	Matthean Redaction		Matt 14:31d Matt 28:17b	Peter Disciples
3. *ἀσύνετος* without understanding	Mark 7:18b	Disciples	Matt 15:16b	Peter
4. The Act of Confessing	Mark 8:29c	Peter	Matt 14:33a	Disciples
5. The Confession *Θεοῦ υἱὸς εἶ* "You are the Son of God."	Mark 8:29c	Peter	Matt 14:33b	Disciples
6. *δέειν . . . λύειν* "bind . . . loose"	Jewish-Christian Tradition Matt 16:19bc	Peter	Matt 18:18bc	Disciples
7. *σκάνδαλον* "Stumbling block"	Q Matt 18:7/Luke 17:1 (Mark 9:42-50)	Disciples	Matt 16:23c	Peter

ing and in danger of scandalizing others. On the positive side, they also shared a common commitment to Jesus as the Messiah as well as the authority to bind and loose.

In some of these cases (#1, 3, 4, 6 & 7), Matthew found half of the equation in one of the traditions available to him. These characterizations he then redactionally balanced, attributing the same action or descriptive term to the other party. In the remaining cases, he originated the common phrases which he then redactionally applied to both Peter and the disciples.

In addition to the examples listed here, there is the double omission about not knowing what to say from Mark 9:6/Matthew 17:4 pertaining to Peter alone and in Mark 14:40c/Matthew 26:43 involving the inner circle of the disciples. There are also several examples of such parallelization which were found already in the traditional materials.[18]

In view of the generally uncomplimentary Petrine profile discernible in Matthean redaction elsewhere, we can undoubtedly surmise what Matthew's editorial purposes were in designing these comparisons. By equating Peter with the disciples as a group, Matthew, in effect, was demoting Peter without destroying him. He was no longer "first," but he was still one of the Eleven, even after his denials and in the post-resurrection community. The evangelist is to be commended for his diplomacy.

Matthew's reasons for wishing to demote Peter in this way undoubtedly become clear when we examine the next circumstance uncovered in our research, Matthew's redactional contrasting of Jesus and Peter. We noted that whenever Jesus and Peter confronted each other, Peter, after a promising beginning, always faltered in the end. He walked on the water momentarily but then slipped beneath the waves (Matt 14:29-30). He could say all the right words in Matthew 16:16, but he still could not understand or live up to their implications (Matt 16:21-23). He could be generous in his offer of remission, and yet not measure up to Jesus' expectation for unlimited forgiveness (Matt 18:21-22). He could have the best of intentions about not denying Jesus (Matt 26:33) and then wilt before the challenges of two little girls and a group

[18]Cf. J. D. Kingsbury, "The Figure of Peter in Matthew's Gospel as a Theological Problem," (1979) 72–74.

of bystanders (Matt 26:69-74). Meanwhile, in each situation, Jesus was the epitome of faithfulness, courage, and consistency. Judging from the effect of Matthew's redaction, then, the goal of the evangelist was to show that even Peter provided no real competition to Jesus, leaving Jesus ultimately to stand unrivaled with all authority, *exousia,* in heaven and on earth (Matt 28:18).

This is as far as our redaction-critical analysis of the role of Peter in MATTHEW took us. Gratefully, it provided us with a cogent and comprehensive explanation of the paradoxical portrayal of Peter in the First Gospel. However, one disturbing consideration remains. One senses that our conclusions, as described, still lack a degree of coherence and cohesiveness. We have identified a complicated collection of sophisticated individual artifices employed by Matthew in pursuing his editorial task, but the relationship of one to another has not always been clear. We have become increasingly aware that the evangelist was capable of a high level of literary art, but we have been unable to comprehend or attach a name to the overall literary strategy he is pursuing. For help in finding an answer to this quandary, we need now to investigate the rubrics of ancient rhetoric.[19]

Rhetorical-Critical Conclusions

The most readily available clue with which to begin this inquiry into the conventions of ancient rhetoric is undoubtedly found in the observation made already in chapters 3 and 6 that the Jewish Christian Petrine traditions in Matthew 16:17-19 and 17:24-27 exhibited many of the characteristics of an ancient Greek encomium.

[19]Helpful works on the subject of ancient rhetoric and rhetorical criticism include Burton L. Mack, *Rhetoric and the New Testament* (1990); George A. Kennedy, *Classical Rhetoric and Its Christian and Secular Tradition from Ancient to Modern Times* (1980). Cf. also his *The Art of Persuasion in Greece* (1963). Donald Lemen Clark, *Rhetoric in Greco-Roman Education* (1957); Stanley F. Bonner, *Education in Ancient Rome* (1977); James J. Murphy, ed., *Quintilian on the Teaching of Speaking and Writing,* translations from Books 1, 2, and 10 of Quintilian's *Institutio Oratoria* (1987); John W. O'Malley, *Praise and Blame in Renaissance Rome* (1979); Philip L. Shuler, *A Genre for the Gospel: The Biographical Character of Matthew* (1982); and Jakob Jonsson, *Humour and Irony in the New Testament* (1965).

An encomium is a form of oratory at least as old as Homer, but it was not identified until Aristotle (384–322 B.C.E.) in the fourth century B.C.E.[20] He listed it under the third general classification of the three types of rhetorical speech: Judicial, Deliberative, and Epideictic. Epideictic referred to orations meant to be performed in public, usually in conjunction with festivals or ceremonies. An encomium, then, was normally a speech in honor of some dignitary, or in recognition of someone's birthday, or in praise of a virtue, or a eulogy at someone's funeral.

As identified by ancient rhetoricians, Isocrates, Cicero, Quintilian, Hermogenes of Tarsus,[21] and others who analyzed the numerous rhetorical forms and developed books of elementary rhetorical exercises for school children, there were three fundamental requirements for any good address: (1) *ethos,* i.e., something which demonstrated the speaker's authority and right to expound his views in public, (2) *pathos,* something which would grab the emotions of the audience, and (3) *logos,* that is, something that would demonstrate reason, or generate thought.[22] The first two were particularly important in epideictic oratory.

Expertise in five techniques were required to accomplish these three goals: (1) invention, (2) arrangement, (3) style, (4) memory, and (5) delivery.[23] The first is undoubtedly the most fascinating for us twentieth-century practitioners, restricted as we are by concerns about accuracy, fears of plagiarism, and excessive emotion. "Invention" meant that since the success or failure of a

[20]Aristotle, *The "Art" of Rhetoric (Ars Rhetorica),* trans. J. H. Freese, Loeb Classical Library (1926). Also in Lane Cooper, *Rhetoric* (1932) 46–55. According to Kennedy, *Classical Rhetoric* (1980), the preconditions for rhetorical speaking and writing were the adoption of the Phoenician alphabet, including the Greek invention of vowels, in the eighth century B.C.E. Two fifth-century Sicilians, Corax and Tisias, began the classification of "technical rhetoric." Aristotle, 384–322 B.C.E., developed the first handbook of classical rhetoric.

[21]Cf. " 'Elenees Egkwmion," *Isocrates Discours,* Georges Mathieu and Emile Bremond, eds. Société D'Édition, Paris, 1963, 153–179. Marcus Tullius Cicero *De Inventione* is found in Cicero's "Rhetorical Treatises." Loeb Classical Library (1949); Marcus Fabius Quintilianus *Institutio Oratoria* is found in the Loeb Classical Library, 4 vols. (1920–1922); Hermogenes *Progymnasmata* is found translated in C. S. Baldwin, *Medieval Rhetoric and Poetic* (1959) 23–38.

[22]Cf. Mack, *Rhetoric* (1990) 36.

[23]Cf. Clark, *Greco-Roman Education* (1957) 67–112.

speech depended so heavily upon the "rhetor's," or orator's, ability to capture the emotions of the hearers, any convention or artifice that one could find or invent which might contribute to the cause was eligible for use. It was a freedom which the more philosophical rhetoricians abhored, but which, according to George Kennedy, nevertheless survived until surprisingly recent times.[24]

Burton Mack provides us with a bare-bones outline of the typical encomium in praise of a human being:[25]

1. Introduction
2. Narration
   Origin/Genealogy/Birth
3. Achievements
   a. Education/Pursuits
   b. Virtues
   c. Deeds
   d. Blessings/Endowments
4. Conclusion
   Honor/Memorial

The speaker, of course, could flesh out this outline by adding any number of rhetorical figures of speech: *Stasis* (an initial statement of the situation), *Synkrisis* (comparison, association), *Prolepsis* (anticipation, designed to add to what is coming), *Anaphora* (repeated identical beginnings of phrases), *Epiphora* (repeated identical ending of phrases), *Paranomasia* (play-on-words, etc.)—anything that would magnify the object of praise.

We previously noted several of these forms in our review of the encomiastic traditions found in Matthew 16:17-19 and 17:24-27.[26]

It is of prime importance for our purposes here, however, to recognize that "encomium," as a rhetorical designation, has as

[24]Kennedy, *Classical Rhetoric* (1980) 110f., says "It was not until the nineteenth century that historians abandoned the convention of writing speeches for characters in their narratives."

[25]Mack, *Rhetoric* (1990) 48.

[26]Cf. 54–56, above.

much to do with form as with content. Two types of encomia, positive and negative, are in fact possible. There are encomia of praise and of dispraise, of *laudandi et vituperandi.*[27] Both were of ancient origin and often used in conjunction with each other.

Encomia of dispraise employed the very same forms and outline as encomia of praise, only to the opposite effect. The goal is to dishonor, to disparage, to cast blame or shame upon a rival or antagonist. Here comparisons result in contrasts. Instead of achievements, the focus is upon failures. Associations with evil persons, vices, and crimes are emphasized. While many of the same figures of speech may be used, invective, woes, and threats are given prominence. Often faint praise or left-handed compliments open up opportunities for ridicule. In fact, encomia of dispraise often begin with brief encomia of praise filled, of course, with irony because, as we all know, "the bigger they are the harder they fall."

D. L. Clark translates the instructions on how to develop a "commonplace," a classic form closely related to an encomium of dispraise, given by a fourth-century C.E. technical rhetorician named Aphthonius:

> Begin with the contrary, analyzing it, not to inform, for the facts are assumed, but to incite and exasperate the auditors. Then introduce a comparison to heighten as much as possible the point you are making. After that introduce a proverb, upbraiding and calumniating the doer of the deed. Then a digression, introducing a defamatory conjecture as to the past life of the accused; then a repudiation of pity. Conclude the exercise with the final considerations of legality, justice, expediency, possibility, decency, and the consequences of the action."[28]

How suggestive and reminiscent of several of the literary dynamics we uncovered in Matthew's redaction of the role of Peter

[27]Cf. John W. O'Malley, *Praise and Blame in Renaissance Rome* (1979) 39; Charles Edgar Little, "On Praise and Blame," in *Quintilian, the School Master* vol. 1 (1951) 122–124; Mack, *Rhetoric* (1990) 48, remarks that ancient Greece fostered a "culture oriented to honor and shame."

[28]Clark, *Greco-Roman Education* (1957) 194ff. Also C. S. Baldwin, *Medieval Rhetoric* (1959) 28–30.

in the First Gospel. Comparisons and contrasts, plays-on-words, defamatory suggestions, and even curses were found there, too. Could Matthew have been employing the art of encomiastic dispraise as his overall strategy? It certainly would appear so. Several scholars have entertained the possibility that Matthew used other rhetorical conventions in similar contexts.[29] Why not here?

Of course, not every detail will fit the classic paradigm. We should not expect it to do so. Matthew's application is of the kind that Kennedy has labled "secondary rhetoric."[30] Primary rhetoric was designed for public speaking. Even when written, the usual form was one of an oration or address.[31] Secondary rhetoric suggests the adaptations which become necessary when the rubrics of oral discourse are adjusted to different art forms and literary genre, e.g., history or drama, or in our case, gospel. Here there is no continuous presentation but a series of pericopes. Here the *ethos* is not vested in the editor, but in Jesus, the recognized authority. Nevertheless, all the essentials are here in terms of forms, sequence, and smaller figures of speech.

In the interest of brevity and clarity we present our analysis in outline and keyword form:

Encomiastic Dispraise of Peter in MATTHEW

Introduction:	The Call of Peter, Andrew, James, and John to become fishers of men (4:18-19)
Genealogy:	The list of the disciples serves as Peter's surrogate family (10:2-4)
Stasis:[32]	"First" (10:2). This word provides a statement of the problem: Peter's proposed rank and privilege

[29]Mack, *Rhetoric* (1990) includes a brief examination of the Sermon on the Mount, Matthew 5–7, 81–85, with a somewhat more detailed look at the pericope on Loving One's Enemies in Matthew 5:43-48 on 53f.; Shuler, *Genre* (1982) attempts (without sufficient detail) to show that Matthew employs the conventions of an encomium in his entire design of the First Gospel.

[30]Kennedy, *Classical Rhetoric* (1980) 5–6.

[31]The oral nature of Paul's letters, mostly dictated, explains why most modern rhetorical-critical research has focused on the Pauline corpus. Cf. the Bibliography in Mack, *Rhetoric* (1990) 103–110.

[32]Perhaps Cicero best characterized this particular form of stasis, calling it an

Contrast 1:	14:22-33. Achievement/Failure
Positive:	Jesus and Peter walk on sea/water
Negative:	Peter sinks, Jesus rebukes him
Comparison 1:	Peter and disciples: "little-faith" (14:31/6:30); "doubt" (14:31/28:17)
Comparison 2:	*Prolepsis:* Disciples confess Jesus as Son of God (14:33), as does Peter in 16:16
Comparison 3:	15:15-16. Peter, as spokesman, asks about defilement
Negative:	Rebuke in second person plural: "Still you are without understanding!"
Contrast 2:	16:13-23, linked by *symploce** with *eimi* Virtues/Vices
Positive:	Peter confesses Christ Encomium in praise of Peter (16:17-19)
Paranomasia:	*Petrws/petra,* 16:18
Negative:	Peter reproves Jesus (16:22) Jesus rebukes Peter (16:23)
Invective:	Association and identification of Peter with Satan, temptation, and human thought
Comparison 4:	Peter and disciples identified with *skandalon* (16:23/18:6-7)
Contrast 3:	17:1-9. Jesus, Moses, and Elijah with Peter, James, and John at the Transfiguration
Positive:	Heavenly voice acknowledges Jesus as God's beloved Son
Negative:	Peter, James, and John are overcome by fear, need to be "touched," healed (17:6-7)
Contrast 4:	17:24-27/18:21-22. Temple Tax
Positive:	Encomiastic association—Peter speaks for Jesus, answers Jesus, identified with Jesus in paying the tax

insinuatio. Cf. Cicero, *Rhetorical Treatises* (1949) 43–49. Kennedy, *Classical Rhetoric* (1980) 93, describes stasis as a form "which by dissimulation or in a roundabout way will steal into the mind of each listener." "First" certainly does so in Matthew 10:2.

*Alternating *anaphora/epiphora*

Negative:	Jesus' correction of Peter's inadequate understanding of forgiveness (18:21-22)
Contrast 5:	26:36-46. Jesus with Peter and sons of Zebedee in Gethsemane
Positive:	Jesus prays
Negative:	Peter and others sleep
Contrast 6:	26:57-75. Jesus and Peter on trial
Positive:	Jesus gives good witness before high authorities
Negative:	Peter denies before two girls and some bystanders
pathos:	Peter weeps bitterly (26:75)
Concluding Contrast 7:	Peter is omitted from the Post-Easter account (28:7/Mark 16:8), while Jesus stands alone with all authority in heaven and on earth (28:18-20)

In addition to these major evidences of Matthew's familiarity with and use of the rubrics of encomiastic dispraise, there are also a number of lesser rhetorical conventions that help us to understand many of the apparent anomalies in Matthean redaction encountered in our research. We see the privilege of invention at work in Matthew's unilateral designation of Peter as the spokesman in Matthew 15:15 and 18:21; also in the selection and location of the Temple Tax account, 17:24-27. There are other instances of *prolepsis,* i.e., anticipatory comments or actions aimed at forestalling credit to someone else or to deepening blame in subsequent developments.[33] Matthew's advance additions of explicit prohibitions of public denial and swearing in Matthew 10:33 and 5:34-37, respectively, are obvious examples. Matthew also used a system of detraction, countering "first" in 10:2 with "first shall be last" in 19:30 and 20:16. Similarly, the privileges accorded Peter in 16:19 are redistributed to all the disciples in 18:18. "Woes" are found redactionally added in 18:7. Irony is a part of all of the comparison/contrasts (*synkrisis*) where it is clear that Peter will not live up to his earlier promise.[34] There is

[33]Cf. Clark, *Greco-Roman Education* (1957) 90f.

[34]As noted occasionally throughout this book, several commentators suspected

typical amplification of Peter's guilt in Matthew's portrayal of him as denying before three different persons instead of two, in fact "before them all," and in punctuating his denials with curses twice instead of once as in MARK. Perhaps we can also detect a kind of "defamatory conjecture," or suggestion, in the "but some doubted" epithet of Matthew 28:17b, signaling that doubters, of the same sort as Peter, are still recognized as present in the community. Beyond everything else, however, the deletion of the Peter reference in Mark 16:7 from Matthew 28:7 is the cruelest cut of all. The greatest insult is to be ignored. Yet, for all practical purposes, that is precisely what happened to Peter in Matthew's depiction of the post-Easter Church.

There is only one redeeming feature, the *pathos* of the Matthew 26:75 comment: "And he went out and wept bitterly." Matthew's addition of "bitterly," *pikrws,* to his MARCAN source pulls at the heartstrings of the reader, suggesting true contrition on Peter's part and therefore the right to continue to be reckoned among the Eleven, even though all of his individual prominence among the disciples has evaporated.

Matthew's use of *pathos* here also reminds us of the important interpretational fact that Matthew's use of the formula of dispraise, even his amplification of Peter's guilt, was not meant to be personally malicious, as a kind of character assasination. Matthew was not worried about Peter per se, but about the inordinate allegiance of his contemporary devotees, as expressed in the encomiastic traditions. Actually, the evangelist was letting Peter down as gently and diplomatically as possible. He is not employing vituperation as he might have, but literally "dis-praise."

Matthew's primary purpose, it now appears, was Christological.[35] Ecclesiology, eschatology, soteriology, and ethics are all sub-

that Matthew was employing irony. Unfortunately, they did not recognize it as part of the larger encomium of dispraise form. Cf. Stock, *Irony?* (1989); H. A. Homeau, "On Fishing for Staters," *The Expository Times,* 85, 11 (1974) 341–342; Myron S. Augsburger, *Matthew* (1982) 213.

[35]There has been an ongoing debate in MATTHEAN studies whether the First Gospel is primarily Christological, Ecclesiological, or Ethical. The ethical element is stressed in the Sermon on the Mount and in the Great Commission: "whatsoever I have commanded, *eneteilameen,* you." The ecclesiological emphasis appears especially in Matthew 18. The concluding enthronement scene in 28:16-20,

sumed under Christology in the First Gospel. The triumphant Christ is all that counts. As Otto Michel and Wolfgang Trilling taught us some time ago, MATTHEW is meant to be read backwards.[36] The evangelist's true target all along consisted in Jesus' closing words: "All power (*exousia*), in heaven and on earth has been given unto Me. Go therefore, and make disciples of all nations (*ta ethnee,* i.e., Gentiles), baptizing them in the name of the Father and of the Son and of the Holy Spirit, teaching them to observe all that I have commanded you; and lo, I am with you always, to the close of the age." This exalted passage in 28:18-20 may be read as a summary of the First Gospel. Jesus is all and everything that the Church in Antioch, and everywhere, truly needs.

Now we can understand Matthew's seemingly helter-skelter depiction of Peter, the addition of Petrine references, the location of the Petrine material, and the apparent gratuitousness of some of the evangelist's denigrations of the first disciple. They were all integral to the rhetorical form of encomiastic dispraise, consistent with Matthew's theological convictions favoring a charismatic polity in Church leadership. First-century readers, such as Ignatius, who had been educated in and made sensitive to such things, would have recognized the convention immediately.

As much as we may not have expected to find these characteristics of ancient Greek encomia in a piece of early Jewish-Christian literature, there they are, witnessing to the pervasiveness of the Hellenistic influence throughout the Mediterranean world in the first century C.E. Cicero (106–43 B.C.E.) had written his influential *De Inventione* a little more than a century earlier.[37]

with Jesus given all authority, *eksousia,* in heaven and earth and promising to be "with you always," however, effectively subsumes all other considerations under Christology.

[36] Otto Michel, "Der Abschluss des Matthäus-evangeliums," *Evangelische Theologie* 10 (1950) 21. Wolfgang Trilling, *Das Wahre Israel, Studien zur Theologie des Matthäus-Evangelium* (1964) 4f. Cf. also Joachim Rohde, *Rediscovering the Teaching of the Evangelists* (1968) 64–73; Benjamin J. Hubbard, *The Matthean Redaction of a Primitive Apostolic Commissioning: An Exegesis of Matthew 28:16-20* (1974).

[37] Cf. p. 135, n. 23, above.

Quintilian (c. 40–96 C.E.) was probably writing his *Institutio Oratoria* at the very same time that Matthew was preparing the First Gospel.[38] Matthew, then, could well have learned the basic principles of rhetoric already as a boy in one of Antioch's Greco-Roman schools. The presence of rhetorical forms imbedded in this Hellenistic Jewish Christian gospel, therefore, should not surprise us in the least.

We have come to the final denouement of the problem of Peter in MATTHEW, arrived at both inductively and deductively, by both redaction- and rhetorical-critical routes. The first evangelist, as diplomatically as he could, subjected the celebrated disciple, Peter, of Jewish Christian tradition, to the denigration of the rhetorical rite of dispraise so that in the end Jesus could stand alone, the singular, living, present, authoritative focus of the Christian community's allegiance, obedience, and hope.

[38]James Murphy, *Quintilian* (1987) xiv–xviii, provides a biographical sketch of Quintilian's life. Born in Spain, apparently the son of a teacher, Quintilian grew up and was educated in the company of rhetoricians. At approximately age thirty-five, he moved to Rome where he quickly gained prominence as a teacher and received a special subsidy from the emperors for his contributions to contemporary education. Pliny the Younger was one of his students. In 88 C.E., Domitian placed him in charge of the "first public school of Rome," effectively making Quintilian the "first teacher" of the empire. He retired in 90 C.E. to write his *Institutio Oratoria* which, he says, took him two years. With the early deaths of his young wife and two young sons, as background, Quintilian dedicated his work, a book on "technical rhetoric" with numerous practice exercises, to "the studious youth" of Rome. Nothing more is heard of Quintilian after Domitian's assasination in 96 C.E.

8

Implications: Peter and Matthew Today

What is the significance for scholarship and for the Church today of the conclusions just reached about Matthew's theological perspective and editorial practice with reference to Peter back in the first century C.E.? That is the challenge confronting us in this final chapter. It is time to replace academic tweeds with the poplin of the preacher; to leave the comfortable confines of exegesis and trespass on the foreign soil of systematics, to lay aside all pretentions of objectivity and assume the role of partisan. A start to the dialog on Church authority, mission, and ministry occasioned by this book needs to be undertaken immediately while the contours of the underlying exegetical issues are still fresh and in focus.

Of course, ours has been only one study, of one Gospel, using essentially one exegetical method. Other analyses of the role of Peter in other Gospels, or even in MATTHEW, employing other methods, could conceivably generate different results. LUKE, for example, seems to have espoused an ecclesiology at some variance from that of the First Gospel.[1] Sweeping, absolutist judgments and dogmatic pronouncements, therefore, are to be

[1]The frequent use of "apostle" in LUKE (six times in the Third Gospel plus twenty-eight times in the first sixteen chapters of ACTS compared to once in MATTHEW and twice in MARK) signals some kind of a conceptual shift. This observation combined with the election of "deacons" in Acts 6:1-6 also indicates incipient stratification in functions, suggesting offices. If there is justification for the idea of Apostolic Succession anywhere in the New Testament, it must be found in LUKE-Acts or the Pastorals. Cf. chap. 1, p. 16, n. 38, above.

avoided. We are interested only in the implications of the Matthean viewpoint as uncovered in our research. They are, without doubt, controversial enough!

1. If our work has been successful, then it is obvious that Matthew failed in his efforts to reduce Peter's attractiveness as a rival to Jesus as head of the Church. Within two decades, Ignatius, Matthew's younger contemporary, had already espoused and was living out a mon-episcopal system of Church government right there in Antioch, even to the extent of claiming the authority of God for his own opinions.[2] Matthew must have died a very disappointed man.

The fact that Ignatius did not base his claims to primacy on the prerogatives of Peter, however, may be significant, especially in view of Origen's later anachronistic pronouncements about Peter serving as the first bishop of that Syrian city.[3] Surely Ignatius knew the history of Peter's prior presence in the vicinity. There are also clear indications that Ignatius was familiar with Matthew's Gospel.[4] Yet he never quoted Matthew 16:17-19 in support of his own ambitions. Was his silence, perhaps, a tacit recognition of Matthew's well-known opposition to the pro-Petrine ecclesiastical traditions extant in the community?

The first evangelist's failure was even more pronounced in the West a little more than a century later. There, whether out of sociological necessity, theological expedience, or Church-political advantage, Peter was posthumously hailed as the first Bishop of Rome beginning the development of a huge hierarchical super-

[2]Cf. Ignatius' letters to the Trallians 5:2 and Philadelphians 7:1-2 in A. C. Coxe, *The Ante-Nicene Fathers,* vol. 1. Schoedel in his commentary on *Ignatius of Antioch* (1985) 205, says: "He shared with many others in the Graeco-Roman world the belief that a sudden loud utterance marked the inrush of the divine." The term "mon-episcopal" is used here instead of "monarchical-episcopal" which would be more appropriate in a discussion or comparison of ecclesial authority with secular royal power and authority.

[3]Cf. chap. 1, p. 14, nn. 30 and 31, above.

[4]W. Schoedel, *Igantius* (1985) 9, prefers to think that Ignatius did not have the written MATTHEW, but was familiar with "tradition primarily only of a Matthean type." J. P. Meier, in Brown and Meier, *Antioch and Rome* (1983) 24, however, makes a reasonably good case for the position that Ignatius had the written MATTHEW available to him.

structure known today as the Petrine Office.[5] Precisely the opposite of what Matthew intended, then, actually materialized in the second- and third-century Church, in both East and West.

2. If our conclusions are correct, this multifaceted Petrine Office, with all its various contemporary denominational expressions, is without foundation as far as MATTHEW is concerned. It would appear to be a gargantuan house of cards built on stilts. Matthew's vision was of an egalitarian brotherhood with the living, present Christ at its head unrivaled by any human surrogate or intermediary. A "proleptic parousia" is John Meier's apt phrase for what Matthew had in mind.[6] That is, the Church was to remain a community where Jesus' coming again was so surely anticipated if not already partially experienced in his death and resurrection, that for all practical purposes he had never left. Christ, then, was the only authority, the only leader, the Church needed.

What resulted over time, however, was something quite different. A vast stratified religious establishment emerged consisting of numerous ecclesial offices and orders with each one gradually appropriating unto itself more and more of the prerogatives of the divine: ecclesiastical predominance, sovereignty over the secular as well as the sacred, disciplinary authority which extended even to matters of life and death, topped off by a kind of assumed magisterial omniscience, theological infallibility, and ecclesial indefectibility.

We may be inclined to excuse as medieval aberrations the sanctimoniousness of many ecclesiastical titles, the pompousness of some clerical vestments, the superciliousness of occasional dicta of episcopal power and privilege, perhaps even the all too frequent cruelty of witch-hunt, interdict, and inquisition, but what

[5]The Petrine Office refers generally to all levels, privileges, and responsibilities of ministry based on the collage of Petrine traditions: his leading role among the disciples, his having been the first to whom the resurrected Christ appeared, his martyrdom in Rome, the concept of the apostolic succession, and the various New Testament passages, especially Matthew 16:17-19, Luke 22:32, and John 21:15-19. Normally the term is used as the equivalent of the episcopal form of Church polity.

[6]Meier, *Vision,* 215, n. 270. Cf. chap. 6, p. 99, n. 17, above. Also his *The Mission of Christ and His Church* (1990) 134–140.

cannot be overlooked are the more contemporary concerns of continuing elitism, chauvinism, patriarchy, and defensive self-interest in the Church at all levels, whether Protestant, Catholic, Orthodox, or Pentecostal, all permitted and even encouraged by a misunderstanding of the Matthean Petrine treatment, all manifesting directly or indirectly the infectious influence of the Matthew 16:17-19 syndrome.

The tendency toward self-interest and self-service seems endemic among us, reaching from the most pious fundamentalist TV evangelist/entertainer, to the occasionally autocratic pastor of a local congregation, to the laypersons in the pew who often, curiously, seem to want to put their pastor on a pedestal. There is none without sin among us. Matthew continues to speak as a corrective to us all, tempering our tendencies toward self-aggrandizement and, thereby, denial of Christ.

If the conclusions arrived at in this book are correct, Matthew would cringe at the effort exerted today to preserve venerable but purely human structures in the Church, at our inclinations to stack one denominationally ethnocentric tradition upon another and claim divine justification for them all. Undoubtedly most tragic is the hurt inflicted upon individuals and entire segments of society by legalistically withholding forgiveness or covering up egregious error all in the name of perpetuating some presumed myth of special ecclesial privilege and authority.

Matthew was not an iconoclast. He saw the continuing need for "prophets and wise men and scribes" (Matt 23:34) who would fulfill the necessary teaching functions in the Church. His concern, however, was that these roles be kept in perspective in view of the solo essential, the lordship of Jesus Christ. It was not the character, but the cult of Peter that Matthew opposed, not Peter's person but his ecclesiastical progeny. Those who revelled in being called rabbi, father, or master (Matt 23:8-10), suggesting some degree of rank, were the ones that Matthew could not countenance, because, as he has Jesus go on to say, "He who is greatest among you shall be your servant; whoever exalts himself will be humbled, and whoever humbles himself will be exalted" (Matt 23:11-12).

In simplest, practical terms, then, what this study teaches is that Matthean Petrine passages may no longer be used to support claims of ecclesiastical preeminence or individual privilege in the Church. There is no ascribed charisma of office in the Church, except for the supreme lordship of Jesus Christ. To use an analogy, this study suggests that the inscription in the cupola of St. Peter's in Rome quoting Matthew 16:18, "You are Peter and upon this rock I will build my church," should be replaced with the commissioning words addressed to Peter in Luke 22:32: " . . . when you have turned again, strengthen your brethren."

3. Speaking more generally, if our analysis has been correct, we need to learn how to read MATTHEW all over again—scholar, priest, and devotional reader alike. The First Gospel must be viewed and understood as a unit with the import of the parts determined by the impact of the whole. The requirements of the form of dispraise dictated that some materials be included which were not intended to be perpetuated, absolutized, or institutionalized. Pious assertions of plenary inspiration must go. As Stock and Van Iersel so bluntly put it, we find here "words (which) mean the opposite of what they seem to say."[7] A sensitivity to Matthean purpose and practice, therefore, is essential. The natural tendency to automatically and indiscriminately project increased value onto redactionally inserted materials has to be curbed. Selective quoting, or proof-texting, out of context, are, of course, completely inappropriate.

As far as one's reading of Petrine passages specifically is concerned, it is clear that prominence does not translate into preeminence in MATTHEW. The opposite, no doubt, would be closer to the truth. Matthew 14:22-33 now emerges as the key passage replacing Matthew 16:17-19. There, in the Walking on the Water episode, in the first major Petrine insertion appropriately composed by the evangelist himself, we find the real paradigm for understanding Peter's role in the First Gospel. Peter is designed to submerge (Matt 14:30-31) while Jesus as the one who saves is exalted as the "Son of God" (Matt 14:33). The identical programmatic is followed in the climactic chapters of the Gospel where Peter is last seen weeping in the shadows (Matt 26:75) while the resurrected Jesus stands on the mountain top, a place of divine

[7]A. Stock, "Ironic?" *Biblical Theology Bulletin* (1987) 66.

revelation, and proclaims his absolute authority in heaven and on earth (Matt 28:16-20). Christology glows more brilliantly against the backdrop of human frailty.

4. Liturgical changes are also in order. The pericopic system, handy as it is both for scholarship and devotional reading, needs to be watched carefully. The various pericopes are often meant to be read in combination rather than in isolation. As we have learned, what Matthew gives in one passage he can also take away in another.

More specifically, the pericopic systems of selected readings used in worship by many denominations should be revamped. For example, the series of readings devised by the Consultation on Common Texts, as employed by Lutheran, Presbyterian, Episcopalian, and Roman Catholic Churches, lists Matthew 16:13-20 as the gospel lesson to be read on the Fourteenth Sunday after Pentecost, series A, and on January 18, the Festival of the Confession of St. Peter.[8] But to focus on that portion without including 16:21-23 with its Satan/stumbling block saying is to distort Matthew's meaning, to perpetuate a theological bias, and in effect to shield the import of the Scriptures from the congregation.

5. The most critical implication of our research, however, is the necessity to reassert Matthew's Christological emphasis and insight. The Church can endure his failure in his secondary purpose to deflate the prestige of Jesus' traditional rivals, but it cannot survive the loss of his primary design and intention, to promote Jesus as the Christ, the Son of the living God. It is one emphasis about which Matthew is unequivocally consistent throughout his Gospel. Both the disciples' and Peter's confessions in 14:33 and 16:16 are unmistakably direct and complete.

In Jesus reside the motive, the model, and the legitimacy for everything else in the Christian life. Eschatology finds its fulfillment in him. He personally constitutes the essence of the Christian ethic. Ecclesiology is but the reflection of Christ's gracious sovereignty. The Church truly is the *Kirk,* the *kyriakon,* "that which has to do with the Lord." Where two or three are gathered together in his name, there he is in their midst (Matt 18:20) and

[8]Cf. *Lutheran Book of Worship* (1978) 27, 31.

only where he is does the Church exist.[9] Prayer becomes genuine and effective when asked in his name (Matt 18:19). The mission to all nations is dependent on his authorization. The reassurance and security of all disciples depends upon the promise of his continuing presence among them . . . and us (Matt 28:20).

According to Matthew, these are the considerations which deserve priority, taking precedence over preoccupations with traditions, structures, personalities, and "the three b's:" bishops, by-laws, and budgets. Required is a new openness to the living Christ as a practical reality in the life of the individual and of the Church. The sovereignty of Christ as head of the whole body needs to be recognized as having priority over denominational self-interest if the ecumenical movement is ever to advance beyond mere cooperation to true community. Needed, too, is an awareness, without any intimations of omniscience on our part, of what the Lord of heaven and earth is saying in and through the scriptures, the insights of sister Churches and Church bodies, world events, ecological warning signs, social problems and opportunities. The Christ needs to be seen in the homeless, the AIDS victim, the illegal alien. His voice needs to be heard above the tumult in South Africa, Northern Ireland, and the uproarious Middle East as well as over the clatter of the New York Stock Exchange. His presence must be felt in every home and in every heart. "All authority is given unto me in heaven and in earth. . . . Behold, I am with you always, unto the end of the age."

* * *

One of my most memorable graduate school experiences occurred when Dr. Frank Beare, at the time professor emeritus of New Testament at Trinity College, Toronto, told our seminar confidentially: "After studying MATTHEW for fifty years, I find I don't like him very much!" His characteristic sly grin took some of the edge off the comment, and as we all knew, he was in the throes of completing his commentary on the First Gospel at that

[9]According to the *Mishna,* trans. Herbert Danby, Aboth 3.2, 450, the presence of ten men was required before synagogue activities could convene. Whether this stipulation pre- or post-dated the composition of MATTHEW, however, is debated. Cf. Jacob Neusner, *The Talmud as History* (1979) esp. 15–18.

very moment.[10] However, I think I know what he meant. When read from a late-twentieth-century perspective, MATTHEW can be very frustrating, even aggravating. The First Gospel appears to vacillate on several crucial issues, not just on the portrait of Peter. In Matthew 5:18 Matthew has Jesus sternly instruct his disciples: " . . . till heaven and earth pass away, not an iota, not a dot, will pass from the law until all is accomplished," and then he blithely proceeds to rewrite Moses' rubrics on divorce (5:30-31/Deut 24:1-4). In Matthew's second discourse (Matt 10:5), Jesus again charges the twelve: "Go nowhere among the Gentiles . . . but go rather to the lost sheep of the house of Israel," but by 10:18, Jesus, by way of Matthean redaction, is already saying: " . . . you will be dragged before governors and kings for my sake, to bear testimony before them and the Gentiles." Similarly, Matthew 23:1 hears Jesus giving this counsel: "The Scribes and the Pharisees sit on Moses' seat; so practice and observe whatever they tell you, but not what they do," but then Matthew has Jesus immediately embark on a merciless series of woes: "Woe to you Scribes and Pharisees, hypocrites . . . !" (Matt 23:13, 23, 27, 29). There is no denying, MATTHEW, and Matthew, can be disconcerting.

However, as we have learned from our own analysis of Matthew's seemingly contradictory portrayal of Peter there can still be reason and rhetoric in the first evangelist's editorial approach when viewed from a first-century C.E. perspective. Jeremias may have been minimally correct in sensing the inadequacy of redaction criticism alone to resolve the complexities of Matthew's approach, but he was in obvious error in his assessment that the juxtaposition of conflicting texts in the First Gospel was "unconcerned."[11] Clearly, the juxtapostion was deliberate, even required by the rubrics of dispraise. The confusion, at least in the case of Peter, thus turns out to have been ours, not the evangelist's.[12]

[10]F. W. Beare, *The Gospel According to Matthew* (1981).

[11]We have finally come to terms with this challenging footnote which, in effect, began this book. Cf. chap. 2, p. 24, n. 2, above.

[12]Contra Meier in Brown and Meier, *Antioch and Rome* (1983) 72. Cf. chap. 2, p. 35, n. 35, above. Meier contends that Matthew has a two-fold concept of the Church, universal and local. (Cf. Bornkamm, chap. 2, p. 31, n. 19, above.)

Our rediscovery of Matthew's editorial technique and purpose give the First Gospel new relevance. It continues to challenge and correct prevailing values and practices, to inspire and motivate us toward a righteousness that exceeds (Matt 5:20), a forgiveness that knows no limit (Matt 18:22), and an allegiance to a Lord who rules heaven and earth (Matt 28:16).

Matthew was surely a professional in his writing and a devout Christian in his thinking—"a scribe trained for the kingdom. . . ." (Matt 13:52). MARK may be more graphic, LUKE easier to read, and JOHN more profound, but in terms of its literary art, comprehensiveness, and enduring cogency MATTHEW deserves its place at the head of its class.

With a salute to Dr. Beare, my various teachers,[13] confreres, and even critics, after nearly twenty years of intently studying MATTHEW, and Matthew, I find that I like them both very much indeed!

He sees Matthew endorsing Peter as head of the universal Church, but finds ambivalence in Matthew's refusal to promote a corresponding head over his local Church. I believe the ambivalence is Meier's own. I find no hint of such ecclesiological bifurcation in Matthew's thought. Christ is the only head of the Church, locally as well as universally (cf. Matt 18:20 and 28:16-20).

[13]Particularly Professor Heinz Guenther at Immanuel College and Seminary, Toronto, who served longer than should have been necessary as advisor for my Th.D. dissertation.

Bibliography

(Authors referred to in the text, plus other works of value for research.)

General Reference Works

Donald Attwater, ed. *A Catholic Dictionary.* Macmillan, New York; 1958.

Aland, Kurt, ed. *Synopsis Quattuor Evangeliorum.* Editio septima. Württembergische Bibelanstalt, Stuttgart; 1971.

Aland, Kurt, Matthew Black, Carlo M. Martini, Bruce M. Metzger, and Allen Wikgren, eds. *The Greek New Testament.* Third edition. United Bible Societies, New York, London, Edinburgh, Amsterdam, Stuttgart; 1975.

Arato, P. "Petrus," *Archivum Historiae Pontificiae.* Facultas Historiae Ecclesiansticae in Pontificia Universitate Gregoriana, Rome; Each year since 1963.

Blass, F. and A. Debrunner. *A Greek Grammer of the New Testament and other Early Christian Literature.* Second edition. A translation and adaptation of the fourth revised and augmented edition of Walter Bauer's *Griechish-Deutsches Wörterbuch zu den Schriften des Neuen Testaments und der übrigen urchristlichen Literatur.* Revised and augmented by F. Wilbur Gingrich and Frederick W. Danker from Walter Bauer's fifth edition of 1958. The University of Chicago Press, Chicago and London; 1979.

Charles, R. H. *The Testaments of the XII Patriarchs.* SPCK, London; 1917.

Coxe, A. Cleveland, ed. *The Ante-Nicene Fathers. The Writings of the Fathers down to* A.D. 325. 9 vols. Wm. B. Eerdmans Publishing Company, Grand Rapids; 1887, reprinted 1971–1973.

Cross, F. L. and E. A. Livingstone, eds. *The Oxford Dictionary of the Christian Church.* Oxford University Press, Oxford; 1957.

Danby, Herbert, ed. *The Mishnah.* Oxford University Press, Oxford; 1933.

Eusebius Pamphilus, *Ecclesiastical History.* Trans. Christian Frederick Cruse. Baker Book House, Grand Rapids; 1955.

Feine, Paul, Johannis Behm, and Werner George Kümmel. *Introduction to the New Testament.* Fourteenth edition. Trans. A. J. Mattill, Jr. Abingdon Press, New York and Nashville; 1965.

Ferm, Vergilius, ed. *An Encyclopedia of Religion.* The Philosophical Library, New York; 1945.

Ghidelli, C. "Bibliographia Biblica Petrina," *La Scuolo Cattolica. Supplemento Bibliographico,* 96, 1968, 62–110.

Josephus, Flavius. *Josephus: Complete Works.* Trans. William Whiston. Kregel Publications, Grand Rapids, Michigan; 1978.

Kittel, Gerhard and Gerhard Friedrich, eds. *Theological Dictionary of the New Testament.* 9 volumes. Trans. and ed. by Geoffrey Bromiley. Wm. B. Eerdmans Publishing Company, Grand Rapids; 1964–1974.

Lutheran Cyclopedia. Erwin L. Leuker, Editor-in-Chief, Concordia Publishing House, St. Louis; 1954.

Lutheran Book of Worship. Augsburg Publishing House, Minneapolis; Board of Publication, Lutheran Church in America, Philadelphia; 1978.

Metzger, Bruce M. *A Textual Commentary of the Greek New Testament.* A companion volume to the United Bible Societies' *Greek New Testament.* Third edition. United Bible Societies, London and New York; 1971.

Kümmel, Werner Georg. *The New Testament; The History of the Investigation of its Problems.* Trans. S. McLean Gilmour and Howard Kee. Abingdon Press, Nashville and New York; 1972.

Migne, J. P., ed. *Patrologiae cursus completus.* Series Graeca. 162 tomes. Lutetiae Parisiorum; 1857–1912.

________. *Patrologiae cursus completus.* Series Latina. 221 tomes. Parisiis; 1844–1864.

Morganthaler, Robert. *Statistik des Neutestamentlichen Wortschatzes.* Gotthelf Verlag, Zurich and Frankfurt am Main; 1958.

Moulton, W. F. and A. S. Geden, eds. *A Concordance to the Greek Testament According to the Texts of Westcott and Hort, Tischen-*

dorf and the English Revisers. Fourth edition revised by H. K. Moulton. T. & T. Clark, Edinburgh; 1970.

New Testament Abstracts. Weston School of Theology, Cambridge, Mass.; three times per year since 1956.

Robinson, James M., ed. *The Nag Hammadi Library in English.* Harper and Row, San Francisco; 1977.

Schneemelcher, Wilhelm, ed. *Edgar Hennecke: The New Testament Apocrypha.* Trans. and ed. by R. McL. Wilson. Westminster Press, Philadelphia; 1964.

Sparks, Jack, ed. *The Apostolic Fathers.* Thomas Nelson, Inc., Nashville and New York; 1978.

The Fathers of the Church. 71 volumes. Various authors and translators. The Catholic University of America, Washington, and Fathers of the Church, Inc., New York; 1947 to the present.

Throckmorton, Burton H. Jr., ed. *Gospel Parallels: A Synopsis of the First Three Gospels.* Thomas Nelson Publishers, Nashville; 1949, 1979.

Holy Bible. Revised Standard Version. Second edition. American Bible Society, New York; Old Testament, 1952, New Testament, 1971.

Holy Bible. New Revised Standard Version. *The New Oxford Annotated Bible with the Apocrypha.* Bruce M. Metzger and Roland E. Murphy, eds. Oxford University Press, New York; 1991.

Commentaries on MATTHEW

Albright, W. F. and C. S. Mann. *Matthew.* The Anchor Bible. W. F. Albright and David Noel Freedman, eds. Doubleday & Co., Garden City; 1971.

Allen, W.C. *A Critical and Exegetical Commentary on the Gospel According to S. Matthew.* The International Critical Commentary. C. A. Briggs, S. R. Driver, and A. Plummer, eds. Charles Scribner's Sons, New York; 1907.

Argyle, A. W. *The Gospel According to Matthew.* The Cambridge Bible Commentary. P. R. Ackroyd, A.R.C. Leaney, and J. W. Packer, eds. Cambridge University Press, Cambridge; 1963.

Augsburger, Myron S. *Matthew.* The Communicator's Commentary. General editor: Lloyd J. Ogilvie. Word Books, Waco; 1982.

Barclay, William. *The Gospel of Matthew.* 2 vols. Second edition. Westminster Press, Philadelphia; 1958.

Beare, Francis Wright. *The Gospel According to Matthew.* Harper and Row, San Francisco; 1981.

Bonnard, Pierre. *L'Évangile selon Saint Matthieu.* Commentaire du Nouveau Testament. Vol. 1. Editions Deachaux et Nestle, Newchatel; 1963.

Edwards, Richard A. *Matthew's Story of Jesus.* Fortress Press, Philadelphia; 1985.

Ellis, Peter F. *Matthew, His Mind and His Message.* The Liturgical Press, Collegeville; 1974.

Fenton, F. C. *The Gospel of Matthew.* The Pelican Gospel Commentaries. D. E. Nineham, ed. Penguin Books. Harmondsworth, Middlesex, England; 1963.

Filson, Floyd V. *A Commentary on the Gospel According to St. Matthew.* Harper's New Testament Commentaries. Henry Chadwick, ed. Harper and Row, New York; 1960.

Gaechter, Paul. *Das Matthäus-Evangelium: Ein Kommentar.* Tyrolia Verlag, Innsbruck; 1964.

Green, H. Benedict. *The Gospel According to Matthew.* New Clarendon Bible. H.F.D. Sparks, ed. Oxford University Press, Oxford; 1975.

Grundmann, Walter. *Das Evangelium nach Matthäus. Theologischer Handkommentar zum Neuen Testament.* Vol. 1. Evangelische Verlagsanstalt, Berlin; 1968.

Gundry, Robert H. *Matthew, A Commentary on His Literary and Theological Art.* Wm. B. Eerdmans Publishing Company, Grand Rapids; 1982.

Hill, David. *The Gospel of Matthew.* New Century Bible. Ronald E. Clements and Matthew Black, eds. The Attic Press, Greenwood, S.C.; 1972.

Johnson, Sherman E. "The Gospel According to St. Matthew." *The Interpreter's Bible.* Vol. 7. George A. Buttrick, ed. Abingdon Press, New York; 1951, 229–625.

Kee, Howard Clark. "The Gospel According to Matthew," *The Interpreter's One Volume Commentary of the Bible.* Charles M. Laymon, ed. Abingdon Press, New York; 1971.

Kingsbury, Jack Dean. *Matthew.* Proclammation Commentaries. Fortress Press, Philadelphia; 1977.

Klostermann, Erich. *Das Matthäusevangelium. Handbuch zum Neuen Testament.* Vol. 4. Second revised edition. J.C.B. Mohr [Paul Siebeck], Tübingen; 1927.

Lohmeyer, Ernst. *Das Evangelium des Matthäus.* Kritisch-exegeticher Kommentar über das Neue Testament. Werner Schmauch, ed. Vandenhoeck & Ruprecht, Göttingen; 1956.

Luz, Ulrich. *Matthew 1–7. A Commentary.* Trans. Wilhelm C. Linss. Augsburg, Minneapolis; 1989.

McKenzie, John L. "The Gospel According to Matthew," *The Jerome Biblical Commentary.* Part II. Raymond Brown, J. A. Fitzmyer, and R. E. Murphy, eds. Prentice Hall, Englewood Cliffs, N.J.; 1968, 62–114.

McNeile, Alan Hugh. *The Gospel According to St. Matthew.* Macmillan & Co., London; 1963.

Meier, John P. *Matthew.* Michael Glazier, Inc., Wilmington; 1980.

Meyer, Heinrich August Wilhelm. *Critical and Exegetical Hand-Book to the Gospel of Matthew.* Translated from the Sixth Edition of the German by Rev. Peter Christie; The translation revised and edited by Frederick Crombie and William Stewart, with a Preface and supplementary notes to the American edition by George R. Crooks. Funk & Wagnalls, New York and London; 1884.

Minear, Paul S. *Matthew, The Teacher's Gospel.* The Pilgrim Press, New York; 1982.

Parker, Pierson. *Good News in Matthew. Matthew in Today's English Version.* Fontana Books. William Collins Sons & Co., Glasgow; 1976.

Patte, Daniel. *The Gospel According to Matthew. A Structural Commentary on Matthew's Faith.* Fortress Press, Philadelphia; 1987.

Plummer, Alfred. *An Exegetical Commentary on the Gospel According to S. Matthew.* Charles Scribner's Sons, New York; 1909.

Schlatter, Adolf. *Das Evangelium nach Matthäus.* Schlatters Erläuterungen zum Neuen Testament. Part 1. Calwer Verlag, Stuttgart; 1947.

Schlatter, D. A. *Der Evangelist Matthäus, Seine Sprache, sein Ziel, seine Selbständigkeit.* Calwer Vereinsbuchhandlung, Stuttgart; 1929.

Schniewind, Julius. *Das Evangelium nach Matthäus.* Das Neue Testament Deutsch: Neues Göttinger Bibelwerk. Gerhard Friedrich, ed. Vol. 2, Paul Althaus and Johannes Behm, eds. Vandenhoeck & Ruprecht, Göttingen; 1950.

Schweizer, Eduard. *The Good News According to Matthew.* Trans. David E. Green. John Knox Press, Atlanta; 1975.

Senior, Donald. *Invitation to Matthew. A Commentary on the Gospel of Matthew with Complete Text from the Jerusalem Bible.* Image Books. Doubleday & Co., Garden City, N.Y.; 1977.

Stendahl, Krister. "Matthew," *Peake's Commentary on the Bible.* Matthew Black and H. H. Rowley, eds. Thomas Nelson & Sons, London; 1962, 769–798.

Strack, Hermann L. and Paul Billerbeck. *Das Evangelium nach Matthäus, Erlautert aus Talmud und Midrasch.* C. H. Beck'sche Verlagsbuchhandlung, München; 1919.

Tasker, R.V.G. *The Gospel According to St. Matthew: An Introduction and Commentary.* The Tyndale New Testament Commentaries. R.V.G. Tasker, ed. Tyndale Press, London; 1961.

Trilling, Wolfang. *The Gospel According to St. Matthew.* 2 vols. Trans. Kevin Smith. New Testament for Spiritual Reading. John L. MacKenzie, ed. Burns & Oates, London; 1969.

Wellhausen, Julius. *Das Evangelium Matthäei.* Georg Reimer, Berlin; 1904.

Williams, A., W. Lukyn, J. Deane, and B. C. Caffin. "Matthew," *The Pulpit Commentary,* II. H.D.M. Spense and Joseph S. Exell, eds. Funk & Wagnalls, New York and London; n.d.

Relevant Books, Monographs and Articles

Abel, Ernest L. "Who Wrote Matthew?" *New Testament Studies,* 17, 1970–1971, 138–152.

Acquinas, Thomas. *Summa Theologiae.* Timothy McDermott, ed. Christian Classics, Westminster, Md.; 1989.

Aland, Kurt. "Wann Starb Petrus? Eine Bemerkung zu Gal. ii.6." *New Testament Studies,* 2, 1955–1956, 267–275.

________. "Petrus in Rome." *Historische Zeitschrift,* 183, 1957, 497–516.

Allen, E. L. "On This Rock," *Journal of Theological Studies,* 5, 1954, 59–62.

Aristotle, "The 'Art' of Rhetoric (Ars Rhetorica)." Trans. J. H. Freese. *Loeb Classical Library.* 1926. Also, Lane Cooper, *The Rhetoric of Aristotle.* Appleton-Century-Crofts, Inc., New York; 1932, 46–55.

Augustine, St. "The Retractions," *The Fathers of the Church,* 60, Book 1, chapter 20. The Catholic University of America, Washington, and Fathers of the Church, Inc., New York; 1947 to the present.

Bacon, Benjamin W. "The Petrine Supplements of Matthew," *The Expositor,* 8th series, 73, January 1917, 1–23.

________. *Studies in Matthew.* Henry Holt and Company, New York; 1930.

Baird, J. A. *Audience Criticism and the Historical Jesus.* Westminster Press, Philadelphia; 1969.

Baldwin, Charles Sears. *Medieval Rhetoric and Peter.* Peter Smith, Gloucester, Mass.; 1959.

Barr, James. *The Semantics of Biblical Language.* Oxford University Press, Oxford; 1961.

Barth, Gerhard. "Matthew's Understanding of the Law," *Tradition and Interpretation in Matthew.* G. Bornkamm, G. Barth, and H. J. Held, eds. Trans. Percy Scott. SCM Press, London; 1963, 58–164.

Baumann, Richard. *Des Petrus Bekenntnis und Schlüssel.* Schwabenverlag, Stuttgart; 1950.

Baur, Ferdinand Christian. *Das Christentum und die Christliche Kirche der Drei Ersten Jahrhunderte.* Verlag und Druck von L. Fr. Fues, Tübingen; 1853.

________. "Die Christuspartei in der korinthischen Gemeinde," 1831, reprinted in F. C. Baur and E. Zeller, eds., "Die Einleitung in das Neue Testament als theologische Wissenschaft," *Theologische Jahrbücher,* 10, 1851, 294–296.

Beare, F. W. *The Earliest Records of Jesus.* Abingdon Press, New York and Nashville; 1962.

________. "The Sayings of Jesus in the Gospel according to St. Matthew," *Studiea Evangelica IV.* Akademie-Verlag, Berlin; 1968.

Bellarminus, Robertus. "Die summo pontifice," *Operum.* Tom. 1, 1620, 58–59.

Benoit, Pierre. "La Primauté de Saint Pierre selon le Nouveau Testament," *Istina,* 2, 1955, 305–334.

________. "Review of Cullmann: Petrus, Junger-Apostel-Martyrer," *Revue Biblique,* 69, 1962, 442–443.

Best, Ernest. "Mark's Use of the Twelve," *Zeitschrift für die Neutestamentliche Wissenschaft,* 69, 1978, 11–35.

________. "Peter in the Gospel According to Mark," *Catholic Biblical Quarterly,* 40, 4, October 1978, 547–558.

Betz, Johannes. "Christus-Petra-Petrus," *Kirche und Überlieferung.* Herder, Freiburg; 1960.

Betz, Otto. "Felsenmann und Felsengemeinde. Eine Parallele zu Mt 16, 17–19 in den Qumranpsalmen," *Zeitschrift für die Neutestamentliche Wissenschaft,* 48, 1957, 49–77.

Black, Matthew. "*ta pasxa* (Mt 26:18), *ta sabbata* (passim), *ta didraxma* (Mt 17:24)," *Melanges Bibliques en homage au R. P. Béda Rigaux.* Duculot, Gembloux; 1970.

Blank, Josef. "The Person and Office of Peter in the New Testament," *Concilium,* 3, 9, 1973, 42–55.

Boff, Leonardo. *Church, Charism and Power.* Trans. John W. Diercksmeier. Crossroad, New York; 1985.

Bonnard, Pierre. "Composition ed Signification Historique de Matthieu XVIII," *De Jésus aux Évangiles. Tradition et Redaction dans les Évangiles synoptiques.* J. Duculot, Gembloux; 1970.

________. "Matthieu, Educateur du Peuple Chretien," *Melanges Bib-*

liques en homage au R. P. Béda Rigaux. J. Duculot, Gembloux; 1970.

Bonner, Stanley F. *Education in Ancient Rome.* University of California Press, Berkely and Los Angeles; 1977.

Boobyer, G. H. *St. Mark and the Transfiguration Story.* T. & T. Clark, Edinburgh; 1942.

Bornkamm, Günther. "The Stilling of the Storm in Matthew," *Tradition and Interpretation in Matthew.* G. Bornkamm, G. Barth, and H. J. Held, eds. Trans. Percy Scott. SCM Press, London; 1963, 52–57.

________. "The Authority to 'Bind' and 'Loose' in the Church in Matthew's Gospel," *Jesus and Man's Hope,* 1, A Perspective Book. Pittsburgh Theological Seminary, Pittsburgh; 1970, 37–50.

________. "The Risen Lord and the Earthly Jesus, Matthew 28:16-20," *The Future of Our Religious Past. Essays in Honour of Rudolf Bultmann.* James M. Robinson, ed. Trans. Charles E. Carlston and Robert Scharlemann. Harper and Row, New York, Evanston, San Francisco, London; 1978.

Braumann, Georg. "Der sinkende Petrus: Matth. 14:28-31." *Theologische Zeitschrift.* (Basel) 22, 1966, 403–414.

Bristol, Lyle O. "Jesus and Peter at Caesarea Philippi," *Foundations.* 5, 1962, 190–205.

Brodrick, James. *Robert Bellarmine, Saint and Scholar.* The Newman Press, Westminster, Md.; 1961.

Brown, John Pairman. "The Form of 'Q' Known to Matthew," *New Testament Studies,* 8, 1960–1962, 27–42.

Brown, Raymond, Karl P. Donfried, and John Reumann, eds. *Peter in the New Testament: A Collaborative Assessment by Protestant and Roman Catholic Scholars.* Augsburg Publishing House, Minneapolis, and Paulist Press, New York, Paramus, Toronto; 1973.

Brown, Raymond and John P. Meier. *Antioch & Rome: New Testament Cradles of Catholic Christianity.* Paulist Press, New York, Ramsey; 1983.

Brown, Schuyler. "The Matthean Community and the Gentile Mission," *Novum Testamentum,* XXII, 3, 1980, 193–221.

Bultmann, Rudolf. *History of the Synoptic Tradition.* Revised edition. Trans. John Marsh. Harper and Row, New York, Hagerstown, San Francisco, London; 1963.

________. "Die Frage nach dem messianischen Bewusstsein Jesu und das Petrus-Bekenntnis," *Rudolf Bultmann: Exegetica: Aufsätze zur Erforschung des Neuen Testaments.* Erich Dinkler, ed. J.C.B. Mohr [Paul Siebeck], Tübingen; 1967, 1-9; reprinted from *Zeit-*

schrift für die Neuentestamentliche Wissenschaft, 19, 1919–1920, 165–174.

________. "Die Frage nach der Echtheit von Mt 16, 17–19," *Rudolf Bultmann: Exegetica: Augsätze zur Erforschung des Neuen Testaments.* J.B.C. Mohr [Paul Siebeck], Tübingen; 1967, 255–277; reprinted from *Theologische Blätter,* 20, 1941, 265–279.

Burgess, Joseph A. *A History of the Exegesis of Matthew 16:17-19 from 1781 to 1965.* Edwards Brothers Inc., Ann Arbor; 1976.

Burnett, Fred W. *The Testament of Jesus Sophia. A Redaction-Critical Study of the Eschatological Discourse in Matthew.* University Press of America, Washington; 1979.

Butler, B. C. *The Originality of Matthew; A Critique of the Two-Document Hypothesis.* University Press, Cambridge; 1951.

Calvin, John. *Institutes of the Christian Religion.* 2 vols. Translated from the Latin and collated with the author's last edition in French by John Allen. Presbyterian Board of Christian Education, Philadelphia; n.d.

Campenhausen, Hans von. *Ecclesiastical Authority and Spiritual Power in the Church of the First Three Centuries.* Trans. J. A. Baker. Stanford University Press, Stanford; 1969.

Carr, Arthur. "The Use of *skandalon* and *skandalizein* in the New Testament," *The Expositor,* 47, 1898, 344–350.

Carroll, Kenneth L. "Thou Art Peter," *Novum Testamentum,* 6, 4, November 1963, 268–276.

Cary, M. and H. H. Scullard. *A History of Rome.* Third edition. St. Martin's Press, New York; 1975.

Cassidy, Richard J. "Matthew 17:24-27—A Word on Civil Taxes," *The Catholic Biblical Quarterly,* 41, 4, 1979, 571–580.

Christ, Felix. "Das Petrusamt im Neuen Testament," *Petrusamt und Papsttum.* Katholisches Bibelwerk Verlag, Stuttgart; 1970, 36–50.

Cicero, Marcus Tullius. "De Inventione," in *Cicero: De Inventione, De Optimo Genere Oratorium, Topica.* Trans. H. M. Hubbell in the *Loeb Classical Library.* Harvard University Press, Cambridge; 1949, 3–345.

Clark, Donald Lemen. *Rhetoric in Greco-Roman Education.* Columbia University Press, New York; 1957.

Clark, Kenneth W. "The Gentile Bias in Matthew," *Journal of Biblical Literature,* 66, March 1947, 165–172.

Clavier, Henri. *"Petros kai petra," Neutestamentliche Studien für Rudolf Bultmann zu seinem siebsigsten Geburtstag,* 2. Berichtigte Auflage. Alfred Töpelmann, Berlin; 1957, 94–109.

________. "Breves Remarques sur les Commentaires Patristiques de Matth. XVI, 18a," *Studia Patristica,* 1, 1957, 253–261.

Clement of Rome. "I Clement," *The Faith of the Early Fathers.* Vol. 1. Trans. W. A. Jurgens. The Liturgical Press, Collegeville; 1970, 6–13.

Coneybeare, Frederick Cornwallis. *Myth, Magic and Morals: A Study of Christian Origins.* Watts & Co., London; 1910.

Congar, Yves M.-J. "Céphas-Cephalè-Caput," *Revue Du Moyen Age Latin,* 8, 1952, 5–42.

Connolly, R. Hugh. *The So-called Egyptian Church Order and Derived Documents.* Cambridge University Press, Cambridge; 1916.

Conzelmann, Hans. *The Theology of St. Luke.* Trans. Geoffrey Buswell. Faber and Faber, London; 1961; German edition, 1953.

________. *History of Primitive Christianity.* Trans. John E. Steely. Abingdon, Nashville and New York; 1973.

Cooper, Lane. *Rhetoric;* 1932.

Cope, O Lamar. *Matthew, A Scribe Trained for the Kingdom of Heaven.* The Catholic Biblical Association of America, Washington; 1976.

Crosby, Michael H. *House of Disciples: Church, Economics & Justice in Matthew.* Orbis Books, Maryknoll, N.Y.; 1988.

Cullmann, Oscar. "Petrus, Werkzeug des Teufels und Werkzeug Gottes," *Oscar Cullmann, Vortrage und Augsätze 1925–1962.* Karlfried Fröhlich, ed. J.C.B. Mohr [Paul Siebeck], Tübingen, and the Zwingli Verlag, Zurich; 1966.

________. *The State in the New Testament.* SCM Press, London; 1957.

________. *Peter: Disciple-Apostle-Martyr.* Second revised and expanded edition. Trans. Floyd V. Filson. SCM Press, London; 1962.

Cyprian, Bishop. "Saint Cyprian, Treatises," *The Ante-Nicene Fathers.* Vol. 5. *The Fathers of the Third Century.* A. Cleveland Coxe, ed. Wm. B. Eerdmans Publishing Company, Grand Rapids; 1971, 421–557.

Davies, W. D. *The Setting of the Sermon on the Mount.* Cambridge University Press, Cambridge; 1966.

Dell, A. "Zur Erklärung von Matthäus 16:17-19," *Zeitschrift für die Neutestamentliche Wissenschaft und die Kunde des Urchristentums,* 17, 1916, 27–32.

Deresser, T. A. (Thaddaeus A. S. Adamo). *Commentatio Biblica in effatum Christi Matth. 18.19.* Bonnae. 1789.

Derrett, J. Duncan M. "Peter's Penny: Fresh Light on Matthew XVII 24-7," *Novum Testamentum,* 6, 1963, 1–15.

________. "Why and How Jesus Walked on the Sea," *Novum Testamentum,* XXIII, 4, 1981, 193–221.

Dietrich, Wolfgang. *Das Petrusbild der Lukanischen Schriften.* Verlag W. Kohlhammer, Stuttgart, Berlin, Köln, Mainz; 1972.

Dinkler, Erich. "Die Petrus-Rom-Frage," *Theologische Rundschau,* 25, 1959, 189–230, 289–335; Also vol. 27, 1961, 33–64.

________. "Die ersten Petrusdarstellungen. Ein archäologischer Beitrag zur Geschichte des Petrusprimates," *Marburger Jahrbuch für Kunstwissenschaft,* 11/12, 1938/39, 1–8.

________. "Peter's Confession and the 'Satan' Saying: The Problem of Jesus' Messiahship," *The Future of Our Religious Past. Essays in Honour of Rudolf Bultmann.* James M. Robinson, ed. Trans. Charles E. Carlston and Robert P. Scharlemann. Harper and Row, New York, Evanston, San Francisco, London; 1971, 169–202.

Dobschütz, Ernst von. "Matthäus als Rabbi und Katechet," *Zeitschrift für die Neutestamentliche Wissenschaft und die Kunde der alteren Kirche,* 27, 1928, 338–348.

Dodd, C. H. "Matthew and Paul," *New Testament Studies.* University Press, Manchester; 1953, 53–66.

Downey, Glanville. *A History of Antioch in Syria from Seleucus to the Arab Conquest.* Princeton University Press, Princeton; 1961.

Dufour, Xavier Leon. "Redactionsgeschichte of Matthew and Literary Criticism," *Jesus and Man's Hope,* 1. A Perspective Book. Pittsburgh Theological Seminary, Pittsburgh; 1970, 9–27.

Dulière, W. L. "La péricope sur le 'Pouvoir des clés,' " *La Nouvelle Clio,* 6, 1954, 73–90.

Easton, Burton Scott. "Critical Note: St. Matthew 16:17-19," *Anglican Theological Review,* 4, 1921/22, 156–166.

Edwards, Richard A. *A Theology of Q.* Fortress Press, Philadelphia; 1976.

Eisler, Robert. *Ieesus Basileus ou Basileusas.* C. Winter, Heidelberg; 1929.

Ehrhardt, Arnold. *The Apostolic Succession in the First Two Centuries of the Church.* Lutterworth Press, London; 1953.

Emerton, J. A. "Binding and Loosing—Forgiving and Retaining," *Journal of Theological Studies.* New Series, 13, 1962, 325–331.

English, E. Schyler. "Was Peter Ever in Rome?" *Bibliotheca Sacra,* 24, 496, October–December 1967, 314–320.

Eno, Robert B. *The Rise of the Papacy,* Michael Glazier, Inc., Wilmington; 1990.

Farmer, Wm. F. "The Post-Sectarian Character of Matthew and its Post-War Setting in Antioch of Syria," *Perspectives in Religious Studies,* III, 3, Fall 1976, 235–247.

Fitzmyer, Joseph A. "Aramaic 'Kepha' and Peter's Name in the New Testament," *Text and Interpretation. Studies in the New Testament presented to Matthew Black.* Ernest Best and R. McL. Wilson, eds. Cambridge University Press, Cambridge; 1979, 121–132.

Ford, J. Massingberd. "Thou Art 'Abraham' and Upon This Rock . . . " *Heythorp Journal,* 6, 1965, 289–301.

Frankemölle, Hubert. "Amtskritik im Matthäus-Evangelium?" *Biblica,* 54, 1973, 247–262.

________. *Jahwebund und Kirche Christi. Studien zur Form- und Traditionsgeschichte des 'Evangeliums' nach Matthäus.* Verlag Aschendorff, Münster; 1974.

Frend, W.H.C. *The Early Church.* Fortress Press, Philadelphia; 1965, 1982.

Fröhlich, Karlfried. *Formen des Auslegung von Matthäus 16:13-18 im lateinischen Mittelalter.* Dissertation zur Erlangung der Doctorwurde der theologischen Fakultät der Universität Basel. Tübingen, 1963.

Fuller, Reginald H. "The 'Thou Art Peter' Pericope and the Easter Appearances," *McCormick Quarterly,* 20, 4, 1967, 309–315.

Gaechter, Paul. "Petrus und Seine Nachfolfe. Zum Petrusbuch von Prof. Oskar Cullmann," *Zeitschrift für Katholische Theologie,* 75, 1953, 331–337.

Gaide, Gilles. "Jésus et Pierre Marchent sur les Eaux," *Assemblées du Seigneur: Catechese des dimanches et dés fêtes,* 50, 1974, 23–31.

________. " 'Tu es le Christ' . . . 'Tu es Pierre,' Mt 16, 13-20," *Assemblées du Seigneur; Catechese des dimanches et dés fêtes,* 52, 1974, 16–26.

Goguel, M. "Tu Es Petrus (Matthew 16:17-19)," *Bulletin, de la Faculte Libre de Theologie Protestante de Paris,* 4, 15, Juillet 1938, 1–13.

Goodspeed, Edgar J. *A History of Early Christian Literature.* Revised and enlarged by Robert M. Grant. Phoenix Books. The University of Chicago Press, Chicago; 1942, 1966.

Goulder, M. D. *Midrash and Lection in Matthew.* SPCK Press, London; 1974.

Grant, Robert M. *Augustus to Constantine.* Harper and Row, San Francisco; 1970.

Grimes, Donald Joseph. *The Papacy and the Petrine Texts: A Study in the History of Biblical Exegesis (A.D. 800–1300).* Ph.D. dissertation submitted to Fordham University in 1981. University Microfilms International, Ann Arbor; 1982.

Guelich, Robert A. *The Sermon on the Mount: A Foundation for Understanding.* Word Books, Waco; 1982.

Gundry, Robert H. "The Narrative Framework of Matthew xvi, 17- 19," *Novum Testamentum,* 7, 1, March 1964, 1–9.

________. *The Use of the Old Testament in St. Matthew's Gospel. With Special Reference to the Messianic Hope.* E. J. Brill, Leiden; 1967.

Hadzega, Julius. "Mt. 16, 16-19 in der neueren Literatur der Orthodoxen," *Theologie und Glaube. Zeitschrift für den katholischen Klerus,* 26, 1934, 458–464.

Haenchen, Ernst. "Die Komposition von Mk vii 27-ix 1 und Par.," *Novum Testamentum,* 6, July 1963, 81–109.

________. "Matthäus 23" and "Petrus Probleme," *Gott und Mensch: Gesammelte Augsätze von Ernst Haenchen.* J.C.B. Mohr [Paul Siebeck], Tübingen; 1965, 29–54 and 55–67.

Haendler, Gert. "Die Drei Grossen Nordafrikanischen Kirchenväter über Mt. 16:18-19," *Theologische Literaturzeitung,* 81, 1956, 361–364.

Hahn, Ferdinand. "Die Petrusverheissung Mt 16, 18f. Eine exegetische Skizze," *Materialdienst des Konfessions-kundlichen Institute Bensheim,* 21, 1970, 8–13.

Hare, Douglas R. A. *The Theme of Jewish Persecution of Christians in the Gospel According to St. Matthew.* Society for New Testament Studies Monograph Series, vol 1, 16. Cambridge University Press, Cambridge; 1967.

Harnack, Adolf von. "Der Spruch über Petrus als den Felsen der Kirche (Matth. 16:17f.)," *Akademie der Wissenschaften, Berlin. Philosophish-Historische Klasse. Stizungsberichte,* 1918, 637–654.

________. "Tatian's Diatessaron und Marcion's Kommentar zum Evangelium bei Ephraem Syrus," *Zeitschrift für Kirchengeschichte,* 4, 1881, 484–485.

________. *Kirchenverfassung,* Berlin, 1910.

Held, Heinz Joachim. "Matthew as Interpreter of the Miracle Stories," *Tradition and Interpretation in Matthew.* Trans. Percy Scott. SCM Press, London; 1963, 165–299.

Henze, Clemens M. "Céphas seu Kephas non est Simon Petrus," *Divus Thomas,* Series 3, vol. 35, 1958, 63–67.

Hermogenes of Tarsus. "Progymnasmata." Cf. Charles Sears Baldwin. *Medieval Rhetoric and Poetic.* Peter Smith, Gloucester, Mass.; 1959, 23–38.

Herrera, Joseph. "Céphas seu Kephas est Simon Petrus," *Divus Thomas.* Series 3, vol. 35, 1958, 481–484.

Hoffmann, Paul. "Der Petrus-Primat im Matthäusevangelium," *Neues Testament und Kirche für Rudolf Schnackenburg.* Joachim Gnilka, ed. Herder, Freiburg, Basel, Wien; 1974.

Hofstetter, Karl. "Das Petrusamt in der Kirche des 1.–2. Jahrhunderts: Jerusalem-Rom," *Begegnung der Christian: Studien evangelischer und katholischer Theologen.* Maximillian Roesle and Oscar Cullmann, eds. Evangelishes Verlagswerk, Stuttgart; Verlag Josef Knecht-Carolusdruckerei, Frankfurt Am Main; 1960.

Homeau, H. A. "On Fishing for Staters: Matthew 17:27," *Expository Times,* 85, 11, August 1974, 340–342.

Hubbard, Benjamin J. *The Matthean Redaction of a Primitive Apostolic Commissioning: An Exegesis of Matthew 28:16-20.* Dissertation Series 19. Society of Biblical Literature, Scholars Press, Missoula; 1974.

Hummell, Reinhart. *Die Auseinandersetzung zwischen Kirche und Judentum im Matthäusevangelium. Beitrage zur evangelischen Theologie.* Band 33. Kaiser Verlag, München; 1966.

Ignatius of Antioch. Cf. *The Apostolic Fathers.* Jack Sparks, ed. Thomas Nelson Inc., Nashville and New York; 1978, 71–119. Also see below Wm. R. Schoedel, *Ignatius of Antioch.*

Immisch, Otto. "Matthäus 16, 18. Laienbemerkungen zu der Untersuchung Dells, ZNW XV, 1914, 1ff." *Zeitschrift für die neutestamentliche Wissenshaft und die Kunde des Urchristentums,* 17, 1916, 18–32.

Irenaeus of Lyons, "Against Heresies," *The Ante-Nicene Fathers,* vol. 1, *The Apostolic Fathers with Justin Martyr and Irenaeus.* A. Cleveland Coxe, ed. Wm. B. Eerdmans Publishing Company, Grand Rapids; 1973, 309–567.

Jeremias, Joachim. *Golgotha.* Verlag von Eduard Pfeiffer, Leipzig; 1926.

________. *The Parables of Jesus.* Charles Scribner's Sons, New York; 1954.

________. *New Testament Theology, I. The Proclamation of Jesus.* SCM Press, London; 1971.

Jonson, Jakob. *Humor and Irony in the New Testament.* Bokautgafa Menningsgarjods, Reykjavik; 1965.

Kähler, Christoph. "Zur Form- und Traditionsgeschichte von Matth. XVI, 17-19, *New Testament Studies,* 23, 1976–1977, 36–58.

Kahmann, J. "Die Verheissung an Petrus; Mt. XVI, 18-19 im Zusammenhang des Matthäusevangeliums," *L'Évangile selon Matthieu. Redaction et Theologie.* M. Didier, ed. Journees Bibliques de Louvain, Louvain; 1970; Ephemeridum Theologicarum Lovaniensium, J. Duculot, Gembloux; 1972, 261–280.

Karrer, Otto. "Apostolische Nachfolge und Primat," *Zeitschrift für Katholische Theologie,* 77, 1955, 129–168.

________. *Peter and the Church. An Examination of Cullmann's Thesis.* Palm Publishers, Montreal; 1963.

Käsemann, Ernst. "Die Anfänge Christlicher Theologie," *Exegetische Versuche und Besinnungen.* Band 2. Vandehoeck & Ruprecht, Göttingen; 1964.

Kattenbusch, Ferdinand. "Der Spruch über Petrus und die Kirche bei Matthäus," *Neutestamentliche Forschungen.* Sonderheft der Theologischen Studien und Kritiken. Verlag Friedrich Andreas Perthes, Stuttgart/Gotha; 1922, 96–131.

Keck, Leander E. "An Exegesis of Matt. 16:13-20," *Foundations,* 5; 1962, 226–237.

Kee, Howard Clark. "The Transfiguration in Mark: Epiphany or Apocalyptic Vision?" *Understanding the Sacred Text: Essays in Honor of Morton S. Enslin, on the Hebrew Bible and Christian Beginnings.* John Reumann, ed. Judson Press, Valley Forge; 1972, 137–152.

Kennedy, George A. *The Art of Persuasion in Greece.* Princeton University Press, Princeton; 1963.

————. *Classical Rhetoric and Its Christian and Secular Tradition from Ancient to Modern Times.* University of North Carolina Press, Chapel Hill; 1980.

Kilpatrick, G. D. *The Origins of the Gospel According to St. Matthew.* Clarendon Press, Oxford; 1946.

Kingsbury, Jack Dean. *Matthew—Structure, Christology, Kingdom.* Fortress Press, Philadelphia; 1975.

————. "The Verb *Akolouthein* ('To Follow') As An Index of Matthew's View of His Community," *Journal of Biblical Literature,* 97, 1, 1978, 56–73.

————. "Observations on the 'Miracle Chapters' of Matthew 8–9," *The Catholic Biblical Quarterly,* 40, 4, October 1978, 559–573.

————. "The Figure of Peter in Matthew's Gospel as a Theological Problem," *Journal of Biblical Literature,* 98, 1, March 1979, 67–83.

————. *Matthew as Story.* Fortress Press, Philadelphia, 1986.

Klein, Günter. "Galater 2, 6–9 und die Geschichte der Jerusalemer Urgemeinde," *Zeitschrift für Theologie und Kirche,* 57, 3, 1960, 275–295.

————. "Die Verleugnung des Petrus. Eine traditionsgeshichtliche Untersuchung," *Zeitschrift für Theologie und Kirche,* 58, 3, 1962, 285–328.

————. "Die Berufung des Petrus," *Rekonstruktion und Interpretation. Gesammelte Augsätze zum Neuen Testament.* Chr. Kaiser Verlag, München; 1969, 11–48.

Klink, Johanna Louise. *Het Petrustype in het Nieuwe Testament en de Oud-Christelijke Letterkunde.* Eduard Ijdo N.V., Leiden; 1947.

Kloppenborg, John S. *The Formation of Q.* Studies in Antiquity and Christianity. Fortress Press, Philadelphia; 1987.

Knight, George A.F. "Thou Art Peter," *Theology Today,* 17, 1, April 1960, 168–180.

Kobayashi, Teruo. *The Role of Peter According to the Theological Un-*

derstanding of Paul, Mark, and Luke-Acts. Ph.D. dissertation submitted to Drew University in 1963. University Microfilms International, Ann Arbor; 1979.

Köhler, W. "Die Schlüssel des Petrus; Versuch einer religionsgeschichlichen Erklärung von Matth. 16, 18.19," *Archiv fur Religionswissenschaft,* 8, 1905, 214–243.

Kreider, Eugene Charles. *Matthew's Contribution to the Eschatological-Ethical Perspective in the Life of the Early Church: A Redaction-Critical Study of Matthew 18.* Ph.D. dissertation submitted to Vanderbilt University in 1976. University Microfilms International, Ann Arbor; 1979.

Krentz, Edgar. *The Historical Critical Method.* Guides to Biblical Scholarship series, Geme M. Tucker, ed. Fortress Press, Philadelphia; 1975.

Krüger, Gustav. "Matthäus 16, 18.19 und der Primat des Petrus," *Theologische Blätter,* 6, 1927, 302-307.

Küng, Hans. *Structures of the Church.* Trans. Salvator Attanasio. Burns & Oates, London; 1964.

________. *On Being a Christian.* Trans. Edward Quinn. Doubleday, Garden City: 1976.

Kwick, Robert J. "Some Doubted," *The Expository Times,* 77, 1965, 181.

Lake, Kirsopp. "Simon, Cephas, Peter," *Harvard Theological Review,* 14, 1921, 95-97.

Lampe, Peter. "Das Spiel mit dem Petrusnamen—Matt. XVI. 18," *New Testament Studies,* 25, January 1979, 227–245.

Launoius, Joannes (Jean de Launoy). "Gulielmo Voello, Epistula VII," *Joannis Launoii, Opera Omnia.* Tome 5, Part 2, Fabri & Barrillot, Coloniae Allobruogum; 1731, 101–115.

Lee, G. M. "Studies in Texts, Matthew 17:24-27," *Theology,* 68, 542, August 1965, 380f.

Légasse, S. "Jésus et l'impôt du Temple," *Science Esprit,* 24, 3, October–December 1972, 361–377.

Lehman, Hans. " 'Du Bist Petrus . . . ' Zum Problem von Matthäus 16:13-26," *Evangelische Theologie,* 13, 1953, 44–67.

Linnemann, Eta. "Die Verleugnung des Petrus," *Zeitschrift für Theologie und Kirche,* 63, 1966, 1–32.

Linton, Olaf. *Das Problem der Urkirche in der Neueren Forschung. Eine kritische Darstellung.* Almquist & Wiksells, Uppsala; 1932.

Little, Charles Edgar. "On Praise and Blame," *Quintilian, the School Master,* vol. 1, 1951.

Liver, J. "The Half-Shekel Offering in Biblical and Post-Biblical Literature," *Harvard Theological Review,* 56, 3, July 1963, 173–198.

Lohmeyer, Ernst. "Die Verklärung Jesu nach dem Markus-Evangelium," *Zeitschrift für neutestamentliche Wissenschaft und die Kunde der alteren Kirche,* 21, 3, 1922, 185–215.

Loisy, Alfred. *L'Évangile selon Marc.* Emile Nourry, Paris; 1912.

_______. "La Confession de Pierre et la Promesse de Jesus (Matth. XVI, 13-23)," *Revue Anglo-Romaine,* 1, 1895, 49–58.

Longenecker, Richard N. *Biblical Exegesis in the Apostolic Period.* Wm. B. Eerdmans Publishing Company, Grand Rapids; 1975.

Ludwig, Joseph. *Die Primatsworte Mt 16, 18.19 in der Altkirchlichen Exegese.* Verlagsbuchhandlung, Münster; 1952.

Lührmann, Dieter. *Die Redaktion der Logienquelle: Wissenschaftliche Monographien zum Alten und Neuen Testaments.* 33, Neukircher Verlag, Neukirchen-Vlüyn, 1969.

Luther, Martin. "On the Papacy in Rome," *Luther's Works,* 39. Trans. Eric W. and Ruth C. Gritsch. Fortress Press, Philadelphia; 1970.

_______. "The Keys," *Luther's Works,* 40. Trans. Earl Bayer and Conrad Bergendoff. Fortress Press, Philadelphia; 1958, 325f.

_______. "Concerning the Ministry," *Ibid.,* 27f.

Luz, Ulrich. "Die Jünger in Matthäusevangelium," *Zeitschrift für die Neutestamentliche Wissenschaft und die Kunde der alteren Kirche,* 62, 3/4, 1971, 141–171.

Maclaren, Alexander. "Peter on the Waves," *Expositions of Holy Scripture. St. Matthew Chaps. IX to XVII.* Baker Book House, Grand Rapids; 1974, reprinted.

Mack, Burton. *Rhetoric and the New Testament.* Guides to Biblical Scholarship series. Dan O. Via, Jr., ed. Fortress Press, Minneapolis; 1990.

Malina, Bruce J. "Normative Dissonance and Christian Origins," *Semeia,* 35, 1986, 35–55.

Maloney, Elliot C. *Semitic Interference in Marcan Syntax.* Society of Biblical Literature Dissertation Series. Edwards Brothers, Ann Arbor; 1974.

Manson, T. W. *The Sayings of Jesus.* SCM Press, London; 1957.

Martin, James P. "The Church in Matthew," *Interpreting the Gospels.* James Luther Mays, ed. Fortress Press, Philadelphia; 1981.

Martin, Raymond A. *Syntactical Evidence of Semitic Sources in Greek Documents.* Septuagint and Cognate Studies, No. 3. Society of Biblical Literature, Missoula; 1974.

Marx, Werner G. "Money Matters in Matthew," *Bibliotheca Sacra: A Theological Quarterly,* 136, 1979, 148–157.

Marxsen, Willi. *Mark the Evangelist. Studies in the Redaction History of the Gospel.* Trans. James Boyce, Donald Juel, Wm. Pohlmann with Roy Harrisville. Abingdon Press, New York and Nashville; 1969.

Mathieu, Georges and Emile Bremond, eds. *Isocrates Discours,* Société D'Edition, Paris; 1963.

Mays, James Luther, ed. *Interpreting the Gospels.* Fortress Press, Philadelphia; 1981.

McElleney, Neil J. "Mt 17:24-27—Who Paid the Temple Tax? A Lesson in Avoidance of Scandal," *The Catholic Biblical Quarterly,* 38, 2, 1976, 178–192.

McKenna, Thomas F. "Matthew on Church Authority," *The Bible Today,* 102, April 1979, 2035–2041.

McKnight, Edgar V. *What is Form Criticism?* Guides to Biblical Scholarship series. Dan O. Via, Jr. ed. Fortress Press, Philadelphia; 1969.

Meier, John P. "Salvation-History in Matthew: In Search of a Starting Point," *The Catholic Biblical Quarterly,* 37, 2, April 1975, 203–215.

________. *The Vision of Matthew. Christ Church and Morality in the First Gospel.* Paulist Press, New York, Ramsey, Toronto; 1978.

Merkel, Helmut. "Peter's Curse," *The Trial of Jesus. Cambridge Studies in honour of C.F.D. Moule.* Ernst Bammel, ed. SCM Press, London; 1970, 66–71.

Michel, O. "Der Abschluss des Matthäus-evangeliums," *Evangelishes Theologie,* 10, 1950, 21ff.

Minear, Paul S. "The Disciples and the Crowds in the Gospel of Matthew," *Anglican Theological Review. Supplementary Series,* 3, 1974, 28–44.

Montefiore, Hugh. "Jesus and the Temple Tax," *New Testament Studies,* 10, 1965, 60–71.

Moule, C.F.D. "Some Reflections on the 'Stone' Testimonia in Relation to the Name Peter," *New Testament Studies,* 2, 1955/56, 56–58.

________. *An Idiom Book of New Testament Greek.* 2nd edition. The University Press, Cambridge; 1963.

Murphy, J. J., ed. *Quintilian on the Teaching of Speaking and Writing.* Excerpts translated from Books 1, 2, and 10 of Quintilian's *Institutio Oratoria;* 1987.

Nau, Arlo J. *A Redaction-Critical Analysis of the Role of St. Peter in the Gospel of St. Matthew.* Th.D. dissertation submitted to the combined Biblical Studies Faculties of the Toronto School of Theology and the University of Toronto; 1983.

Neusner, Jacob. *The Talmud as History.* Gate Press, Westmont, Quebec; 1979.

Nober, P. "Petrus," *Elenchus Bibliographicus. Biblica.* Pontificium Institutum Biblicum, Rome; each year since 1955.

O'Connor, Daniel. Wm.. *Peter in Rome: The Literary, Liturgical and Archeological Evidence.* Columbia University Press, New York and London; 1969.

Oepke, Albrecht. "Der Herrnspruch über die Kirche Mt 16:17-19 in der neuesten Forschung," *Studia Theologica,* 3, Oslo, 1950, 110–165.

O'Malley, John W. *Praise and Blame in Renaissance Rome.* Duke University Press, Durham, N.C.; 1979.

Orton, David E. *The Understanding Scribe.* Journal for the Study of the New Testament, Supplement Series 25. Sheffield Academic Press, Sheffield, Great Britain; 1989.

Pelikan, Jaroslav. *The Emergence of the Catholic Tradition (100–600).* Vol. 1 in the series: *The Christian Tradition: A History of the Development of Doctrine.* The University of Chicago Press, Chicago and London; 1971.

Perrin, Norman. *What is Redaction Criticism.* Guides to Biblical Scholarship series. Fortress Press, Philadelphia; 1969.

Pesch, Rudolf. "Die Verleugnung des Petrus. Eine Studie zu Mk 14, 54. 66-72 (und Mk 14, 26-31)," *Neues Testaments und Kirche, für Rudolf Schnackenburg.* Joachim Gnilka, ed. Herder, Freiburg, Basel, Wien; 1974, 42–62.

________. "The Position and Significance of Peter in the Church of the New Testament. A survey of Current Research," *Concilium,* 64, *Papal Ministry in the Church.* Hans Küng, ed. Herder and Herder, New York; 1971, 21–35.

________. *Simon-Petrus: Papste und Papsttum.* Band 15. Anton Hiersemann, Stuttgart, 1980.

Pesch, Wilhelm. "Die sogenannte Gemeindeordnung Mt 18," *Biblische Zeitschrift,* Neue Folge 7, 1963, 220–235.

Pfatteicher, Philip H. *Festivals and Commemorations.* Augsburg Publishing House, Minneapolis; 1980.

Pope Pius XII, *Divino Afflante Spiritu.* An encyclical letter on Promotion of Biblical Studies. National Catholic Welfare Conference, Washington; 1953, 1-27.

Quast, Kevin. *Peter and the Beloved Disciple.* Journal for the Study of the New Testament, Supplement Series 32. JSOT Press, Sheffield; 1989.

Quintilianus, Marcus Fabius. *Institutio Oratoria.* Cf. Loeb Classical Library, 4 vols. 1920–1922. Cf. also Charles Edgar Little, ed. *Quintilian, The School Master,* vol 1. George Peabody College for Teachers, Nashville; 1951.

Ramm, Bernard L. "The Exegesis of Matt. 16:13-20 in the Patristic and Reformation Period," *Foundations,* 5, 3, July 1962, 207–216.

Reiche, Bo. *The New Testament Era.* Trans. David E. Green. Fortress Press, Philadelphia; 1968.

Riddle, Donald W. "The Cephas-Peter Problem, and a Possible Solution," *Journal of Biblical Literature,* 59, 1940, 169–180.

Riesenfeld, Harald. *Jesus Transfiguré.* Hakan Ohlssons Boktryckeri, Lund; 1947.

Rigaux, Béda. "St. Peter in Contemporary Exegesis," *Concilium,* 27. *Progress and Decline in the History of Church Renewal.* Roger Aubert, ed. Paulist Press, New York and Glen Rock, N.J.; 1967.

Ringger, Johannes. "Das Felsenwort. Zur Sinndeutung von Mt 16, 18, vor allem in Lichte der Symbolgeschichte," *Begegnung der Christen. Studien evangelischer und katholischer Theologen.* Maximillian Roesle and Oscar Cullmann, eds. Evangelisches Verlagswerk, Stuttgart; Verlag Josef Knecht-Carolusdruckerei, Frankfurt Am Main; 1960.

Robinson, James M. and Helmut Koester. *Trajectories through Early Christianity.* Fortress Press, Philadelphia; 1971.

Rohde, Joachim. *Rediscovering the Teaching of the Evangelists.* Trans. Dorothea M. Barton. SCM Press, London; 1968.

Sanders, E. P. and Margaret Davies. *Studying the Synoptic Gospels.* SCM Press, London; Trinity Press International, Philadelphia; 1989.

Saunders, D. J. "The Confession of Peter," *Theological Studies,* 10, 4, 1949, 522–540.

Schmid, Josef. "Petrus 'Der Fels' und die Petrusgestalt der Urgemeinde," *Begegnung der Christen. Studien evangelischer und katholischer Theologen.* Maximillian Roesle and Oscar Cullmann, eds. Evangelisches Verlagswerk, Stuttgart; Verlag Josef Knecht—Carolusdruckerei; 1960, 347–359.

Schmithals, Walter. *The Office of Apostle in the Early Church.* Trans. John E. Steely. Abingdon Press, Nashville and New York; 1969.

Schoedel, William R. *Ignatius of Antioch.* Hermeneia—A Critical and Historical Commentary on the Bible. Helmut Koester, ed. Fortress Press, Philadelphia; 1985.

Schultz, Siegfried. *Q, Die Spruchquelle der Evangelisten.* Theologischer Verlag, Zurich; 1972.

Schweizer, Eduard. "Observance of Law and Charismatic Activity in Matthew," *New Testament Studies,* 16, 3, 1970, 213–230.

________. "The 'Matthean' Church," *New Testament Studies,* 20, 2, 1974, 216.

________. "The Gospel of Matthew," *Jesus and Man's Hope,* II. Donald G. Miller and Kikran Y. Hadidian, eds. A Perspective Book. Pittsburgh Theological Seminary, Pittsburgh; 1971, 339–341.

Seitz, Oscar J. F. "Upon This Rock: A Critical Re-examination of Matt 16, 17-19," *Journal of Biblical Literature,* 69, 1950, 329–340.

Sell, Jesse. "Simon Peter's 'Confession' and the Acts of Peter and the Twelve Apostles," *Novum Testamentum,* XII, 4, 1979, 344–356.

Senior, Donald P. *The Passion Narrative According to Matthew; A Redactional Study.* Leuven University, Leuven; 1975.

Shuler, Philip L. *A Genre for the Gospels. The Biographical Character of Matthew.* Fortress Press, Philadelphia; 1982.

Slingerland, H. Dixon: "The Transjordanian Origin of St. Matthew's Gospel," *Journal for the Study of the New Testament,* 3, 1979, 18–28.

Smith, Terrence V. *Petrine Controversies in Early Christianity.* J.C.B. Mohr [Paul Siebeck], Tübingen; 1985.

Stählin, Wilhelm. "Petrus und die Petriner," *Quatember,* 18, 1953/54, 29–32.

Stanley, David. "Kingdom to Church. The Structural Development of Apostolic Christianity in the New Testament," *Theological Studies,* 16, 1955, 1-29.

________. "An Ecumenical Quest for the Historical Peter," *Interpretation,* 29, 3. 1975, 300–302.

Stanton, Graham. *The Interpretation of Matthew.* SPCK, London; Fortress Press, Philadelphia; 1983.

Stauffer, Ethelbert. "Petrus und Jacobus in Jerusalem," *Begegnung der Christen. Studien evangelischer und katholischer Theologen.* Maximillian Roesle and Oscar Cullmann, eds. Evangelisches Verlagwerk, Stuttgart; Verlag Josef Knecht—Carolusdruckerei, Frankfurt Am Main; 1960, 361-372.

Stein, Robert H. "What is Redaktionsgeschichte?" *Journal of Biblical Literature,* 88, 1969, 45–56.

Stendahl, Krister. *The School of St. Matthew, and Its Use of the Old Testament.* Second edition. CWK Gleerup, Lund; n.d.

Stock, Augustine. "Is Matthew's Presentation of Peter Ironic?" *Biblical Theology Bulletin,* 17, 1987.

Stockmeier, Peter. "Das Petrusamt in der frühen Kirche," *Petrusamt und Papsttum.* Katholisches Bibelwerk, Stuttgart; 1970, 61–79.

Strathmann, Hermann. "Die Stellung des Petrus in der Urkirche. Zur Frühgeschichte des Wortes an Petrus Matthäus 16:17-19," *Zeitschrift für Systematische Theologie,* 20, 1943, 223–282.

Strecker, Georg. *Der Weg der Gerechtigkeit. Untersuchung zur Theologie des Matthäus.* Dritte, durchgesehene und erweiterte Auflage, Vandenhoeck & Ruprecht, Göttingen; 1971.

________. "Die Geschichtsverständnis des Matthäus," *Evangelische Theologie,* 26, 1966, 57–74.

Streeter, Burnett Hillman. *The Four Gospels: A Study of Origins.* Macmillan & Co. Ltd., London; 1964.

________. *Oxford Studies in the Synoptic Problem.* Clarendon Press, Oxford; 1911.

Stroth, Friedrich Andreas. "Von Interpolationem im Evangelium Matthäe," *Reportorium für Biblische und Morganländische Litteratur,* 9, Leipzig; 1781.

Sutcliffe, Edmund F. "St. Peter's Double Confession in Mt 16:16-19," *The Heythorp Journal,* 3, 1962, 31–41, with an additional note on 275f.

Tagawa, Kenzo. "People and Community in the Gospel of Matthew," *New Testament Studies,* 16, 2, 1970, 149–162.

Taylor, Vincent. *The Gospel According to St. Mark.* Second edition. Macmillin, St. Martin's Press, London; 1966.

Tertullian, "Adversus Marcionem," *The Ante-Nicene Father,* vol. III, *Latin Christianity, Its Founder: Tertullian.* A. Cleveland Coxe, ed. Wm B. Eerdmans Publishing Company, Grand Rapids; 1973, Part II, 219–474.

Thompson, William G. *Matthew's Advice to a Divided Community, Mt. 17:22–18:35.* Analecta Biblica. Biblical Institute Press, Rome; 1970.

________. "Reflections on the Composition of Mt 8:1–9:34." *Catholic Biblical Quarterly,* 33, 1971.

________. "An Historical Perspective in the Gospel of Matthew," *Journal of Biblical Literature,* 93, 2, 1974, 243–262.

Tillard, J.M.R., *The Bishop of Rome.* Michael Glazier, Inc., Wilmington; 1983. Translated from the French, *Éditions du Cerf,* by John de Satgé.

Tillborg, Sjef von. *The Jewish Leaders in Matthew.* E. J. Brill, Leiden; 1972.

Thyen, H. *Studien zur Sündenvergebung.* Furschungen zur Relgion und Literatur des Alten und Neuen Testaments, 96, Vandenhoeck & Ruprecht, Göttingen; 1970.

Trilling, Wolfgang. "Die Taufertradition bei Matthäus," *Biblische Zeitschrift,* 19, 2, 1959, 271–289.

________. *Hausordnung Gottes. Eine Auslegung von Matthäus 18.* Patmos-Verlag, Düsseldorf; 1960.

________. *Das Wahre Israel. Studien zur Theologie des Matthäus-Evangelium.* Kösel-Verlag, München; 1964.

________. "Ist die katholische Primatslehre schriftgemäss? Exegetische Gedanken zu einer wichtigen Frage," *Petrusamt und Papsttum.* Katholisches Bibelwerk; Stuttgart; 1970, 51–60.

Turner, C. H. "1. St. Peter in the New Testament," *Theology,* 13, 74, August 1926, 66–78; "2. St. Peter and St. Paul in the New Testament and in the Early Church," *Theology,* 13, 76, October 1926, 190–204.

Van Der Loos. *The Miracles of Jesus.* E. J. Brill, Leiden; 1968.

Vögtle, Anton. "Messiasbekenntnis und Petrusverheissung. Zur Komposition Mt. 16:13-23 par.," *Biblische Zeitschrift,* N.F. 1, 1957, N.F. 2, 1958, 85–103.

________. "Zum Problem der Herkunft von 'Mt 16, 17-19,' " *Orientierung an Jesus. Zur Theologie der Synoptiker.* Herder, Freiburg; 1973, 372–393.

Volkmar, Gustav. *Die Religion Jesu,* 1857.

Walker, Rolf. *Die Heilsgeschichte im ersten Evangelium.* Vandenhoeck & Ruprecht, Göttingen; 1967.

Wallace, David H. "An Exegesis of Matt. 16:13-20," *Foundations,* 5, 1962, 217–225.

White, R.E.O. *The Mind of Matthew.* Westminster Press, Philadelphia; 1971.

Wilcox, Max. "Peter and the Rock: A Fresh Look at Matthew XVI. 17-19," *New Testament Studies,* 22, 1975/76, 73–88.

Wrede, William. *The Messianic Secret.* Trans. J.C.G. Grieg. James Clarke & Co., Ltd., Cambridge and London; 1971; German edition, 1901.

Zimmermann, Heinrich. "Die Innere Struktur der Kirche und das Petrusamt nach Mt 18," *Catholica,* 30, 1976, 168–183.

Index of Authors

(Names may appear more than once on the pages listed. Additional authors, not referred to in the text, may be listed in the Bibliography.)

Index of Matthean References